Classic Miniature Vehicles
MADE IN FRANCE

Dr. Edward Force

With Price Guide
and Variations List

1469 Morstein Road, West Chester, Pennsylvania 19380

The names and trade marks of the various brands of miniature vehicles mentioned in this book, those of the makes of real vehicles they represent, and those of products advertised on them, are the copyrighted names and registered trade marks of those brands and products.

We are interested in hearing from authors with book ideas on related topics.

Published by Schiffer Publishing, Ltd.
1469 Morstein Road
West Chester, Pennsylvania 19380
Please write for a free catalog.
This book may be purchased from the publisher.
Please include $2.00 postage.
Try your bookstore first.

Contents

MADE IN FRANCE

The history of miniature vehicle production in France is a long, varied, and significant one. It began in the twenties, and as it developed, three firms stood out: A.R., which concentrated on models of Peugeot; C.D., which stressed Renaults; and Citroen, which naturally made models of their own products. The first such models were made of cast lead or similar metallic alloys, but it was not long before another material came into the picture: a mixture of plaster and flour.

This might seem odd, but if even Citroen used plaster and flour to make miniature cars, it must have had its advantages, and one obvious advantage is that it cost considerably less than lead. And it must be pointed out that the models in question were not made by the millions and sold as toys, as many modern-day brands are. These models, whether lead or plaster, were generally made in small quantities, and though some of them must have seen service as toys, others were used as showroom models, where they were not subjected to rough handling. For that matter, a lead model is no less safe than a plaster one in the hands of a determined youngster.

Two firms that began by making plaster-and-flour models in pre-war days later became well-known manufacturers of diecast cars in the post-war era: C.I.J. and J.R.D. At the same time, though, two firms that were to play a major role in the development of diecast models in France entered the picture: Solido in 1931-32, and the French branch of Dinky Toys in 1933-34. Neither brand will be discussed in this book; Dinky Toys are already the subject of a book by this author, and Solido's story would fill a book all by itself. A book on the older Solido models has not been written to date, though Bertrand Azema has written a superb book on the newer Solido products.

Somewhere along the way, a little-known firm known by the initials S.R. also appeared on the scene, making an assortment of small-scale models on a variety of subjects, from a 1914 Grand Prix Mercedes to warships on wheels. As the pioneers, A.R., C.D., and Citroen, faded out of the picture, Solido and Dinky grew and flourished, and those two firms were the first to revive when World War II ended. So the situation remained until the mid-fifties, when France erupted with manufacturers of diecast and plastic miniature cars.

This golden age began in 1953, when the firm of Norev produced its first plastic models, taking its business name from that of its proprietor, M. Veron, spelled backward. In 1954 the C.I.J. firm, now settled, if I remember correctly, in a new factory in an industrial park, introduced its Europarc series, appropriately named after the firm's new location. Quiralu began to produce its diecast models in 1955, and Gege introduced a small series of plastic-bodied models in 1956. In 1957 Desormeaux produced the first of its two cast lead old-timers, Jadali brought out a series of small-scale diecast models, and the time-honored firm of Solido introduced a series of fine-quality ¼3-scale diecast models that was to become one of the world's classic series of miniature vehicles.

The following year, 1958, saw the introduction of the diecast J.R.D. series, the RAMI old-timers, two picturesque P.R. vans, and the plastic models of J.E.P. and Cle. In 1959 they were joined by a series of France Jouets (F.J. for short) trucks, small-scale diecast models from Midget Toys and Les Routiers, and the first plastic Minialuxe models, while 1961 brought the first Safir old-timers, two of which had previously been made by Jadali.

This was the situation that we old-timers knew when we started collecting. Solido models, which had set a new standard of quality for the rest of the manufacturers to aim at, were available in America, most French Dinky Toys were imported to the USA along with their British brethren, Norev models were fairly easy to get, and so were RAMI; beyond that, one had to know someone in Europe and have something to trade, or find one of the few mail-order houses on the Continent that sold brands like C.I.J. and J.R.D. It was a challenge at times, but that was part of the fun—finding collectors in other countries to swap with, and finding models in your own country to swap with them.

The years went by, the quality got better, and the majority of the manufacturers went out of business or at least stopped producing model cars. Then in 1966 an event took place that went all but unnoticed at the time but was to lead to major developments: The firm of Railroute introduced its Majorette series of Matchbox-size models.

The previous French models had been either O or HO gauge, with Norev's 500 series and a plastic line by Jouef having joined those already mentioned in the smaller scale, not to mention the tiny Gitanes series. But nobody in France had as yet produced models in a scale or size between those two. Majorette models caught on, though for some time neither the retailers nor the collectors took them too seriously. They showed, though, that there was a market for Matchbox-size models in France.

As the sixties came to an end, Safir expanded its production from its original series of picturesque diecast old-time cars to include modern racing and sports cars, often with plastic bodies and diecast chassis; some of them were made to O gauge, while others were smaller, though not usually as small as HO gauge. And collectors of racing car models were enthusiastic about the first Faracars model, that of an Indianapolis STP turbine car, that appeared in 1969. Alas, it was the only Faracars model ever issued.

In the seventies the major developments in French miniature car production were in the area of white metal and resin kits, and ready-made limited editions—a subject outside the scope of this book. But a few important things happened in the field of traditional miniature cars. Safir bought some of the F.J. dies and produced a number of model trucks and Jeeps, often in both metal and plastic. In 1971 Norev introduced its first diecast cars, which were soon to dominate that firm's production, though Norev still makes plastic models as well. Around 1973 the heavy equipment firm of Poclain produced plastic models of their own products, and in 1976 we read that a new firm, Eligor, was taking over production of the pre-war car models that Norev had made a few years before. Before seeing this note in a hobby magazine, I had not been aware of a link between Norev's plastic old-timers and Eligor's diecast models, but soon Eligor had established itself on the market, where it holds a respected position to this day—though one is never quite sure whether to call it French or Swiss.

Early in the eighties, just before Matchbox changed hands, the collecting world was stunned to hear that Solido, in financial trouble, was being bought by, of all people, the makers of Majorette. This move resulted not only in the survival of the time-honored Solido brand, but in its products becoming better distributed—or so it seemed to us on this side of the ocean—and less expensive. Inflation soon had its effect on prices, but other brands, such as Eligor, appear to have been affected a lot more by inflation. Majorette's merchandising expertise was certainly good for business, and it did not come as too much of a shock when we learned later in the eighties that Norev had become affiliated with Solido and Majorette.

This trio dominates the traditional side of diecast miniature vehicle production in France today. Each brand retains its own identity, but all three stand to gain from the practical policies that direct their progress into the future. Aside from them and Eligor, there are firms such as Verem and Cofradis, which produce models that Solido used to make or special versions of Solido models, plus a variety of firms making limited-edition ready-made models or kits.

The purpose of this book shall be to trace the histories and production of those firms that have played a part in the French miniature vehicle story between the twenties and the modern times of resin and white metal. As noted above, French Dinky Toys have been dealt with elsewhere, Solido and its sister by adoption, Majorette, deserve separate treatment, and Eligor, Verem, and other firms are too new. This leaves some two dozen firms, some of which produced hundreds of models, others just a handful, and still others only one or two, for us to examine here. In some cases we know every model that the firm produced; in others, very little is known of the company's production, and in any case you are invited to contribute information to fill holes in what is known about the manufacturers and their products.

There is relatively little already in print on the subject. The Greilsamer-Azema *Catalogue Mondial des Modeles Reduits Automobiles* offers lists and photographs of French products through 1966, and a series of articles by Mike Richardson on C.I.J. models can be found in *Modellers' World,* beginning in the April, 1973 issue. The same journal offers Jean-Michel Roulet's article on Quiralu in the October, 1976 issue. M. Roulet's book, *Les Dinky Toys et Dinky Supertoys Francais,* and Bertrand Azema's *Solido,* are two of the best books ever written on our hobby. French Dinky Toys are also covered in my own **Dinky Toys,** published by Schiffer Publishing Ltd. in 1988, and *Argus de la Miniature,* in October of 1990, published an excellent Norev guide which has been of much use in preparing the Norev section of this book. In addition, useful and enlightening information on the lesser-known brands (as well as their better-known brethren) has appeared in Paolo Rampini's *Encyclopedia of 1/43 Model Cars 1900-1975* and in the pages of *Ma Collection.* I would like to express my gratitude to the compilers of these books and journals for their pioneering work, without which this book would be a lot shorter.

As for the details to be listed, we shall try to strike a happy medium between too much and too little. On the one hand, it is impossible to list every minute detail of some models; on the other, we try to state the basic facts about each model, as far as those facts are known to us, and to provide pictures of as many models as possible. The words "no data" are an invitation to those of you who can provide additional information on those models—or have the models themselves to spare, for models that fill holes in my collection are always welcome.

In describing individual models, we begin with the diecast metal parts, usually the main body or major components of it, then minor pieces; next come plastic, sheet metal, rubber, and other parts, running gear, paint work, decals or labels. The length of the model is given in millimeters, and its year of introduction (and deletion, if we know it) are noted, not to mention its catalog number.

The list of variations will be a very simple one, usually consisting of body colors—and even there I am the first to admit that many of the models listed in this book were issued in more colors than I know of. Here again, your contribution of data will be much appreciated. The book will also include the inevitable price guide, which will try to offer parameters between which a model or a series of models can be valued. The prices stated are intended to refer to mint boxed models—though in some cases one will never find a boxed model, and in a few cases even a mint specimen is impossible to find.

The higher price is what a collector who absolutely has to have that particular model might be willing to pay; the lower price is what a collector might be willing to pay simply because he likes the model. I must add that some of the stated values are no more than guesses on my part, so please do not take them for gospel!

At this point I would like to express my thanks to all those who helped to make this book possible: to all my sources of models over my nearly thirty years of collecting, from French collectors such as Philippe Moro to dealers such as Danhausen Modelcar, John Gay, Eric Waiter, and James Wieland, who has often turned me loose in his stocks and information, and who has lent me more than two dozen models from his own collection for photographing, as well as Nelson Adams, who has lent even more models from his collection; to my frequent companion and helper at toy shows, The Rev. Charles Gelbach; to Pat, Lisa, and Ellen for giving me the time to write this book; to Peter Schiffer and all his crew, especially photographer Doug Congdon-Martin, for bringing it to you;—and not least to you for buying and reading it. I owe more than thanks to a fellow collector from whom I obtained several of the HO scale models included here and was never able to repay fully in kind; if he will get in touch with me, I'll do my best to square the deal.

Having said that, we can begin to look at the individual brands and their products. Once you have had that look, please feel free to contact me if you have additional data to offer or questions to be answered.

Dr. Edward Force
42 Warham Street
Windsor CT 06095

Row 1: **AR Peugeot 201 Roadster (x2), Peugeot 301 Limousine (x2), Taxi.**
Row 2: **AR Bluebird, Peugeot 202 Sedan, Peugeot 601 Sedan, Renault Paris Bus.**
Row 3: **AR Renault Tank (x2), Steam Roller, Traction Engine, Disc Harrow.**
Row 4: **AR Latil Open and Covered Farm Trucks, AA Gun Truck, Dump Truck, Tank Truck.**

Row 1: **AR Peugeot Dump, Vat, Cable, Lumber and Farm Trucks.**
Row 2: **AR Peugeot Milk, Barrel, Fire and Mail Trucks and Army Ambulance.**
Row 3: **CD Renault 4040 CV Ambulance, Renault Vivaquatre.**
Row 4: **CD Chenard & Walcker Wrecker, Latil Box Van, Renault Army Ambulance, Renault Open Truck.**

Row 1: **SR (or similar) Truck & Trailer (x2), two Self-Propelled Guns.**
Row 2: **SR two Warships, Model T Ford, Motorcycle & Sidecar, Caisson & Cannon.**
Row 3: **SR Mercedes Grand Prix, Single- and Double-deck Buses, Yellow Taxi, Open Truck, Ladder Truck, Car (open rear seat).**
Row 4: **SR Sports Roadster, Touring Cars (+ & - rear doors), Town Car (x2), Steam Shovel, Car (covered rear seat), anon. Two-Seater, Whistle Car.**

Row 1: **Citroen lead B14 Torpedo, B14 Coupe, sheet metal Coupe, lead B14 Sedan (x2).**
Row 2: **Citroen plaster Prime Mover, Sedan, Tanker, CIJ Hose Truck, Ladder Truck.**
Row 3: **Citroen Petite Rosalie, anon. Gun Car, three sheet metal cars (2nd "CR 1904," 3rd "II 235," not listed in text).**
Row 4: **Sheet metal Grand Sport, Juvaquatre, Celtaquatre, Coupe (not listed in text).**

Row 1: **CIJ 3/1 DeRovin, 3/3 Facellia (x2), 3/5 Panhard Dyna Junior (x2).**
Row 2: **CIJ 3/2 Etoile Filante, 3/4 Citroen ID19 Break, 3/10 Citroen 11CV, 3/12 Mercedes 220.**
Row 3: **CIJ 3/6 Citroen Ami 6, 3/7 Simca 1000, 3/8 Simca 1000 Police, 3/9 Simca Bertone, 3/10 Volkswagen.**
Row 4: **CIJ 3/15 Chrysler Windsor (x2), 3/16 Plymouth Belvedere (x2).**

Row 1: **CIJ 3/20 & 4/20 Panhard BP Tanker, 3/24 & 3/21 Renault Shell Tankers.**
Row 2: **CIJ 3/25 Renault 7-Ton Truck (x2), 3/26 Truck Trailer, 3/30 Fire Engine.**
Row 3: **CIJ 3/27 & 3/27T Caravans, 3/41 Citroen ID19 Ambulance.**
Row 4: **CIJ 3/42 Renault Prairie, 3/43 Renault Savane, 3/44 Renault Colorale, 3/45 Renault Prairie Taxi.**

14

Row 1: **CIJ #? Renault Tractor, 3/31 Sugar Beet Trailer, 3/33 Renault Tractor & 3/37 Tipping Trailer (= 3/34).**
Row 2: **CIJ 3/32 Seed Trailer, 3/33 Renault Tractor & 3/36 Sling Cart (= 3/39).**
Row 3: **CIJ 4/50 Renault Cattle Truck & 3/28 Cattle Trailer, 3/80 Renault Dump Truck, 3/35 Tank Trailer.**
Row 4: **CIJ 4/76 Saviem Covered Truck (x2), 4/77 Covered Trailer, 3/89B Citroen Brandt Van.**

Row 1: **CIJ 3/40 Renault Bus (x2), 3/50 Alpine Coupe (x2).**
Row 2: **CIJ 3/46 Peugeot 403 Break, 3/56E Ambulance, 3/46H with windows, 3/46P Police Car.**
Row 3: **CIJ 3/51 Renault Frégate (x2), 3/48 (x2) & 4/48 Renault 4CV.**
Row 4: **CIJ 3/47 Panhard Dyna (x2), 3/52 Renault Frégate Grand Pavois, 3/49 Renault 4CV Police Car.**

Row 1: **CIJ 3/66 Renault Dauphinoise, 3/69 Dauphinoise Police, 3/67 Renault 300 KG Van, 3/68 300 KG Mail Van, 3/76 Citroen 2CV Mail Van.**
Row 2: **CIJ 3/56 Renault Dauphine, 3/56 Dauphine Taxi (x2), 3/57 Dauphine Police, 3/58 Renault Floride.**
Row 3: **CIJ 3/54 Panhard Dyna (x2), 3/54T Panhard Taxi, 3/55 Renault Colorale Ambulance.**
Row 4: **3/53 Renault Domane, 3/53A Domane Ambulance, 3/65 Renault Police Pickup & Trailer.**

Row 1: **CIJ 3/91 & 3/93 Renault Police Vans, 3/90 Renault Estafette Van, 3/92 Estafette Bus (x2).**
Row 2: **CIJ 3/60 Renault 1000 KG Van, 3/60A Astra Van, 3/60B Boucherie Van, 3/60P Mail Van.**
Row 3: **CIJ 3/60S Shell Van, 3/60T PTT Van & Trailer, 3/61 Ambulance.**
Row 4: **CIJ 3/61M Army Ambulance, 3/62 SNCF Bus, 3/62N Teindre Mettoyer Van, 3/63 Police Van.**

Row 1: **CIJ 3/95 Renault Fire Truck, 3/70 Renault Covered Semi, 3/83 Renault Wrecker.**
Row 2: **CIJ Renault Shell Tanker, 4/69 Saviem Shell Tanker.**
Row 3: **CIJ 4/70 Saviem Mobil Tanker, 4/71 Saviem BP Tanker.**
Row 4: **CIJ 4/78 Saviem Dumper, 3/73 Renault Logger, 4/80 Saviem Dumper.**

19

Row 1: **CIJ 4/75 Saviem Cable Carrier, 3/76A Boat Trailer.**
Row 2: **CIJ 3/81 Renault Crane Truck, 3/82 Renault Shovel Truck, 4/81 Berliet Garbage Truck.**
Row 3: **CIJ 3/94 Renault Bottle Truck, 4/73 Saviem Cement Truck, 3/84 Berliet Weitz Crane.**
Row 4: **CIJ 3/75 Renault Atomic Pile Transporter.**

Row 1: **CIJ 3/97 Saviem Missile Launcher, 4/72 Somua Transformer Truck.**
Row 2: **CIJ 3/98 Renault Radar Truck, 3/96 Renault Searchlight Truck & Generator Trailer, 4/74 Saviem Army Truck.**
Row 3: **CIJ 3/99 Renault Gun Truck, 4/68 Saviem Army Tanker.**

Front: CIJ 1/1 Fouga, 1/2 Norécrin, 1/12 Noratlas, 1/10 Caravelle.
Rear: CIJ 1/16 Douglas DC 6, 1/11 Douglas DC 7, 1/14 Breguet Deux Ponts, 1/15 Boeing 707.

Row 1: **Jouef Citroen DS19, Panhard Dyna, Peugeot 203 (x2), Peugeot 403, Simca Ariane, Simca Aronde.**
Row 2: **Jouef Panamericaine, Chausson Bus, Farmall Tractor, Porsche 911S, Ferrari GTO.**
Row 3: **Gulliver Renault Celtaquatre, Berliet Diesel Truck, Berliet Bus.**
Row 4: **Vebe Truck & Trailer, Tank Truck, Dump Truck (not listed in text).**

Row 1: **Cle 1 Peugeot 203, 2 Citroen 11CV, 3 Peugeot 403, 6 Simca P60, 11 Renault Dauphine.**
Row 2: **Cle 12 Renault Caravelle Coupe, 13 Caravelle Cabriolet, 16 Panhard Dyna, 21 Peugeot 403 Break, 24 Peugeot 404 Red Cross.**
Row 3: **Cle 20 Fiat 600, 25 Citroen Ami 6, 26 Renault R4L, 27 Simca 1000, #? Simca 1300.**
Row 4: **#? Peugeot 404 Cabriolet, Peugeot 404 Coupe, 18 Citroen 1200 KG Fire Van & Ambulance, #? Citroen 2CV Van.**

Row 1: **Cle 202 Peugeot 1895, 203 Peugeot 1895 Vis-à-vis, 204 Gauthier-Wehrlé 1897, 205 Renault 1900 Coupe, 207 De Dion-Bouton 1900 Coupe.**

Row 2: **Cle 206 De Dion-Bouton 1900 Vis-à-vis (x2), 210 Peugeot 1905 5CV (x2), 109 Georges Richard 1902, 212 Lion-Peugeot 1908 (x2).**

Row 3: **Cle 213 Hispano-Suiza 1922 (x2), 216 Isotta-Fraschini 1926, 217 Bentley 1927 Tourer (x2).**

Row 4: **Cle 218 Mercedes SS 1928, 219 Mercedes SSK 1929 (x2), 220 Bentley 1929 Le Mans, 221 Packard 1930 Sport Phaeton.**

Row 1: **Cle 222 Packard 1930 Roadster, 223 Rolls-Royce 1931 Phantom (x3), 215 Panhard 1926.**
Row 2: **Cle Ferguson, Lotus (x2), Ferrari and BRM racing cars.**
Row 3: **Cle Chapparal, McLaren, Matra-BRM, Ferrari 330P2, 214 Citroen 1923 Ambulance.**
Row 4: **Cle Porsche Carrera 6, Berliet Box Van, Flat Truck with Box, Bottle Truck, Flat Truck, 211 Sizaire-Naudin 1906.**

Row 1: **FJ 101 Berliet Tank Truck, 103 Covered Truck, 104 Dump Truck, 105 Grocery Truck.**
Row 2: **FJ 106 Berliet Street Sweeper, 107 Cement Mixer, 108 Crane Truck, 109 Garbage Truck.**
Row 3: **FJ 110 Berliet Overhead Truck, 111 Farm Truck, 112 Pipe Truck, 113 Glass Truck.**
Row 4: **FJ 114 Berliet Crane Truck, 115 Tow Truck, 116 Bucket Truck.**

Row 1: **FJ 204 Pacific Transformer Carrier.**
Row 2: **FJ 202 Pacific Pipe Carrier.**
Row 3: **203 Pacific Rocket Launcher, 201 Pacific Heavy Crane Truck.**

Row 1: **FJ 205 Pacific Cement Truck.**
Row 2: **FJ 206 Pacific Atomic Cannon Truck with AA Guns.**
Row 3: **FJ 208 Pacific Atomic Cannon Truck with Searchlight.**

Row 1: **FJ 301 GMC Ambulance, 303 AA Gun Truck, 304 Lance Rocket Truck, 305 Rocket Carrier.**
Row 2: **FJ 302 GMC Covered Truck, #? Dump Truck & Trailer, 306 Dump Truck with Shovel.**
Row 3: **FJ #? GMC Lumber Truck, Radar Truck, Searchlight Truck, Tank Truck.**
Row 4: **FJ 401 Dodge Army Truck, 402 Troop Carrier, 403 Covered Army Truck, 404 AA Gun Truck.**

Row 1: **FJ 405 Dodge Radar Truck (x2), 406 Searchlight Truck (x2), Open Trailer.**
Row 2: **FJ 407 Dodge Fire Truck, 408 Lance Rocket Truck, 409 Ambulance Truck, 603 Army Jeep (= 501) & Open Trailer.**
Row 3: **FJ 601 Jeep & Antitank Gun, 602 Jeep & Generator, 502 Covered Jeep, Lance Rocket Trailer.**
Row 4: **FJ 507 Fire Jeep, 505 Radar Jeep, 506 Searchlight Jeep, 508 Police Jeep, Searchlight Trailer.**

Row 1: **FJ 701 Berliet Stradair Dump Truck, 702 Grocery Truck, 703 Tow Truck, 704 Glass Truck.**
Row 2: **FJ 706 Stradair Street Sweeper, 708 Coca-Cola Truck, JRD 106 Citroen 1200 KG Police Van, 107 Citroen Red Cross Van.**
Row 3: **JRD 108 Citroen 2CV EDF Van (x2), 109 2CV Fire Van, 110 Citroen 2CV (x2).**
Row 4: **JRD 111 Citroen 2CV Van (x2), 113 Citroen 1200 KG Esso Van, 117 2CV Road Service Van, 118 2CV Air France Van.**

Row 1: **JRD 112 Citroen 11CV (x2), 114 Citroen P55 Covered Truck (x2).**
Row 2: **JRD 116 Citroen DS19, 121 Berliet Total Tanker, 122 Unic Antar Tanker.**
Row 3: **JRD 120 Berliet Kronenbourg Semi, 123 Unic with Railroad Car.**
Row 4: **JRD 124 Izoard Circus Train.**

Row 1: **JRD 125 Berliet Weitz Crane, 134 Berliet Bottle Truck, 131 Berliet Garbage Truck.**
Row 2: **JRD 126 Unic Hafa Van, 132 Berliet Antargaz Semi.**
Row 3: **JRD 130 Unic Liquid Transporter, 133 Berliet Fire Truck, 128 Unic Milk Truck.**
Row 4: **JRD 127 Unic Transports Internationaux Van & 129 Fruehauf Trailer.**

Row 1: JRD 152 Citroen DS19 Cabriolet (x2), sheet metal Citroen Cabriolet, 154 Citroen Ami 6.
Row 2: JRD 151 Peugeot 404, 153 Mercedes-Benz 220S, 115 Citroen Army Truck & Trailer.
Row 3: JRD 155 Simca 1000, JEP 1611 Panhard Dyna (x2), 1612 Peugeot 403.
Row 4: JEP 1613 Simca Versailles (x2), 1614 Citroen DS19, 1615 Renault Dauphine.

Row 1: **Minialuxe 1 Ford Model T 1909 (x2), 2 Packard 1912 (x2), 6 Citroen 1925 B2.**
Row 2: **Minialuxe 3 Ford Model T 1911 (x2), 4 Renault Paris-Madrid (x2), 6 Citroen 1925 B2.**
Row 3: **Minialuxe 5 Renault 1907 Landau (x2), 7 Renault Taxi de la Marne (x2), 9 Peugeot 1906 Torpedo.**
Row 4: **Minialuxe 13 Oldsmobile 1902, 8 Peugeot 1906 Double Phaeton (x3), 9 Peugeot 1906 Torpedo.**

Row 1: **Minialuxe 14 Peugeot 1892 Victoria, 15 Autocar 1903 (x3), 16 Peugeot 1891 Vis-à-vis.**
Row 2: **Minialuxe 10 Renault 1910 Truck, 11 Ford Model T 1915 (x2), 12 Ford Model T 1907 (x2).**
Row 3: **Minialuxe 17 Panhard 1895, 18 Panhard 1891 (x2), 19 Panhard 1914 Skiff (x2).**
Row 4: **Minialuxe 20 Balda 1895, 22 Peugeot 1892, 24 Panhard 1892 Coupe (x2), 25 Peugeot 1892 Vis-à-vis, 27 Park Royal 1912 Landau.**

Row 1: **Minialuxe 21 Renault 1906 Grande Remise (x2), 26 Jamieson 1902, 28 Austin 1911 Van (x2).**
Row 2: **Minialuxe 23 Renault 1914 Army Truck, 30 Panhard 1905 Roi des Belges (x2), 31 De Dion-Bouton 1912.**
Row 3: **Minialuxe 29 Lanchester 1908, 32 Lorraine-Dietrich 1905, 34 Peugeot 1906 Double Phaeton.**
Row 4: **Minialuxe 101 Delaunay-Belleville 1911, 102 Muller 1913, 103 Clément-Bayard, 104 Hills 1839 Locomotive, 1/32 scale Peugeot 403.**

Row 1: **Minialuxe S-1 Siata-Fiat 1500TS (x2), S-2 BMW 1500 (x2).**
Row 2: **Minialuxe S-3 Simca 1300 (x2), S-4 Ford Consul, S-6 Fiat 124.**
Row 3: **Minialuxe S-5 Peugeot 204 (x2), S-8 Volvo 144, S-9 Citroen Ami 6 Break.**
Row 4: **Minialuxe S-10 Renault R16 (x2), S-12 Porsche 911S Targa (x2).**

Row 1: **Minialuxe S-11 Citroen Dyane, S-13 Renault R10 Major (x2), S-16 Jaguar E-Type Coupe.**
Row 2: **Minialuxe S-14 Matra Djet (x2), BMW 1500 with Skis, Alpine-Renault A310.**
Row 3: **Minialuxe Citroen 11CV, Citroen SM, Citroen CX 2200, Citroen GS.**
Row 4: **Minialuxe Citroen Ami 6, Citroen DS19 Taxi, Citroen DS19, Citroen DS21 Police.**

Row 1: **Minialuxe Matra MS80, Mercedes-Benz W196 (x3).**
Row 2: **Minialuxe Gordini Formula 1 (x2), Jaguar D-Type (x2).**
Row 3: **Minialuxe Ferrari 312B (x2), Ford Mark IV (x2).**
Row 4: **Panhard PL17 Cabriolet (x2), Panhard PL17 Citroen Dyane Mehari.**

Row 1: **Minialuxe Hotchkiss-Gregoire, Ford Anglia, Ford Taunus 17M, Peugeot 203U.**
Row 2: **Minialuxe Peugeot 403, Peugeot 404, Peugeot 504 (x2).**
Row 3: **Minialuxe Peugeot 604, Peugeot 604 with Roof Rack, Simca Aronde, VW K-70.**
Row 4: **Minialuxe Renault 5 (x2), Vespa 2CV, Renault Ondine, Renault Ondine Police Car.**

Row 1: **Minialuxe Renault Floride, Simca Oceane, Simca Plein Ciel, Simca 1100 Special, Week-End Canoe Trailer.**

Row 2: **Minialuxe Renault 17TS (x2), Renault 30TS (x2).**

Row 3: **Minialuxe Minibus (x2, flanking) Simca 1000 (x2).**

Row 4: **Minialuxe Renault Estafette Taxi, Simca 1000 Police Car, Police Motorcycle & Sidecar, Renault Estafette Police Van.**

Row 1: **Minialuxe C-2 Berliet Paris Bus, Somua Paris Bus.**
Row 2: **Norev 98 Saviem Paris Bus (x2).**
Row 3: **Norev 98 & 1602 Saviem Paris Bus.**

Row 1: **Norev 1 Simca 9 Aronde, 1 Opel Rekord, 3 Citroen 15-Six (x2).**
Row 2: **Norev 2 Citroen Ami 6 Break, 2 Ford Vedette (x3).**
Row 3: **Norev 3 Renault 16, 4 Panhard Dyna (x2), 4 Panhard PL17 Break.**
Row 4: **Norev 5 Simca Aronde Elysée (x2), 5 Peugeot 204, 6 Peugeot 201 1930.**

Row 1: **Norev 6 Simca Versailles (x2), 7 Simca Trianon, 7 Peugeot J7 Van.**
Row 2: **Norev 8 Peugeot 172R, 9 Renault R10, 10 Renault Juvaquatre, 12 Maserati 2000S (x2).**
Row 3: **Norev 11 Renault Amiral, 11 Alfa Romeo Giulietta (x3).**
Row 4: **Norev 12/13 Mercedes-Benz W196 (x3), 14 Ford Vedette Ambulance.**

Row 1: **Norev 13 Renault Dauphine (x2), 16 Porsche Carrera (x3).**
Row 2: **Norev 8/14 Peugeot 203 (x4), 18 Vespa 400.**
Row 3: **Norev 15 Citroen 15 Police Car, 15 Peugeot 403 (x2), 18 Monteverdi 375L.**
Row 4: **Norev 14 Renault 8 Gordini (x2), 22 Volkswagen 1600TL (x2), 27 Citroen 2CV AZ.**

Row 1: **Norev 5 Renault 4CV (x4), 19 Jaguar Mark X.**
Row 2: **Norev 17 Renault 4CV (x3), 20 Fiat 500 Jardinière, 21 Peugeot 203 with Skis.**
Row 3: **Norev 21 Simca Ariane Miramas, 21 Mercedes-Benz 250SE, 22 Panhard Dyna with Skis (x2).**
Row 4: **Norev 22 Chrysler 180, 22 Simca Aronde (x3).**

Row 1: **Norev 23 Renault Grand Pavois (x3), 24 Simca 5 1936 (x2).**
Row 2: **Norev 24 Jaguar 2.4, 23 Simca 1200 (x2), 27 Citroen SM.**
Row 3: **Norev 22/25 Lancia Aurelia (x4), 26 Citroen 2CV Van.**
Row 4: **Norev 25 Peugeot J7 Bus (x2), 16 Citroen 2CV Van (x3).**

Row 1: **Norev 28 Peugeot 404 Break (x2), 29 Panhard PL17 (x2).**
Row 2: **Norev 29 Citroen 11A (x2), 30 Simca 1300 (x2).**
Row 3: **Norev 31 DAF Variomatic (x2), 33 Rolls-Royce Silver Shadow (x2).**
Row 4: **Norev 32 Peugeot 204 Break, 32 Simca Oceane (x2), 33 Simca Plein Ciel.**

Row 1: **Norev 34 Ford Vedette Wrecker (x2), 35 Simca Versailles (x2).**
Row 2: **Norev 35 Citroen Rosalie (x2), 37 DKW Junior, 39 Panhard 35CV 1927 (x2).**
Row 3: **Norev 36 Fiat 1100D (x2), 42 Renault Estafette Van (x2), 39 Simca Beaulieu.**
Row 4: **Norev 40 Simca Chambord (x2), 38 Fiat 2300 (x2).**

Row 1: **Norev 40 Citroen ID19 Ambulance (x2), 41 Simca Marly Ambulance, 49 Mercedes-Benz 220SE.**
Row 2: **Norev 48 Citroen DS19 (x2), 47 Chrysler New Yorker (x2).**
Row 3: **Norev 43 Ford Taunus 17M (x2), 46 Citroen 5CV (x2), 47 Simca 1501.**
Row 4: **Norev 44 Volvo P1800, 45 Fiat 1500, 50 Renault Dauphine, 53 Renault 4L (x2).**

Row 1: **Norev 51 Peugeot 404, 58 Lancia Flaminia, 64 Opel Kapitän, 52 Renault Floride.**
Row 2: **Norev 67 Ford Anglia, 54 Citroen Ami 6, 56 Citroen 2CV AZ Luxe, 57 Simca 1000, 66 Fiat 1500 Cabriolet.**
Row 3: **Norev Renault Alpine A110 (x2), 61 Fiat 600, 60 BMW 700LS, 65 Renault R4 Van.**
Row 4: **Norev 62 Volkswagen 113 (x2), 63 Volkswagen 1500, 55 Renault Estafette Bus.**

Row 1: **Norev 68 Renault R8 (x2), 68 Renault R8 Gordini, 74 Ford Consul 315, 77 Ford Taunus 12M.**
Row 2: **Norev 69 Chevrolet Corvair, 74 Morris Mini-Minor (x2), 71 Peugeot 404 Coupe (x2).**
Row 3: **Norev 70 BMW 2000, 76 Panhard PL17, 72 Panhard 24CT, 80 Fiat 2300 Coupe.**
Row 4: **Norev 78 Renault NN1 (x2), 81 Citroen 1200 KG Van, 79 Simca 1500, 73 Simca 1000 Coupe.**

Row 1: **Norev 83 Morris 1100, 89 Austin 1100 (x2), 90 MG 1100, 82 Citroen 3CV Van.**
Row 2: **Norev 84 Ford Cortina, 86 Simca 1500 Break, 89 Peugeot 304, 85 Panhard 24BT.**
Row 3: **Norev 87 Citroen ID19 Break, 88 Citroen DS19 Cabriolet (x2), 139 Citroen Ami 8.**
Row 4: **Norev 120 Army Land Rover & Trailer, 137 Citroen Mehari, 92 Chrysler New Yorker & Boat Trailer.**

Row 1: **Norev 95 Berliet Auto Transporter.**
Row 2: **Norev 100 Saviem Cattle Truck, 101 Saviem Garbage Truck, 102 Saviem Milk Tanker.**
Row 3: **Norev 97 Berliet Ladder Truck, 111 Continental Bulldozer, 128 Richier Roller.**

Row 1: **Norev 103 BMW 2000 & Horse Trailer, 104 Peugeot 504 & Matra.**
Row 2: **Norev 94 Simca 1100 & Voilier, 105 Renault Tractor & Cattle Trailer.**
Row 3: **Norev 106 Renault Tractor & Cargo Trailer (x2).**
Row 4: **Norev 108 Mercedes-Benz 250SE & Porsche, 109 Fiat Dino & Ferrari GTB.**

Row 1: **Norev 112 Power Shovel, 114 Berliet Excavator Truck**
Row 2: **Norev 113 Berliet Dump Truck, 116 Berliet Bucket Truck, 117 Renault R-86 Tractor.**
Row 3. **Norev 126 Mercedes-Benz Cement Truck, 127 Richier Grader.**

Row 1: **Norev 131 Saviem Cherry Picker (x2), 220 Saviem Fire Tanker.**
Row 2: **Norev 125 Mercedes-Benz Truck & Trailer, 124 Mercedes-Benz Truck.**
Row 3: **Norev 133 Saviem Racing Car Transporter (x3).**

Row 1: **Norev 91 Simca Chambord & Henon Caravan, 93 Peugeot 404 & Digue Caravan.**
Row 2: **Norev 141 Porsche 911 Targa (x2), 142 Ferrari 275GTB (x2).**
Row 3: **Norev 140 Renault R12, 143 Matra 530A, 144 Triumph TR5, 148 Fiat 124.**
Row 4: **Norev 145 Lancia Flavia, 146 Fiat 525 (x2), 147 Peugeot 204 Coupe.**

Row 1: **Norev 149 Porsche Carrera 6 (x2), 174 Ligier JS3, 161 CD Le Mans, 156 Jaguar E-Type Coupe.**
Row 2: **Norev 150 Mercedes SSK (x3), 151 Simca 1100, 157 Citroen Dyane.**
Row 3: **Norev 158 Citroen DS21, 158 Citroen DS21 Police, 160 Peugeot 504, 163 Fiat Dino Coupe.**
Row 4: **Norev 152 Land Rover Police, 153 Land Rover Pickup, 159 Peugeot 404 Van, 154 Land Rover Wrecker, 155 Land Rover Expedition.**

Row 1: **Norev 167 Renault 15TS, 168 Renault 17TS, 162 Renault R6, 179 Alfa Romeo Montreal, 169 Citroen GS.**
Row 2: **Norev 171 Alpine A220, 172 Mercedes-Benz C-111, 181 Alfa Romeo 33, 180 Porsche 917.**
Row 3: **Norev 177 Opel GT, 188 Peugeot 104, 178 Renault 5, 183 Lancia Stratos, 182 Porsche 917.**
Row 4: **Norev 173 Ligier JS2 (x2), 170 Maserati Ghibli, 176 Alpine A310.**

Row 1: **Norev 186 Ferrari 246GTS, 184 Porsche Carrera RSR, 190 Renault 14TL with Luggage, 175 Mercedes-Benz 350, 191 Chevron B23.**
Row 2: **Norev 189 Matra Bagheera (x2), 201 Lola T294, 192 Ferrari 312P, 195 De Tomaso Pantera.**
Row 3: **Norev 193 Fiat X1/9 (x4), 215 Fiat X1/9 Abarth.**
Row 4: **Norev 196 Matra MS670 short, 197 MS670 long (x2), 198 Alpine A440.**

Row 1: **Norev 199 Mercedes-Benz Truck with Crane (x2), 230 BMW Police Motorcycle.**
Row 2: **Norev 233 Peugeot J7 Mail Van, 245 J7 Police Van, 252 J7 Ambulance, 251 J7 Road Service Van.**
Row 3: **Norev 246 Renault Estafette School Bus, 247 Citroen 1200 KG Police Van, 248 Peugeot J7 Bus with Skis, 254 Renault Estafette Van.**
Row 4: **Norev 212 Peugeot 504 Press Car & Cycles, 210 Peugeot J7 Ambulance & Lifeboat.**

Row 1: **Norev 205 Renault 16TX Taxi, 207 Citroen CX 2200, 211 Citroen ID19 Ambulance & Cycles, 214 Peugeot 504 Police.**

Row 2: **Norev 216 Renault 17TS Rally, 202 Renault 5 Driving School, 217 Renault 5 Rally, 240 Renault 5 Doctor, 218 Alpine A310 Rally.**

Row 3: **Norev 239 Alpine A310 Police, 222 Peugeot 504 Safari, 223 Simca 1308GT, 228 Renault 20TL.**

Row 4: **Norev 241 Renault R4 Fire, 344 Citroen ID19 Ambulance (x2), 341 Renault R4 Fire.**

Row 1: **Norev 356 Citroen 2CV6, 362 Volkswagen 1300, 332 Peugeot 204 Break, 389 Peugeot 304, 337 Citroen Mehari.**
Row 2: **Norev 317 Renault Tractor (x2), 326 Citroen 2CV Van, 512 Renault 30TS & Motorcycle Trailer.**
Row 3: **Norev 533 Peugeot 604 & Caravan, 541 Mercedes-Benz Ambulance & Police Motorcycles.**
Row 4: **Norev 521 Saviem, 522 DAF & 523 Volvo Milk Tankers.**

Row 1: **Norev 530 Saviem, 531 DAF & 532 Volvo Overhead Trucks.**
Row 2: **Norev 515 Saviem, 516 DAF & 517 Volvo Bottle Trucks.**
Row 3: **Norev 508 Saviem, 509 DAF & 510 Volvo Crane Trucks.**

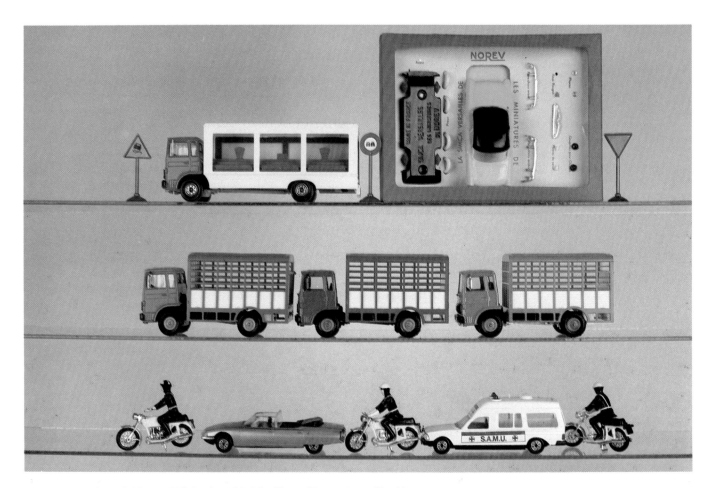

Row 1: **Norev 518 Saviem Mobile Shop, Simca Versailles kit.**
Row 2: **Norev 527 Saviem, 528 DAF & 529 Volvo Cattle Trucks.**
Row 3: **Norev 1509 Citroen Présidentielle & Escort, 874 Mercedes-Benz Ambulance & Escort (= 541, 506)**

Row 1: **Norev 601 Matra Formula 2 (x3), 700 Renault R4 Coca-Cola Van, 711 Renault R4 Van.**
Row 2: **Norev 603 DKW Junior, 606 Simca 1500, 604 Volkswagen 1500, 607 Fiat 1500.**
Row 3: **Norev 613 Volkswagen 1300, 701 Peugeot 404 Coupe, 702 Fiat 2300 Coupe, 703 Simca 1000 Coupe.**
Row 4: **Norev 704 Ford Taunus 12M, 705 Ford Cortina, 706 Fiat 124, 707 Simca 1100S.**

Row 1: **Norev 709 Mercedes-Benz C-111, 713 Lancia Stratos, 711 Renault 5, 710 Ligier JS3, 712 Porsche 917.**
Row 2: **Norev 708 Volkswagen 1600TL, 712 Alpine A310, 722 Citroen 2CV6, 761 Renault 14TL, 718 Ligier JS2.**
Row 3: **Norev 757 Peugeot 604, 714 Bertone Camargue, 762 Renault 20TL, 794 Citroen BX.**
Row 4: **Norev 780 Talbot Horizon, 781 Renault 18TL, 764 Porsche 924, 773 Ford Fiesta, 801 Peugeot 204 Coupe.**

Row 1: **Norev 803 Opel Rekord, 806 Citroen DS21, 807 Citroen SM, 808 Chrysler 180.**
Row 2: **Norev 804 Peugeot 304, 805 Renault R12, 806 Ligier JS3, 807 Talbot 1100S (x2).**
Row 3: **Norev 805 Renault 18TL Police, 811 Opel GT, 808 Renault 5, 810 Citroen GS, 812 Alpine A310.**
Row 4: **Norev 809 Alpine A220, 809 Mercedes-Benz C-111 (x3).**

Row 1: **Norev 815 Alfa Romeo 33, 821 Mercedes-Benz 350SL, 816 Alfa Romeo Montreal, 820 Maserati Ghibli.**
Row 2: **Norev 818 Ligier JS2 (x3), 818 Ligier JS2 Le Mans.**
Row 3: **Norev 822 Renault 15TS, 823 Renault 17TS (x3).**
Row 4: **Norev 824 Ferrari 246GTS, 825 Matra Simca Bagheera (x2), 829 De Tomaso Pantera.**

Row 1: **Norev 832 Matra MS670 short, 813 Lola T294, 833 Matra MS670 long, 835 Ferrari 312P, 834 Chevron B23.**
Row 2: **Norev 826 Peugeot 104 (x2), 836 Fiat X1/9, 839 Porsche Carrera RSR (x2).**
Row 3: **Norev 840 Alpine A440, 843 Citroen 2CV6, 846 Renault 17TS Rally, 847 Fiat X1/9 Abarth, 850 Renault 5 Driving School.**
Row 4: **Norev 838 Citroen SM Présidentielle, 841 Renault 16TX, 842 Peugeot 504, 845 Citroen CX 2200.**

Row 1: **Norev 849 Peugeot 504 Police, 852 Renault 16TX Taxi, 853 Volvo 264 Taxi, 856 Renault 30TS.**
Row 2: **Norev 851 Matra Simca Bagheera with Skis, 853 Renault 5 Rally, 854 BMW Turbo, 855 Alpine A310 Rally, 858 Alpine A442.**
Row 3: **Norev 857 Peugeot 604 (x3), 859 Peugeot 504 Safari.**
Row 4: **Norev 863 Lancia Stratos Alitalia, 860 Simca 1308GT, 861 Renault 14TL (x2), 864 Porsche 924.**

Row 1: **Norev 871 Alpine A310 Police, 865 Renault R4 Fire, 866 Renault R4 Police, 867 Renault R4 Mail, 872 Renault 18TL Police.**

Row 2: **Norev 870 De Tomaso Pantera, 868 BMW 633CF (x2), 869 BMW 633 Prototype.**

Row 3: **Norev 862 Renault 20TL, 881 Renault 18TL (x3).**

Row 4: **Norev 876 Simca 1308 Europe 1, 875 Renault 5 Doctor, 878 Volkswagen Golf (x2), 877 Ligier JS2 Le Mans.**

Row 1: **Norev 879 Peugeot 305 (x2), 880 Talbot Horizon, 882 Citroen Visa, 885 Porsche 924 Police.**
Row 2: **Norev 892 Ford Escort (x5).**
Row 3: **Norev 886 Volvo 264 (x3), 893 Talbot Solara.**
Row 4: **Norev 888 Alfa Romeo 6 (x4).**

Row 1: **Norev 887 Ford Mustang (x2), 890 Mercedes-Benz 280 (x2).**
Row 2: **Norev 884 VW Golf ADAC, 883 VW Golf Police, 891 Renault Fuego (x2), 895 Citroen BX.**
Row 3: **Norev 897 Renault 18TL, 898 Renault 9, 899 VW Golf Rally.**
Row 4: **Norev 889 Peugeot 505 (x2), 896 Volvo 264 Wagon (x2).**

Row 1: **Norev 400 Citroen BX, 401 Ligier JS2 (x3), 402 Matra Simca Bagheera (x3).**
Row 2: **Norev 404 Citroen GS (x3), 405 Peugeot 504 (x3), 415 Talbot 1510SX.**
Row 3: **Norev 406 Citroen CX (x3), 409 Renault 4L (x2), 410 Mercedes-Benz Ambulance (x2).**
Row 4: **Norev 407 Renault 12 (x4), 408 Citroen Dyane (x2), 412 Bertone Trapeze.**

Row 1: **Norev 411 Maserati Boomerang (x3), 413 Renault 30TS, 414 Peugeot 604 (x3).**
Row 2: **Norev 416 BMW 633CSI (x2), 417 Fiat 131 (x2), 419 Renault 14 (x2), #? Simca 1308.**
Row 3: **Norev 420 Peugeot 305SR (x2), 422 Renault 18GTS, 423 Volvo 264, 424 Ford Mustang, 809 BMW 2002.**
Row 4: **Norev 425 Mercedes-Benz 280SE, 428 Citroen Visa (x2), 430 Alfa Romeo 6, 431 Peugeot 505SR, 432 Fiat Ritmo, #? Renault 4L Fire.**

Row 1: **Norev 429 VW Golf, 437 Renault Fuego, 813 Porsche 911S (x2), 816 Ford Capri, 861 Renault 17, 421 Simca Horizon.**

Row 2: **Norev 854 Porsche 917, 438 Ford Escort, 871 Renault 5 (x3), 883 Citroen DS21 (x2).**

Row 3: **Norev 433 Volvo Crane Truck, 434 Volvo Fire Truck, 435 Volvo Tanker (x3), 436 Volvo Covered Truck.**

Row 4: **Norev 440 Volvo Milk Truck, 441 Volvo Propane Truck, 442 Volvo Ladder Truck, 446 Renault Cement Truck, 447 Renault Bucket Truck, 448 Renault Dump Truck.**

Row 1: **Norev 452 Renault Garbage Truck, 460 Chevrolet Camper, 461 Fire Truck, 462 Covered Truck, 464 Wrecker, 465 Pickup.**
Row 2: **Norev 466 Chevrolet Airport Truck, 467 Cattle Truck, 468 Pickup with Motorcycle, 525 Unic Auto Carrier.**
Row 3: **Norev 521 Unic Cement Truck, 522 Unic Milk Tanker, 523 Unic Propane Truck.**
Row 4: **Norev 525 Unic Titan Semi, 527 Unic Tanker, 528 Saviem Bus (x3).**

81

Row 1: **Norev 501 Simca Ariane, 501 Simca Versailles (x2), 502 Simca Aronde, 503 Citroen 2CV, 504 Citroen DS19, 505 Mercedes 220SE, 506 Panhard PL17, 507 Renault 4CV.**
Row 2: **Norev 508 Renault Dauphine, 509 Renault Estafette, 510 Renault Caravelle, 511 Renault 4L, 512 Citroen Ami 6, 513 Renault R4 Van (x2), 517 Peugeot 404 & Trailer, 518 Peugeot 404.**
Row 3: **Norev 514 Renault 8, 515 Citroen Van (x3), 516 Peugeot 403 Van, 519 Simca 1000, 529 Simca 1500 (x3).**
Row 4: **Norev 530 Panhard 24CT, 531 Renault 16 (x2), 532 Peugeot 204 (x3), 420 Unic Dumper (x2).**

Row 1: **Quiralu 1 Simca Trianon (x2), 4 & 7 Peugeot 402.**
Row 2: **Quiralu 2 Simca Versailles (x4).**
Row 3: **Quiralu 3 Simca Régence (x4).**
Row 4: **Quiralu 10 (x2) & 11 Simca Marly Break, 12 Simca Marly Ambulance.**

Row 1: **Quiralu 14 Porsche Carrera (x4), 19 Velam Isetta.**
Row 2: **Quiralu 8 & 9 (x2) Mercedes-Benz 300SL, 17 Rolls-Royce.**
Row 3: **Quiralu 15 Jaguar XK140 (x3), 17 Rolls-Royce.**
Row 4: **Quiralu 17 Rolls-Royce (x4).**

Row 1: **Quiralu 26 Berliet Dump Truck, 27 Covered Trailer.**
Row 2: **Quiralu 20 (x2) & 21 Renault Etoile Filante, 16 Messerschmitt.**
Row 3: **Quiralu 18 Vespa 400 (x3), 16 Messerschmitt (x2).**
Row 4: **22 Peugeot Primagaz Van, 23 Peugeot Thomson Van, 24 Peugeot Army Ambulance, old Hose Reel.**

Row 1: **Rami 1 Renault Taxi de la Marne, 2 De Dion-Bouton Vis-à-vis, 2 Motobloc, 3 Lion-Peugeot, 4 Citroen 5CV, 5 De Dion Cab.**
Row 2: **Rami 6 Bugatti 35, 7 Citroen B2, 8 Sizaire & Naudin, 9 Rochet-Schneider, 10 Hispano-Suiza.**
Row 3: **Rami 11 Gobron-Brillié, 12 Gauthier-Wehrlé, 13 Packard Landaulet, 14 Peugeot Coupe, 17 Panhard Marquise.**
Row 4: **Rami 15 Ford Model T, 16 Ford Tourer, 18 Panhard Ballon, 19 Hautier Electric, 20 Delaunay-Belleville.**

Row 1: **Rami 21 Georges Richard, 22 Scotte Steamer, 23 Renault Tonneau, 24 Lorraine-Dietrich, 25 Panhard Tonneau.**
Row 2: **Rami 26 Delahaye Phaeton, 27 Audibert & Lavirotte, 28 Léon Bollée, 29 SPA, 31 Luc Court.**
Row 3: **Rami 30 Amédée Bollée, 32 Brasier Landaulet, 33 Berliet, 34 Mieusset, 35 De Dion-Bouton.**
Row 4: **36 Lacroix de Laville, 37 Delage Torpedo, 38 Mercedes SSK.**

Row 1: **Safir 1 Peugeot Vis-à-vis, 2 Peugeot 1898 Victoria, 3 Peugeot 1899 Victoria, 4 Peugeot 1896, 5 Decauville, 6 Delahaye.**
Row 2: **Safir 7 Renault Paris-Vienna, 8 Ford Model T, 9 Citroen Taxi, 10 Renault Coupe, 11 Citroen Fire Truck.**
Row 3: **Safir 12 Citroen Ambulance, 13 Citroen Mail Truck, 14 Fiat 1901, 15 Mercedes 1901, 16 Renault 1899.**
Row 4: **Safir 17 Panhard 1898, 18 Peugeot 1900, 19 Peugeot Toit Bois, 22 & 23 Citroen Taxis.**

Row 1: **Safir 24 Renault Town Car, 101 Gregoire Triple Berline, 26 Unic Taxi.**
Row 2: **Safir 30, 31, 32 & 33 Lola T70.**
Row 3: **Safir 34 & 35 Lola T70, 40 & 41 Porsche 917.**
Row 4: **Safir 42, 43, 44 & 45 Porsche 917.**

Row 1: **Safir 50, 51, 52 & 53 Porsche 917.**
Row 2: **Safir 54 & 55 Porsche 917, 60 & 61 Ferrari 512M.**
Row 3: **Safir 62, 63, 64 & 65 Ferrari 512M.**
Row 4: **Safir 70, 71, 72 & 73 Porsche 917.**

Row 1: **Safir 74 & 75 Porsche 917, 82 & 83 Tyrrell P34.**
Row 2: **Racing Porsche 917 long (x4).**
Row 3: **Racing Porsche 917 short (x4).**
Row 4: **Racing Lola T70 (x4).**

Row 1: **Safir Berliet Covered (x2), Dump & Fire Trucks.**
Row 2: **Safir Berliet Garbage & Stake Trucks, Stradair Circus & Bottle Trucks.**
Row 3: **Safir Stradair Wrecker, Mercedes-Benz Cement, Covered & Crane Trucks.**
Row 4: **Safir 80 Ferrari 312T2, Mercedes-Benz Tanker (x3), 81 Ligier JS5.**

Row 1: **Safir Berliet Covered Truck & Trailer, Fire Truck & Trailer, 3 Love Jeep.**
Row 2: **Safir Mercedes-Benz Tanker & Trailer, Covered Truck & Trailer, 1 Taxi Jeep.**
Row 3: **Safir Stradair Circus Truck & Trailer, Circus Jeep, 4 Red Cross Jeep, Fire Jeep.**
Row 4: **Safir Dodge Wrecker, Circus Truck, Fire Truck (x2), Police Jeep.**

Row 1: **Safir Dodge USSR Rocket Truck & Trailer, Israeli Jeep & Trailer, USSR Jeep & Cannon.**
Row 2: **Safir Dodge USSR Radar Truck, USSR AA Gun Truck (x2), USSR Truck & Cannon.**
Row 3: **Safir Dodge US Radar Truck, Israeli Jeep, Dodge US Searchlight Truck, USSR Jeep, Dodge Israeli Searchlight Truck.**
Row 4: **Safir Dodge Ambulance, USA Jeep, Dodge French Army Truck, US Ranger Jeep, US Ambulance Truck.**

Row 1: **Safir Ferrari (x2), Honda (x2) & Lotus (x2) Racers.**
Row 2: **Safir STP Lotus (x2), Matra (x2) & McLaren (x2) Racers.**
Row 3: **Safir BRM (x3) & Tyrrell (x4) Racers.**
Row 4: **Safir Matra (x5) & March (x3) Racers.**

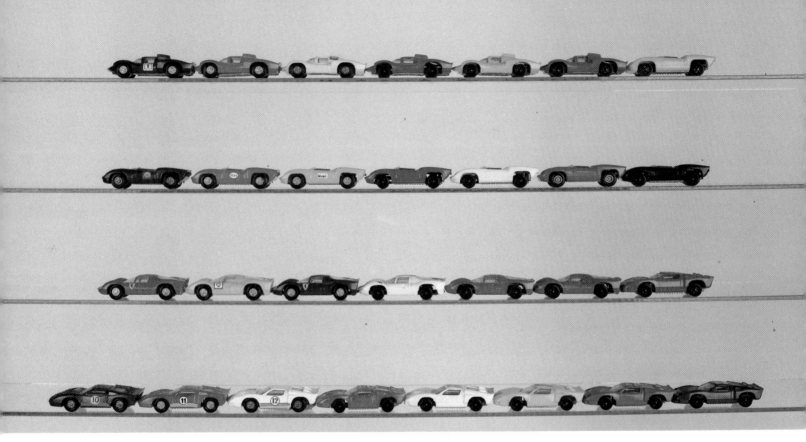

Row 1: **Safir Chapparal 2D (x6), Lola T-70.**
Row 2: **Safir Lola T-70 (x7).**
Row 3: **Safir Ferrari P4 (x6), Ford GT II.**
Row 4: **Safir Ford GT II (x8).**

Row 1: **Safir Citroen 2CV (x4), Saviem Dump Truck (x2).**
Row 2: **Safir Land Rover Safari (x4), Saviem Box Van (x2).**
Row 3: **Safir Renault Estafette Van (x4), Saviem Garbage Truck (x2).**
Row 4: **Safir Saviem Flat Trucks with Rocket (x2), Airplane, Site Hut, & Boat (x2).**

Row 1: **Safir Porsche 917 short (x3) & long (x3).**
Row 2: **Safir Ferrari 512S (x3), Matra 650 (x3).**
Row 3: **Les Routiers 3 Berliet Dumper, 4 Citroen Wrecker, 11 Renault Byrrh Tanker, 5 Citroen Dumper, 7 Richier Roller, Safir Matra 650.**
Row 4: **Jadali 51 Esso Tanker, 55 Compressor, 56 Roller, #? Ford Model T, Gitanes Renault Mail Van, Citroen 2CV, Aston Martin, Gordini.**

Row 1: **Bourbon Poclain GY120 Shovel (2 types).**
Row 2: **Bourbon Poclain TY45, Poclain TY45 Shovel, Bourbon Poclain LY2P Shovel.**
Row 3: **Bourbon Berliet Tanker, Poclain TC45 Shovel.**

Row 1: **Salza Peugeot Van, Aspro Ambulance, Peugeot Loudspeaker Van, Jeep.**
Row 2: **Cofalu Kart, Peugeot 404, Salza Peugeot 203, Peugeot 404.**
Row 3: **Joustra Meiller Excavator, 4002 Meiller Dumper, PR Waterman & Savon Le Chat Vans.**

Row 1: **Bonux Isotta-Fraschini 1902, Peugeot 203, Roller, Double-deck Bus, Peugeot 1898, anon. Jeep.**
Row 2: **Shell Ferrari, JF Record Car, anon. Sedan, Four-Seat Roadster.**
Row 3: **Anon. Simca 9, green Sports Coupe, Renault 1908, Bugatti Le Mans, pink Sports Coupe.**
Row 4: **Anon. Cisitalia, Bugatti Formula 1, Motorcycle, Renault Frégate, Fastback Sedan.**

Row 1: **Midget Toys 1 Flat Truck, 2 Lumber Semi, 3 Quarry Dumper, 4 Tractor, 5 Open Semi, 6 Panhard, Citroen DS19.**
Row 2: **Midget Toys Vespa 400 (x2), 1/43 Vespa 400 (x2), 14 Crane Truck, Transformer Carrier, Jaguar D-Type, Vanwall.**
Row 3: **CIJ M1 Somua Bus, M2 Peugeot 403, M3 Renault Van, M4 Renault Dumper, M5 Renault Tanker, M6 Renault Ambulance, M7 Renault 1000 KG Van, M8 Renault Dauphine.**
Row 4: **CIJ M9 Simca Ariane, M10 Renault Army Ambulance, three RD Marmande balsa models (not listed in text).**

Row 1: **JP Cars 11 Delahaye Racer (x2), 14 Racing Car, 18 Petite Rosalie, 19 Rosalie.**
Row 2: **JP 13 Maserati, 12 Bugatti Le Mans, 15 Peugeot 402 Cabriolet, 33 Renault Nervasport.**
Row 3: **JP 21 Citroen CR Roadster, 22 Moteur Flottant version, 24 Citroen C4 Sedan, 26 Citroen Barrel Truck, 27 Citroen Livestock Truck.**
Row 4: **JP 34 Renault Fire Truck, 35 Renault Street Sprinkler, 37 Renault Coal Truck, 38 Renault Open Truck.**

Row 1: **JP Cars 36 Renault Brewery Truck, 101 Citroen Fire Truck, 42 Citroen Fire Ambulance, Rhodanienne Army Ambulance.**
Row 2: **Gege Simca Aronde, Citroen DS19, Peugeot 403, BS Simca Ariane.**
Row 3: **Del Lion-Peugeot 1908, Voison 1934, Fiat 1926 Torpedo, Citroen B2 1925, Lancia Lambda 1925.**
Row 4: **Del Renault Paris-Vienna 1902, Desormeaux Le Zebre 1910 & Citroen 5CV 1923, Les Rouliers Renault Etoile Filante, Faracars 101 STP Turbine.**

THE EARLY BRANDS

It is impossible to say much about the earliest French manufacturers of miniature vehicles, for very little is known of their histories. A.R. probably began production in the early twenties and may have continued into the early fifties, but its best models were made between 1930 and 1939; it specialized in models of Peugeot, some of which were probably used as showroom models. A.R. products, usually part lead and part tinplate, include some fine models which are extremely rare today. Judging from their relative lack of rarity, the firm's series of Peugeot 301 trucks may well have been produced into the early postwar years; they all use the same cast chassis-cab unit, with a wide variety of tin rear bodies. Some A.R. models have tin baseplates, and their wheels vary from disc types of cast lead or other materials to cast hubs with rubber tires. Other than the 301 trucks, some of which must still go for two-figure amounts, and perhaps one or two other items, A.R. models should be worth over $100 each, but I cannot be more precise than that.

C.D. began production in the mid-twenties and continued for about a decade. This firm specialized in Renault models plus those of other French marques such as Delage, Delahaye, Bugatti, Hotchkiss, Rosengart, and Chenard & Walcker. Values of C.D. models should generally be somewhere over $100 each.

The firm of Citroen made their own models of their own cars and trucks, not only of lead but also of sheet metal and a material soon adopted by other manufacturers as well: plaster and flour. Two firms whose best days were yet to come, C.I.J. and J.R.D., also produced plaster-and-flour models in pre-war days. As for their values, your guess may well be better than mine–in fact, I'd rather not guess.

Even less is known of another firm, S.R., and we cannot even arrive at a more-or-less complete list of their products, but will list what we know to be theirs and add such models as bear a resemblance to them in workmanship. As for values, they should generally be well below $100, but again I'd rather not guess.

As scant as our data on pre-war French models is, we cannot offer very thorough listings of the individual models, for in many cases we do not even have a photograph to work from. Thus this list will of necessity be a fragmentary one.

A.R.

AIRPLANE
High wing monoplane, cast fuselage and wheels, tin wings and propeller.

AUTOGIRO
Cast body and hubs, tin rotor and propeller, rubber tires. Are hubs and tires original?

BLUEBIRD 126 mm
Record car, cast body with driver, unpainted cast wheels.
    1. Light blue body.

DISC HARROW 86 mm
Cast front and rear frames, unpainted discs, spoked wheels, two white plastic spacers.
    1. Light blue frames.

LATIL ANTI-AIRCRAFT GUN TRUCK 83 mm
Cast chassis, gun, mount, and wheels, tin seats and rear, wire trigger.
    1. Olive body parts, gun, mount, and wheels.

LATIL COVERED FARM TRUCK 85 mm
Cast cab-chassis, red wheels, black tin seats and rear, gray cover.
    1. Black body parts.

LATIL DUMP TRUCK
Cast chassis, black roofed cab and unpainted wheels, green tin tipper parts.
    1. Red chassis, black cab.

LATIL FARM TRUCK 85 mm
Same as covered farm truck minus top.
    1. Black body parts.

LATIL FIRE LADDER TRUCK
Same chassis unit as above. No other data.

LATIL TANK TRUCK
Cast chassis, tank, black roofed cab and unpainted wheels.
    1. Red chassis and tank, black cab.

PEUGEOT ANDREAU COUPE
Streamlined car with tail fin, cast body, grille, and hubs, tin base, rubber tires. Light green, maroon or gray body.

PEUGEOT ANDREAU LIMOUSINE
Streamlined car with tail fin, cast body, grille, and hubs, tin base, rubber tires. Pale blue body.

PEUGEOT COACH
Existence questionable.

PEUGEOT DARL'MART CABRIOLET
Streamlined sports roadster, cast body and hubs, rubber tires.

PEUGEOT 201 COUPE
No data.

PEUGEOT 201 LIMOUSINE
No data.

PEUGEOT 201 ROADSTER 81 mm
Open two-seater, cast body, black chassis, grille-headlights, dash-windshield-steering wheel, wheels, and spare, "Peugeot 201" on grille. Red, yellow, green or blue body.

PEUGEOT 202 SEDAN 88 mm
Sedan, cast body and hubs, white tires. Cream body.

PEUGEOT 301 CONVERTIBLE COUPE
Cast body and matching hubs, rubber tires, rear spare, tan convertible top, red or green body.

PEUGEOT 301 LIMOUSINE 90 mm
Sedan with cast body, unpainted grille and wheels, or cast hubs and white tires. Three basic casting types; some versions have lettering on roof: "Roues Avants Independantes Peugeot." Red, green, blue, or gray & blue body, black tin chassis.

PEUGEOT 301 ROADSTER
May not be A.R. product; resembles other 301 types but has no headlights. Red body, cast wheels.

PEUGEOT 301 STREAMLINED COUPE
Similar to convertible coupe, with slightly less squarish lines, spare faired into rear. Yellow, blue-green, or gray body.

PEUGEOT 302
Existence questionable.

PEUGEOT 402 FUSEAU SOCHAUX
Two-door fastback, cast body, grille, and hubs, open front wheels, tin base, rubber tires, name on spare wheel cover. Red, light green, green, or brown body.

PEUGEOT 402 FUSEAU SOCHAUX
As above but with covered front wheels.

PEUGEOT 601 TWO-DOOR SEDAN 105 mm
Two-door with cast body, chassis, grille, and hubs, white rubber tires, tin base panel holds axles in place; two-tone red, green, blue, or gray body and chassis (chassis darker).

PEUGEOT 301 AMBULANCE VAN 82 mm
Cast cab-chassis and wheels, light gray tin rear and cover, red cross labels.
1. Light gray cab-chassis and wheels.

PEUGEOT 301 ARMY TRUCK
Cast cab-chassis and wheels, tin rear.

PEUGEOT 301 BARREL TRUCK 90 mm
Cast cab-chassis and wheels, light green tin rear, three tan wooden barrels.
1. Light green cab-chassis and wheels.

PEUGEOT 301 CABLE TRUCK 90 mm
Cast cab-chassis and wheels, green tin rear body with brackets for red wooden spool, wire crank.
1. Green cab-chassis, rear body, and wheels.

PEUGEOT 301 CRANE TRUCK
Cast cab-chassis and wheels. No other data.

PEUGEOT 301 DUMP TRUCK 92 mm
Cast cab-chassis and wheels, green tin tipper and opening tailboard.
1. Maroon cab-chassis and wheels.

PEUGEOT 301 ELEVATOR TRUCK
Cast cab-chassis and wheels. No other data

PEUGEOT 301 FARM TRUCK 89 mm
Cast cab-chassis and wheels, green tin rear body.
1. Maroon cab-chassis and wheels.

PEUGEOT 301 FIRE TRUCK 95 mm
Cast cab-chassis and wheels, red tin rear body with ladder racks, unpainted ladder.
> 1. Red cab-chassis and wheels.

PEUGEOT 301 LUMBER TRUCK 98 mm
Cast cab-chassis and unpainted wheels, light blue tin rear body, three dowels.
> 1. Light blue cab-chassis.

PEUGEOT 301 MAIL TRUCK 85 mm
Cast cab-chassis, rear body, and wheels, yellow-on-black "Postes" labels.
> 1. Light green cab-chassis, body, and wheels.

PEUGEOT 301 MILK TRUCK 90 mm
Cast cab-chassis and wheels, light blue tin rear body holding five unpainted cast milk cans.
> 1. Light blue cab-chassis and wheels.

PEUGEOT 301 MIRROR TRUCK
Cast cab-chassis and wheels. No other data.

PEUGEOT 301 TANK TRUCK
Cast cab-chassis and wheels. No other data.

PEUGEOT 301 VAN
Probably same components as ambulance and mail truck.

PEUGEOT 301 VAT TRUCK 88 mm
Cast cab-chassis and wheels, light blue tin rear body, tan wooden vat.
> 1. Light blue cab-chassis and wheels.

PLOW
Questionable–may be same model as disc harrow.

RENAULT 1914
Existence questionable.

RENAULT PARIS BUS 97 mm
Cast body and unpainted wheels, tin roof.
> 1. Green body, cream roof.

RENAULT PARIS BUS 97 mm.
Cast body, roof with signboard, and unpainted wheels.

RENAULT TANK 63 mm
Cast body and unpainted wheels, white rubber tracks. Turret cast in, does not rotate.
> 1. Red body.

STEAM ROLLER
Cast body, front roller mount, and rollers.
> 1. Red body and rollers.
> 2. Dark blue body, silver rollers.

TAXI 67 mm
Cast body and wheels. With or without window posts. Resembles Tootsietoy Yellow Cab.
> 1. Silver body.

TOWING TRACTOR
Cast body and spoked wheels. Resembles pre-war Tootsietoy tractor, but is not a copy.

TRACTION ENGINE 73 mm
Cast body with driver, unpainted spoked wheels.
  1. Red body.

C.D.

Less is known about C.D. than about A.R. The following is a composite of what has been published and what little I know. In most cases, I can do no more than list the models.

BUGATTI SPORTS CAR

CHENARD & WALCKER AMBULANCE

CHENARD & WALCKER LIMOUSINE
Appears to have cast body and disc wheels.

CHENARD & WALCKER "RICARD" VAN

CHENARD & WALCKER WRECKER 85 mm
Cast body, chassis, and unpainted wheels, silver grille.
  1. Blue body, red chassis.

DELAGE LIMOUSINE

DELAHAYE AMBULANCE
Appears to have cast body, chassis, and disc wheels; light body with dark stripe bearing lettering.

DELAHAYE FIRE TRUCK

DELAHAYE LIMOUSINE

DELAHAYE TORPEDO

DELAHAYE VAN

FORD MODEL T

HOTCHKISS LIMOUSINE

LATIL FARM TRUCK

LATIL VAN 92 mm
Box van with cast body, chassis, and unpainted wheels. Light green body, red chassis.

MG RECORD CAR

PANHARD TRACTOR

PEUGEOT SANS SOUPAPE

RENAULT 40 CV BERLINE 94 mm
Four-window sedan with cast body, chassis, and wheels. Two-tone blue body shown is probably repainted.
  1. Red body, black chassis.

RENAULT 40 CV COUPE

RENAULT 40 CV LIMOUSINE
Six-window sedan with cast body, apparently chassis and hubs, rubber tires. Probably similar to Berline above.

RENAULT 40 CV TORPEDO

RENAULT 40 CV AMBULANCE
Cast body and chassis, red cross and Tricolor labels, wheels and tires not original as shown.
    1. Gray body, cream roof, black chassis.

RENAULT 40 CV ARMY AMBULANCE 85 mm
Cast body, top, and spoked wheels, red cross labels. Completely different model from ambulance listed just above.
    1. Olive body, top, and wheels.

RENAULT 40 CV DUMPING SEMI-TRAILER TRUCK

RENAULT 40 CV FLAT SEMI-TRAILER TRUCK

RENAULT 40 CV HEAVY FLAT TRUCK

RENAULT 40 CV LIGHT FLAT TRUCK

RENAULT 40 CV HIGH-SIDE STAKE TRUCK

RENAULT 40 CV LOW-SIDE STAKE TRUCK

RENAULT 40 CV MAIL TRUCK

RENAULT 40 CV OPEN TRUCK 95 mm
Haven't seen it listed but have seen the model; open truck with cast body, chassis, and unpainted wheels. Green body, black chassis.

RENAULT 40 CV "SAPONITE" VAN

RENAULT 40 CV WRECKER

RENAULT VIVAQUATRE COUPE

RENAULT VIVAQUATRE LIMOUSINE 99 mm
Sedan with cast body including chassis, cast hubs, white tires. Yellow-green body, black chassis.

ROSENGART SUPER TRACTION FASTBACK

ROSENGART SUPER TRACTION ROADSTER

CITROEN
    All models are of Citroens, all to 1/43 scale. The first models listed are cast in lead, followed by plaster-and-flour and sheet metal models. At least one of each will be shown.

CITROEN B 14 COUPE 85 mm
Coupe with cast body, hood-grille, chassis, wheels, and spare. Black body, red roof, unpainted grille, black and white wheels.

CITROEN B 14 FOUR-WINDOW SEDAN

CITROEN B 14 SIX-WINDOW SEDAN 88 mm
Sedan with cast body, hood-grille, chassis, wheels, and spare. Blue upper body, maroon lower body, silver grille, gold radiator shell, or cream upper, red lower body, black chassis, unpainted grille, black and white wheels.

CITROEN B 14 STAKE TRUCK

CITROEN B 14 TORPEDO 85 mm
Open 4-seater with cast body, hood-grille, chassis, wheels, and spare. Light gray body, gray hood, black chassis, black and white wheels.

CITROEN B 14 TOWN CAR

Plaster and Flour Models:

CITROEN C4 CABRIOLET, Moteur Flottant

CITROEN C4 COUPE

CITROEN C4 CONVERTIBLE COUPE

CITROEN C4 4-WINDOW SEDAN

CITROEN C4 6-WINDOW SEDAN

CITROEN C4 CATTLE TRUCK

CITROEN C4 COAL TRUCK

CITROEN C4 FIRE TRUCK

CITROEN C4 LADDER TRUCK

CITROEN C4 PRODUCE TRUCK

CITROEN C4 SAND TRUCK

CITROEN C4 TANK TRUCK

CITROEN C4 VAT TRUCK

CITROEN ROSALIE CABRIOLET

CITROEN ROSALIE CABLE TRUCK

CITROEN ROSALIE FIRE ENGINE

CITROEN ROSALIE FIRE TRUCK

CITROEN ROSALIE MILK TRUCK

CITROEN ROSALIE SEMI-TRAILER TRUCK

CITROEN ROSALIE STAKE TRUCK

CITROEN ROSALIE WRECKER

CITROEN P45 BUS

CITROEN P45 DUMP TRUCK

CITROEN P45 FIRE TRUCK WITH LADDER

CITROEN P45 FIRE TRUCK WITH 4 MEN

CITROEN P45 SACK TRUCK

CITROEN P45 SAND TRUCK

CITROEN P45 STREET SWEEPER

CITROEN P45 TANK TRUCK

CITROEN P45 WRECKER

CITROEN P45 SEMI WITH CRATES

CITROEN P45 SEMI WITH PRODUCE

CITROEN P45 SEMI WITH SAND

CITROEN P45 MILK TANKER SEMI

CITROEN P45 GAS TANKER SEMI

1/43 Sheet Metal Models:
CITROEN ROSALIE CABRIOLET

CITROEN ROSALIE COUPE

CITROEN ROSALIE FAUX CABRIOLET

S.R. AND OTHERS

Some of these were definitely made by S.R., while others are not marked with a maker's name but resemble S.R. products in terms of workmanship. Some still have their original finish, or at least traces thereof, others have been repainted, still others have lost their finish.

BUS   55 mm
Single-deck bus with cast body, roof, and spoked hubs, "Compagnie Generale des Omnibus" lettering cast in, S.R. cast inside.
1. Silver body.

CANNON   95 mm
Cast chassis, gun, and two spoked wheels, spring-operated gun.
1. Light gray chassis, gun, and wheels.

CAISSON   63 mm
Cast body, opening lid, and two spoked wheels. Cannon hooks on.
1. Light gray body, lid, and wheels, brown tongue.

CAR WITH COVERED REAR SEAT   46 mm

Car with cast body including rear roof, spoked wheels, and steering wheel, S.R. cast on bottom.
1. Unknown original color.

CAR WITH OPEN REAR SEAT   62 mm
Car with cast body, spoked wheels, and base of something in open space between front and rear seats, S.R. cast on bottom.
1. Unknown original color.

DOUBLE-DECK BUS   60 mm
Cast body and four spoked wheels, "General" lettering cast in, S.R. cast inside.
1. Light gray body and wheels.

FORD MODEL T   75 mm
Open tourer with cast body, spoked wheels, and steering wheel, S.R. cast inside.
1. Gold body, wheels, and steering wheel.

LADDER TRUCK   60 mm
Cast body, spoked wheels, and steering wheel, S.R. cast inside. "Ladders" may just be stake sides.
1. Unknown original color.

MERCEDES 1914 GRAND PRIX CAR   60 mm
Racer with cast body and cream spoked wheels; may have had driver or steering wheel.
1. Red body.

MOTORCYCLE AND SIDECAR   87 mm
Cast cycle, sidecar, and three spoked wheels.
1. Red cycle, sidecar, and wheels.

OPEN TRUCK   63 mm

Cast body, spoked wheels, and steering wheel.
  1. Bronzed body?, gold grille.

SELF-PROPELLED GUN 86 mm
Cast body, gun, and spoked wheels, spring-operated gun.
  1. Gold body, gun, and wheels.

SELF-PROPELLED GUN 55 mm
Identical to above but smaller, S.R. cast inside.
  1. Light gray body, gun, and wheels.

SPORTS ROADSTER 62 mm
Cast body, wheels, and steering wheel, S.R. cast inside.
  1. Blue body, black interior and fenders, gold grille (repainted).

STEAM SHOVEL 56 mm
Cast chassis, cab-boom, shovel, and spoked wheels.
  1. Dark gray chassis and other parts.

TANK 138 mm
Army tank with cast body, turning turret, tail, dummy tracks, and spoked wheels, S.R. cast inside. (Biggest and best S.R. I've ever seen!)
  1. Cream, tan, dark green, and black camouflage paint.

TOURING CAR 57 mm
Tourer with cast body including closed rear doors, spoked wheels, probably steering wheel.
  1. Silver body.

TOURING CAR 58 mm
Tourer with cast body without rear doors, spoked wheels, no sign of steering wheel.
  1. Black body?

TOWN CAR 52 mm
Two similar models. Cast body and disc or spoked wheels.
  1. Brown body, gold disc hubs (repainted).
  2. Bronzed body, spoked hubs, S.R. cast inside.

TRUCK CAB AND TRAILER 105 mm
Cast cab, trailer, and unpainted wheels, silver trailer bed, brown tin cover. Also found without cover, but was it issued that way? Resembles cast lead Citroen models, possibly may be one.
  1. Maroon cab and trailer, black fenders.
  2. Blue cab, black fenders, green trailer.

WARSHIP 84 mm
Cast body with curved sides, three spoked wheels.
  1. Light gray body and wheels.

WARSHIP 74 mm
Cast body with flat sides, four wheels.
  1. Gray body and wheels.

YELLOW TAXI 60 mm
Taxi with cast body and wheels, black roof, and interior, "Yellow Taxi" lettering cast on doors.
  1. Yellow body (repainted; exists in other colors).

  Two other early French cars, a two-seater with sloping nose and tail, and an unusual open car that is actually a whistle, will also be shown. I have no idea who made them. A few sheet metal models from pre-war days will also be shown in the photos. The pre-war C.I.J. and J.R.D. plaster-and-flour models will be listed in the chapters on those brands.

C.I.J.

The initials of C.I.J. stand for Compagnie Industrielle du Jouet. The firm made large-scale tin toy cars in the twenties and began to produce 1/43 scale models of plaster and flour about 1933. While some were made completely of plaster and flour, others, notably truck models, had tinplate chassis, the wheels were either cast metal or a combination of metal hubs and rubber tires. We are not at all sure that our list of these models is complete, but can only offer what we know—or at least suspect.

In 1938 the firm made at least one 1/43 scale cast lead model. This was a Renault Vivagrand Sport coupe, pictures of which appeared in "Ma Collection" some years ago.

In 1950 the firm began to make diecast models. Production continued until 1964 and included some very interesting and highly prized items: some fine models of French trucks, tractors, and farm equipment, and even two models of American sedans. On the other hand, some C.I.J. diecast models were plagued with metal fatigue, while others—notably the 3/30 fire engine—were mere caricatures instead of scale models.

The name "Europarc" was subsequently added to that of C.I.J. Though I cannot substantiate it, I seem to recall reading that the firm moved its factory to a new industrial park called Europarc, but as no one else has mentioned this, I may well be mistaken.

Early C.I.J. diecast models usually had plain sheet metal bases; some bore only the name of the car, while later models' bases include the firm's name as well as that of the model. Early models often had cast one-piece metal wheels; later models ran on conventional cast hubs and black or white rubber tires, and included typical features such as clear plastic windows and opening doors. Since some models were produced over a period of years during which new wheel types and other features were introduced, it is quite possible that they exist in more than one form, but I can only list what I know to exist. Additional information, as always, will be much appreciated.

In 1963 C.I.J. absorbed J.R.D. and produced a number of J.R.D. models unchanged except for the occasional new body color or application of tape with the C.I.J. name to the base. At least one of these hybrids, though, has a completely plain base, and some of them that left the factory with blue CIJ tape have since lost it. As C.I.J. closed its doors a year after absorbing J.R.D., these hybrid models are not plentiful.

Most C.I.J. catalog numbers begin with 3/, this apparently being their usual series of model cars and trucks. A few issues begin with 4/ instead; some of these are motorized versions of the 3/ series models, while others are variations of 3/ types. The firm also made diecast airplanes, their numbers prefixed with 1/, a small number of accessories with other prefixes,and a series of HO scale models whose catalog numbers begin with the letter M.

PLASTER AND FLOUR MODELS
Value $50 and up. See J. P. Cars for reissues of some of these models.
BUGATTI RACING CAR 1/43 1934

BUGATTI 'TANK' SPORTS CAR 1/43 1938

CITROEN BOUBOULE RACING CAR 1/43 1933

CITROEN PETITE ROSALIE 1/43 1933

CITROEN ROSALIE 1/43 1933

CITROEN ROSALIE TYPE 3 1/43 1933

DELAHAYE RACING CAR 1/43 1935

MG SPEED RECORD CAR 1/43 1935

RENAULT BREWERY TRUCK 1/43 1935

RENAULT CLOSED VAN 1/43 1935

RENAULT COAL TRUCK 1/43 1935

RENAULT DUMP TRUCK 1/43 1935

RENAULT FIRE TRUCK 93 mm 1/43 1935
Hose truck with one-piece body including black and silver driver and fireman, three hose reels, silver grille, red sheet metal chassis, unpainted hubs, white tires, Renault decals.
    1. Red body and chassis.

RENAULT HOSE TRUCK 91 mm 1/43 1935
Ladder truck with one-piece body including black and silver driver and fireman, silver grille, red sheet metal ladder, mount and chassis, unpainted hubs, white tires, Renault decals.
    1. Red body and chassis.

RENAULT FLAT TRUCK 1/43 1935

RENAULT NERVASPORT 1/43 1935

RENAULT SACK TRUCK 1/43 1935

CAST MODELS
RENAULT VIVA GRAND SPORT 1/43 1938
Sport coupe, cast body and wheels or hubs with rubber tires.
    1. Two-piece windshield and rear window, cast wheels.
    2. One-piece windshield and rear window, cast wheels.
    3. One-piece windshield and rear window, hubs and tires.

AIRCRAFT
Fuselage length x wingspan. Value $40 and up.
1/1 FOUGA 53 x 66 mm
Jet fighter plane, single casting, blue canopy and wing tanks, roun-

dels.
    1. Silver body.

1/2 NORÉCRIN 42 x 61 mm
Small monoplane, single casting, blue canopy, wing tips, and stripes.
    1. White body.

1/10 SE 210 CARAVELLE 104 x 115 mm
Jet airliner, body casting plus unpainted landing gear, blue and white "Caravelle" and trim.
    1. White upper fuselage and tail, rest of plane silver.

1/11 DOUGLAS DC 7 103 x 117 mm
Four-propeller airliner, body casting plus unpainted landing gear, blue "DC 7" and windows, red trim.
    1. White body.

1/12 NORATLAS 71 x 107 mm
Twin-boom plane, body casting plus unpainted landing gear, roundel decals, blue and red stripes, blue windows.
    1. Silver body, white upper cabin.

1/14 BREGUET DEUX PONTS 98 x 114 mm
Four-engine plane, body casting plus unpainted landing gear, tin propellers, blue trim and "Air France" logo.
    1. White upper fuselage, silver lower fuselage and wings.

1/15 BOEING 707 125 x 135 mm
Four-engine jetliner, body casting plus unpainted landing gear, silver engines, blue windows, red trim.
    1. White body.

1/16 DOUGLAS DC 6 103 x 117 mm

Four-engine plane, body casting plus unpainted landing gear, tin propellers, yellow and blue "UAT Aeromatique" logo and trim, black F-B GTX lettering.
    1. White upper fuselage, silver lower fuselage and wings.

1/20 CARAVELLE AIR FRANCE 104 x 115 mm
Same casting etc. as 1/10, "Air France" logo.
    1. White upper fuselage, silver lower fuselage and wings.

1/30 BOEING 707 AIR FRANCE 125 x 135 mm
Same casting etc. as 1/15, "Air France" logo.
    1. White upper fuselage, silver lower fuselage and wings.

1/43 SCALE DIECAST MOTOR VEHICLES

3/1 DE ROVIN 91 mm 1954
Open two-seater, cast body, silver tin chassis, tin frame with clear plastic windshield, turned hubs, white tires, silver grille, headlights, and trim, red taillights. Value $75-95.
    1. Black body.
    2. Light purple body.

3/2 RENAULT ÉTOILE FILANTE 109 mm 1957
Record car with cast body, blue tin chassis, plastic driver, clear windshield, turned hubs, black tires, white name decal, red and white trim. Value $80-95.
    1. Blue body.

3/3 FACEL VEGA FACELLIA 96 mm 1958/60
Hardtop convertible, cast body, tin chassis, plastic interior and windows, removable hardtop, turned hubs, black tires, silver bumpers, grille, and headlights, red taillights. Value $75-95.
    1. Metallic maroon body.

2. Metallic gray body.

3/4 CITROEN ID19 ESTATE CAR 114 mm 1958/59

Wagon, cast body and chassis, plastic interior, clear windows, turned hubs, black tires, silver grille, bumpers, headlights, and trim, red and yellow taillights. Value $75-95.
1. Orange and white body, blue interior.
2. Two-tone blue body, ? interior.

3/5 PANHARD DYNA JUNIOR 90 mm 1954

Two-seater, cast body, silver gray tin chassis, cream top, black windshield frame, silver gray hubs, white tires, cream cast-in folded top, red seats, silver grille, bumper, and headlights, red taillights, painted-on door lines. Value $75-95.
1. Red body.
2. Blue body.

3/6 CITROEN AMI 6 90 mm 1964

Four-door sedan, cast body, matching tin chassis, clear plastic windows, red interior, turned hubs, black tires, silver bumpers and headlights, red taillights, suspension. Value $50-65.
1. Light green and white body.
2. Two-tone blue body.

3/7 SIMCA 1000 SEDAN 86 mm 1962/63

Four-door sedan, cast body, tin chassis, clear plastic windows, orange interior, turned hubs, black tires, silver grille, bumpers, and headlights, red taillights, suspension. Value $50-65.
1. Light blue body.

3/8 SIMCA 1000 POLICE CAR 86 mm 1963

Same casting and parts as 3/7 plus red roof light, white "Police" lettering. Value $50-65.

1. Black body, white fenders and roof.

3/9 SIMCA 1000 COUPE BERTONE 89 mm 1964

Two-door coupe, cast body, opening hood, doors and trunk, black tin chassis, clear plastic windows, blue interior, turned hubs, black tires, silver bumper and headlights, yellow (or red?) taillights. Value $50-65.
1. Red body.
2. Blue body.

3/10 VOLKSWAGEN 92 mm 1954

Two-door sedan, cast body, tin chassis, red hubs, white tires, silver bumper and headlights, red taillights. Value $60-75.
1. Cream body.
2. Metallic gray-green body.
3. Metallic gray body.

3/10 CITROEN 11CV 103 mm 1964/65

Reissued JRD #112; no changes. Value $50-65.
1. Gray body.
2. Black body.

3/12 MERCEDES-BENZ 220 SEDAN 104 mm 1959

Four-door sedan, cast body, metallic gray tin chassis, silver radiator shell, bumpers, headlights, and hubs, white tires, red or yellow taillights. Value $60-75.
1. Red body.
2. Gray body.

3/13 PEUGEOT 404 SEDAN 111 mm 1965

Reissued JRD #151, no changes. Value $50-65.
1. White body.
2. Red body.

3/15 CHRYSLER WINDSOR SEDAN 111 mm 1956
Four-door sedan, cast body, silver gray tin chassis, turned hubs, white tires, silver grille, bumpers, trim, and headlights, red taillights. Value $125-150.
  1. Light green body, dark green roof.
  2. Light blue body, dark blue roof.

3/16 PLYMOUTH BELVEDERE SEDAN 113 mm 1957
Four-door sedan, cast body, silver gray tin chassis, turned hubs, white tires, silver grille, bumpers, trim, and headlights, red or yellow taillights. Value $125-150.
  1. Red body, cream roof and trim.
  2. Blue body, cream roof and trim.

3/20 PANHARD B.P. TANK TRUCK 100 mm 1951
Tanker, cast body, silver gray tin chassis, turned hubs, black tires, yellow or green "BP Energic Energol" decals, yellow trim, silver grille and bumpers. Small scale. Value $60-75.
  1. Green body, yellow logo.
  2. Green body, green logo on yellow panel.

3/21 RENAULT SHELL TANK TRUCK 100 mm 1952
Tanker, cast body, silver gray tin chassis, turned hubs, black tires, black fenders and lower sides, "Shell" decals, silver grille, bumpers, catwalks, and headlights. Small scale. Value $60-75.
  1. Red cab, yellow tank.

3/23 BERLIET GLR 19 TANK TRUCK 139 mm 1959
Tanker, cast cab, tank, and chassis, silver hubs, black tires, unpainted tin ladders. Value $70-85.
  1. No other data.

3/24 BERLIET GLR 19 SHELL TANKER 139 mm 1959
Same castings and parts as 3/23 plus red "Shell" decals, black chassis and fenders, silver grille and headlights. Value $70-85.
  1. Red cab, yellow-orange tank.

3/25 RENAULT 7-TON COVERED TRUCK 105 mm 1953
Truck, cast body, matching tin cab base, lighter rear cover, wire tow hook, red hubs, black tires, silver emblem, bumper and headlights. Value $50-65.
  1. Green body, light green top.
  2. Gray body, light gray top.

3/26 RENAULT COVERED TRUCK TRAILER 84 mm 1953
Four-wheel trailer, cast body, matching tin axle mounts/hitch, lighter cover, red hubs, black tires. $40-50.
  1. Green body, light green cover.

3/27 CARAVAN TRAILER 147 mm 1959
Caravan, cast body, tin chassis/hitch and interior, turned or chromed hubs, black or white tires. Value $50-65.
  1. Cream body, red roof.

3/27T CARAVAN TRAILER 147 mm 196_
Same basic model as above, but with blue tinted plastic roof panel. Value $50-65.
  1. Red and white body.
  2. Green and white body.

3/28 CATTLE TRAILER 120 mm 1962
Two-wheel trailer, cast body, tailgate and black chassis, tin hitch and bar, silver hubs, black tires. Value $50-65.
  1. Yellow body and tailgate, red stakes.

3/30 FIRE ENGINE 100 mm 1959
Open truck, cast body, silver chassis and hubs, black tires, ladder, plastic figures, no other data. Not a scale model, just a toy. Value $100-125.
    1. Red body.

3/31 SUGAR BEET TRAILER 110 mm 1959
Tipping trailer, cast body, tailgate and red hubs, black tires, green tin chassis and tipping lever. Value $50-65.
    1. Red body and tailgate.

3/32 SEED TRAILER 155 mm 1959
Open four-wheel trailer, tin body and axle mounts/hitch, orange cast hubs, black tires. Value $50-65.
    1. Orange body and mounts, green body panels.

3/33 RENAULT E-30 FARM TRACTOR 100 mm 1959
Tractor, cast body, front axle mount, rear axle, and hubs, black tires, plastic driver, cast-in "E-30" emblem, silver grille and headlights. Value $100-125.
    1. Orange body and parts.

3/34 RENAULT E-30 TRACTOR & TRAILER 210 mm 1959
Set of 3/33 Tractor and 3/37 Trailer. Value $150-175.
    1. Orange tractor, orange and green trailer.

3/35 WATER TANK TRAILER 108 mm 1959
Trailer, tin tank and chassis, black straps, cast hubs. black tires, yellow plastic spigots, rubber hose. Value $50-65.
    1. Green tank, orange-red chassis and hubs.

3/36 SLING CART TRAILER 156 1959
Trailer, cast frame and hubs, black tires, chains holding log.
    1. Orange frame and hubs. Value $50-65.

3/37 TIPPING FARM TRAILER 110 mm 1959
Trailer, tin body, mount, chassis and tipping lever, orange cast hubs, black tires. Value $50-65.
    1. Orange body and parts.

3/38 RENAULT TRACTOR & TIPPING TRAILER 210 mm 1959
Set of 3/33 Tractor and 3/37 Trailer. Different from 3/34?
    1. Orange tractor, orange and green trailer. Value $150-175.

3/39 RENAULT TRACTOR AND SLING CART TRAILER 250 mm 1959
Set of 3/33 Tractor and 3/36 Trailer. Value $150-175.
    1. Orange tractor and trailer.

3/40 RENAULT BUS 127 mm 1954
Single-deck bus, cast body, silver tin chassis, unpainted ladder, red plastic hubs, white tires, silver grille, bumpers, trim and headlights. Value $75-95.
    1. Cream body, red fenders and trim.
    2. Cream body, green fenders and trim.
    3. Cream body, blue fenders and trim.

3/41 CITROEN ID19 AMBULANCE 114 mm 1964
Wagon, cast body and chassis (= 3/4), blue plastic working dome light, clear and opaque windows, turned hubs, black tires, "Croix-Rouge Francaise" and red cross decals. Value $85-95.
    1. Blue body, pale blue roof.

3/42 RENAULT PRAIRIE 97 mm 1953

Three-door wagon, cast body, silver tin chassis, yellow plastic hubs, white tires, silver grille, bumpers and headlights, red taillights. Six windows. Value $50-60.
  1. Dark blue body.

3/43 RENAULT SAVANE 97 mm 1953

Three-door wagon, cast body, silver tin chassis, turned hubs, white tires, silver grille, bumper and headlights, perhaps red taillights. Four windows. Value $50-60.
  1. Tan body.

3/44 RENAULT COLORALE 97 mm 1953

Light van, cast body, matching tin chassis, silver hubs, white tires, silver grille, bumpers and headlights, red taillights.
  1. Dark green body. Value $50-60.

3/45 RENAULT PRAIRIE TAXI 97 mm 1955

Same casting and parts as 3/42, with red plastic hubs, plus silver meter, red "Taxi" decal. Value $50-60.
  1. Red upper, black lower body.
  2. Yellow upper, black lower body.
  3. Cream upper, black lower body.

3/46 PEUGEOT 403 BREAK 100 mm 1955

Wagon, cast body, metallic gray or matching tin chassis, turned hubs, black tires, no windows, silver gray bumpers and headlights, red taillights. Value $50-65.
  1. Green body.
  2. Gray body.

3/46E PEUGEOT 403 AMBULANCE 100 mm 1962

Same casting and parts as 3/46, plus blue working dome light, partly opaque windows, blue-on-white "Secours Routier Francais" decals. Value $75-85.
  1. Light gray body and base (has been called ivory).

3/46H PEUGEOT 403 BREAK 100 mm 1958

Same casting and parts as 3/46 plus clear plastic windows. Value $50-65.
  1. Green body.

3/46P PEUGEOT 403 POLICE CAR 100 mm 1960

Same casting and parts as 3/46 plus amber working dome light, partly opaque windows, white "Police" decals. Value $50-65.
  1. Black body and base.

3/47 PANHARD DYNA 130 80 mm 1950

Four-door sedan, cast body, silver tin chassis, silver cast wheels or red plastic hubs and white tires, silver grille, bumpers and headlights. Value $60-75.
  1. Green body.
  2. Dark blue body.

3/48 RENAULT 4CV 78 mm 1950

Four-door sedan, cast body, matching or metallic gray silver hubs, white tires, silver grille, bumpers and headlights, red or yellow taillights. Two body castings; first has 6-bar grille, no rear lights; second has 3-bar grille, taillights. Value $60-75.
  1. Red body.
  2. Orange body.
  3. Blue body.
  4. Gray body.

3/49 RENAULT 4CV POLICE CAR 78 mm 1950

Same basic model as 3/48, with cream hubs, plus wire antenna, white

"Police" decals. Two casting types: first has cutaway doors, second has straight edge between door and window. Value $65-75.

    1. Black body, white roof and fenders.

3/50 RENAULT ALPINE COUPE 80 mm 1958/59
Sports coupe, cast body, metallic gray tin chassis, turned hubs, black tires, clear plastic windows, silver bumpers and headlights, red taillights. Value $50-65.

    1. Pale gray body (has been called ivory).

    1. White body, red and black racing number and stripe decals.

3/51 RENAULT FRÉGATE 80 mm 1951
Four-door sedan, cast body, silver tin chassis, turned or yellow plastic hubs, white tires, silver grille, bumpers, and headlights, +/- red taillights. Two castings: first type grille has four horizontal bars, two lights; second type (1956) has oval grille, no small lights. Value $50-65.

    1. Dark gray-blue body, first casting.

    2. Dull green body, new casting.

    3. Gray body, new casting.

3/52 RENAULT FRÉGATE GRAND PAVOIS 102 mm 1958
Four-door sedan, cast body, metallic gray tin chassis, turned hubs, white tires, silver grille, bumpers, and headlights, yellow taillights. Value $50-65.

    1. Gray upper, red lower body.

3/53 RENAULT DOMANE BREAK 102 mm 1958
Wagon, cast body, metallic gray chassis, turned hubs, white tires, clear plastic windows, silver grille, bumpers, and headlights. Value $50-65.

    1. Light red body, yellow and brown woodwork.

3/53A RENAULT DOMANE AMBULANCE 102 mm 1960
Same casting and parts as 3/53 plus opaque rear windows, blue crosses on white circles on doors and flag. Value $70-85.

    1. Blue body, white top and hood.

3/54 PANHARD DYNA 54 101 mm 1955
Four-door sedan, cast body, metallic gray tin chassis, silver bumpers, headlights, and hubs, white tires, red taillights. Value $60-75.

    1. Light green body.

    2. Dull blue body.

3/54T PANHARD DYNA TAXI 101 mm 1958
Same casting and parts as 3/54 plus silver meter, white "Taxi" decal. Value $60-75.

    1. Black upper, red lower body.

3/55 RENAULT COLORALE AMBULANCE 97 mm 1956
Same casting and parts as 3/44, with silver hubs, white tires, plus red "Ambulance: decal, white flag with blue cross. Value $70-85.

    1. Cream body, white side panels.

3/56 RENAULT DAUPHINE 85 mm 1956
Four-door sedan, cast body, metallic gray tin chassis, silver bumpers, headlights, and hubs, white tires, red taillights. Clear plastic windows added in 1957. Value $50-65.

    1. Dark blue body.

    2. Yellow body, black roof and trim.

3/56T RENAULT DAUPHINE TAXI 85 mm 1958
Same casting and parts as 3/56 including windows, plus cast taxi sign and meter, red-on-white "Taxi" decals. Value $50-65.

    1. Red upper, black lower body.

    2. Green upper, pale yellow lower body.

3/57 RENAULT DAUPHINE POLICE CAR 85 mm 1958

Same casting and parts as 3/56 including windows, plus red dome light, wire antenna, white "Police" decals. Value $50-65.
    1. Black body, white roof and fenders.

3/58 RENAULT FLORIDE 100 mm 1960

Hardtop coupe, cast body, chassis and opening hood, black plastic removable top, clear windows, red interior and taillights, silver bumpers, headlights, and hubs, black tires. Value $50-65.
    1. Rose red body.
    2. White body, black top.
    3. Aqua body, black top.

3/60 RENAULT 1000 KG VAN 100 mm 1955

Van, cast body, tin opening rear doors, metallic gray chassis, red hubs, black tires, silver bumper and headlights. Value $50-60.
    1. Gray body, no logo.
    2. Cream and green body, "Primistere" logo (1957).

3/60A RENAULT 1000 KG ASTRA VAN 100 mm 1957

Same casting and parts as 3/60, turned hubs, green and white "Astra Margarine" decals. Value $85-95.
    1. Yellow body.

3/60B RENAULT 1000 KG BOUCHERIE VAN 100 mm 1960

Same casting and parts as 3/60, black hubs, yellow and red "Boucherie" decals. Value $85-95.
    1. Blue body, white roof, dark blue stripe.

3/60P RENAULT 1000 KG MAIL VAN 100 mm 1957

Same casting and parts as 3/60, black hubs. Value $85-95.
    1. Dark green body, gold "Postes" decals.
    2. Yellow body, German mail decals, no other data.

3/60PB RENAULT 1000 KG BELGIAN MAIL VAN 100 mm 1957

Same casting and parts as 3/60, Belgian mail decals. Value $120-130.
    1. Red body.

3/60S RENAULT 1000 KG SHELL VAN 100 mm 1956

Same casting and parts as 3/60, black hubs, red "Shell" decals. Value $85-95.
    1. Red cab, dark yellow rear body.

3/60T RENAULT 1000 KG VAN & TRAILER 190 mm 1957

Same casting and parts as 3/60 plus cast trailer, gray tin chassis, black hubs, two poles and wire in trailer, red and yellow "PTT" decals. Value $110-120.
    1. Gray van and trailer.

3/61 RENAULT 1000 KG AMBULANCE 107 mm 1955

Casting and parts similar to 3/60, open rear side windows, metallic gray tin chassis, opening rear doors, black rear step, silver hubs, white tires, red cross and "Ambulance Municipale" decals. Was it issued with interior and stretchers (see 3/61M)? Value $100-115.
    1. White body.

3/61M RENAULT 1000 KG ARMY AMBULANCE 107 mm 1959

Same casting and parts as 3/61, +/- cream interior and stretchers, with red crosses on white panels. Value $100-115.
    1. Olive body.

3/62 RENAULT 1000 KG BUS 100 mm 1955

Casting and parts similar to 3/60, open wide windows, metallic gray chassis, black rear step, silver hubs, white tires, black "SNCF" decals, silver bumper and headlights. Value $85-95.

1. Light gray body.
2. Tan body.

3/62N RENAULT 1000 KG BUS 100 mm 1955
Same casting and parts as 3/62, red-yellow-blue-black "Teindre" and "Nettoyer" logo decals. Value $85-95.
1. Yellow body.

3/63 RENAULT 1000 KG POLICE VAN 100 mm 1955
Same casting and parts as 3/61, metallic gray chassis, black rear step, red hubs, white tires, white "Police" decals. Value $75-85.
1. Dark blue body.

3/65 RENAULT POLICE PICKUP AND TRAILER 215 mm 1962
Pickup, cast body, matching tin chassis, gray tin cover and interior, blue and yellow tin trailer, red flags, cast roof lights and sign, silver grille, bumpers, and hubs, black tires, "Police" and Tricolor decals, two figures. Value $100-110.
1. Dark blue pickup body.

3/66 RENAULT DAUPHINOISE BREAK 84 mm 1956/57
Three-door wagon, cast body, metallic gray tin chassis, silver grille, bumpers, headlights, and hubs, black tires. Value $50-60.
1. Light gray body.

3/67 RENAULT 300 KG VAN 84 mm 1957
Light van, cast body, metallic gray tin chassis, silver grille, bumpers, headlights, and hubs, black tires. Value $50-60.
1. Gray body.

3/68 RENAULT 300 KG MAIL VAN 84 mm 1957
Same casting and parts as 3/67, yellow and black "Postes" decals.

Value $65-75.
1. Blue-green body.

3/68PB RENAULT 300 KG BELGIAN MAIL VAN 84 mm 1957
Same casting and parts as 3/67, Belgian mail decals. Value $95-110.
1. Red body.

3/69 RENAULT DAUPHINOISE POLICE CAR 84 mm 1957
Same casting and parts as 3/66, black chassis, silver hubs, plus wire antenna, Tricolor decal. Value $60-75.
1. Dark blue body.

3/70 RENAULT SEMI-TRAILER TRUCK 190 mm 1955
Semi, cast cab and chassis, green tin semi body, chassis, rest (with unpainted wheels) and spare rack, light green cover, red hubs, black tires, spare wheel, silver headlights. Value $75-85.
1. Green cab and semi.

3/72 RENAULT SEMI-TRAILER TANK TRUCK 200 mm 1958
Semi, cast cab, chassis and tank, black semi chassis and rest (with unpainted wheels), red spare rack, silver headlights and hubs, black tires, spare wheel, black fenders and bumper, red taillights and "Shell" logo. Value $100-110.
1. Red cab, yellow tank.

3/73 RENAULT SEMI-TRAILER LOG TRUCK 204 mm 1956
Semi, cast cab and chassis, blue tin semi and spare rack, chains, logs, silver headlights and hubs, black tires, spare wheel. Value $80-90.
1. Blue cab and semi.

3/75 RENAULT ATOMIC PILE TRANSPORTER ca. 400 cm 1957
Cast cab, two light gray tin trailer units, cab base, and spare rack, red-white-blue tin cylinder with "E. D. F. Marcoule" logo and other lettering, silver emblems, headlights and hubs, black tires, black-on-yellow "Bourgey & Montreuil" decals on cab. Value $175-195.
    1. Gray cab and trailers.

3/76 CITROEN 2CV MAIL VAN 93 mm 1965
Light van, JRD #111 reissue, cast body, black tin chassis, gray hubs, black tires, blue decals and trim, orange and green advertising labels, silver grille and headlights, blue CIJ on base. Value $75-85.
    1. Yellow body.

3/76A SAILBOAT ON TRAILER 125 mm 1964
Cast trailer frame, black tin chassis, silver hubs, white tires, pale blue and white plastic boat, silver centerboard, white sails. Value $50-60.
    1. Red and black trailer.

3/77 BERLIET SEMI-TRAILER TRUCK 200 mm 1965
JRD #120 reissue, all details apparently unchanged, including Kronenbourg logo. Value $100-120.
    1. Red body.

3/78 UNIC CAB AND TRAILER WITH RAILROAD CAR 259 mm 1965
Reissue of JRD #123, apparently unchanged. including Kronenbourg logo. Value $125-150.
    1. Red and cream cab, cream trailer and railroad car.

3/79 SAVIEM BOTTLE TRUCK 157 mm? 1965
Apparently reissue of JRD #134.
    1. Unchanged from JRD version?

3/80 RENAULT DUMP TRUCK 102 mm 1955
Dumper, cast cab-chassis, green tin tipper, tailgate, tipping lever, and cab base, red hubs, black tires, silver headlights and emblem. Value $75-85.
    1. Green body.

3/81 RENAULT OR SAVIEM CRANE TRUCK 140 mm 1956
Crane truck, cast cab-chassis (Renault until 1964, then Saviem), tin cab base, cabin, boom, scoop, and unpainted hook, winch with line, red hubs, black tires, silver emblem and headlights. Value $85-95.
    1. Orange cab and crane parts.
    2. Green and yellow, no other data.

3/82 RENAULT OR SAVIEM SHOVEL TRUCK 140 mm 1958
Power shovel truck, cast cab-chassis (Renault until 1964, then Saviem), matching tin cab base, painted cabin, unpainted arm and shovel, crank and control lines, silver emblems, headlights, and hubs, black tires. Value $85-95.
    1. Cream cab-chassis, red cabin.
    2. Blue cab-chassis, orange cabin.

3/83 RENAULT WRECKER 125 mm 1964
Wrecker, cast cab-chassis, red rear bed, red tin winch and boom, gray cab base, spare rack and hubs, black tires, spare wheel, line and hook, silver emblem and headlights, black-on-yellow "Bourgey & Montreuil" decal. Value $85-95.
    1. Red and green body.
    2. Gray and red body.

3/84 BERLIET WEITZ MOBILE CRANE 180 mm 1964/65
Reissue of JRD #125 with "Sablieres de la Loire" logo. Value $90-100.

1. Red body, yellow crane, black mount, blue tin shovel.

3/88   RENAULT EXCAVATOR
No data.

3/89   CITROEN 1200 KG POLICE VAN   100 mm   1964/65
Reissue of JRD #106, presumably unchanged. Value $60-75.
1. Black and white body.

3/89B   CITROEN 1200 KG VAN   100 mm   1965
Same castings and parts as 3/89, plain black tin chassis, yellow hubs, black tires, black "Brandt" logo decals and trim. Value $85-95.
1. Blue lower, yellow upper body.

3/90   RENAULT ESTAFETTE VAN   90 mm   1961
Van, cast body, sliding and opening doors, and hubs, black tires, metallic gray tin chassis, clear plastic windows, cream interior, blue trim, silver grille, bumpers, and headlights, red taillights. Value $65-75.
1. Cream body and hubs.
2. Orange body, ? hubs.
3. Blue body, ? hubs.

3/91   RENAULT ESTAFETTE POLICE VAN   90 mm   1963
High-roof van, cast body, sliding and opening doors, tin chassis, blue hubs, black tires, clear plastic windows, cream interior, amber dome light, black grille, silver headlights, red taillights, white and black "Police" decals. Value $70-80.
1. Blue body, white fenders, cream roof.

3/92   RENAULT ESTAFETTE BUS   92 mm   1961
Minibus, cast body, sliding and opening doors, matching tin chassis, clear plastic windows, cream interior, cast or turned hubs, black tires, silver headlights, red taillights, black and white "Hostellerie du Cheval Blanc" logo decals. Value $65-75.
1. Dark yellow body, black grille, bumpers and trim.
2. Pale green body, dark green roof, grille, bumpers and trim.

3/93   RENAULT ESTAFETTE POLICE BUS   90 mm   1962
Minibus, cast body, sliding and opening doors, dark blue tin chassis, blue hubs, black tires, clear plastic windows, cream interior, red roof light, wire antenna, "Gendarmerie Nationale" and Tricolor decals, silver headlights, black grille and bumpers. Value $70-80.
1. Dark blue body.

3/94   RENAULT 2.5 TON BOTTLE TRUCK   122 mm   1963
Flat truck, cast cab, rear bed, and black chassis, tin tailboards, red hubs, black tires, clear plastic windows, yellow cases, green bottles, white headlights, black front bumper, red and white "Evian" logo decals. Value $90-100.
1. Red and white body.

3/95   RENAULT 2.5 TON FIRE ENGINE   133 mm   1963
Fire truck, cast cab and black chassis, red plastic rear body and hubs, white tires, clear windows, unpainted tin aerial ladder and mount, red and white hose reels with tin handles, black bumper, silver headlights. Value $110-125.
1. Red body.

3/96   RENAULT SEARCHLIGHT TRUCK & TRAILER   198 mm   1963
Army truck, cast cab and black chassis, olive plastic rear body, mount, light and hubs, black tires, clear windows, olive tin trailer with opening side panels and battery, wires, controls, silver hubs, soldier figure. Value $100-110.
1. Olive body.

3/97 SAVIEM MISSILE LAUNCHER 222 mm 1964
Truck, cast cab and chassis, blue sheet metal trailer, black rack, red plastic rocket, clear truck windows, blue hubs, black tires, chrome trim, black and silver grille, silver headlights, plastic figure. Value $90-100.
1. Blue truck and trailer.
2. Olive truck and trailer.

3/98 RENAULT 2.5 TON RADAR TRUCK 121 mm 1964
Army truck, cast cab and black chassis, olive plastic rear body, mount, soldier figure and hubs, black tires, clear windows, tin and screen radar dish, unpainted metal controls, silver headlights. Value $90-100.
1. Olive body.

3/99 RENAULT 2.5 TON GUN TRUCK 158 mm 1964
Army truck, cast cab, rear body, and black chassis, olive tin gun parts, clear plastic windows, olive hubs, black tires, unpainted controls, black bumper, silver headlights. Value $90-100.
1. Olive body.

3/? RENAULT FARM TRACTOR 98 mm ?
Shorter, higher, and squarer tractor than 3/30, cast body, chassis, and hubs, tin front axle mount and rear fenders, black tires, plastic driver, silver headlights and caps, "Renault" decals. Value $110-125.
1. Orange body, chassis and hubs.

4/20 PANHARD B.P. TANK TRUCK 100 mm
Mechanical version of 3/20, with motor. Value $75-85.
1. Green body.

4/21 RENAULT SHELL TANKER 100 mm
Mechanical version of 3/21, with motor. Value $75-85.
1. Red cab, yellow tank.

4/30 FIRE ENGINE 100 mm
Mechanical version of 3/30, with motor. Value $125-150.
1. Red body.

4/42 RENAULT PRAIRIE 97 mm
Mechanical version of 3/42, with motor. Value $65-75.
1. Dark blue body?

4/43 RENAULT SAVANE 97 mm
Mechanical version of 3/43, with motor. Value $65-75.
1. Tan body?

4/44 RENAULT COLORALE 97 mm
Mechanical version of 3/44, with motor. Value $65-75.
1. Dark green body?

4/45 RENAULT PARIRIE TAXI 97 mm
Mechanical version of 3/45, with motor. Value $65-75.
1. Colors?

4/47 PANHARD DYNA 80 mm
Mechanical version of 3/47, with motor. Value $70-80.
1. Colors?

4/48 RENAULT 4CV 78 mm
Mechanical version of 3/48, with motor. Value $70-80.
1. Gray body.

4/50 RENAULT 2.5 TON CATTLE TRUCK 122 mm 1959
Truck, cast cab, rear body, opening tailgate, and two-piece chassis, clear plastic windows, silver hubs, black tires, yellow tin bar, silver headlights. $75-85.
1. Red cab, yellow rear body and tailgate, red stakes.

4/51 RENAULT FRÉGATE 92 mm
Mechanical version of 3/51, with motor. Value $60-70.
1. No data.

4/68 SAVIEM ARMY TANK TRUCK 205 mm 1962/63
Tanker semi, cast cab, black chassis, and semi body, black tin semi chassis and rests (with silver wheels), clear plastic windows, olive hubs, black tires and catwalk, Tricolor decals. Value $90-100.
1. Olive cab and semi.

4/69 SAVIEM SHELL TANKER 205 mm 1962
Same castings and parts as 4/68, orange hubs, red Shell emblem decals. Value $110-125.
1. Yellow and red cab and semi.

4/70 SAVIEM MOBIL TANKER 205 mm 1964
Same castings and parts as 4/68, silver hubs, red-white-blue Mobil decals. Value $110-125.
1. Red cab and semi.

4/71 SAVIEM B.P. TANKER 205 mm 1959
Same castings and parts as 4/68, silver hubs, yellow catwalk, green and yellow BP decals. Value $110-125.
1. White cab, white and green semi.

4/72 SOMUA TRANSFORMER CARRIER 228 mm 1960
Truck, cast cab and gray chassis, gray tin trailer, light blue plastic transformer, clear parts and windows, silver hubs, black tires, black and silver grille, silver headlights. Value $110-125.
1. Yellow cab, gray chassis and trailer.

4/73 SAVIEM CEMENT TRUCK 128 mm 1964
Truck, cast cab and black chassis, black tin rear bed, red sign and ladder, clear plastic windows, light gray vats, black caps, silver hubs, black tires, black and silver grille, silver headlights, yellow "Ciment" logo. Value $85-95.
1. Red cab, black chassis and bed.

4/74 SAVIEM COVERED ARMY TRUCK 118 mm 1965
Truck, cast cab and black chassis, olive tin rear body, cover and seats, black tow hook, clear plastic windows, black hubs and tires, silver headlights, plastic driver and soldier figures. Value $80-90.
1. Olive cab and rear.

4/75 SAVIEM CABLE CARRIER 302 mm 1960
Flat semi, cast cab, semi, ramps, and black cab chassis, clear plastic windows, gray reels and bases, gold simulated cable, winch, line, chains, gray hubs, black tires, black and silver grille, silver headlights, red taillights. Value $100-115.
1. Blue and yellow cab and semi.

4/76 SAVIEM COVERED TRUCK 110 mm 1965
Truck, cast cab, black chassis, matching tin rear body, green cover, clear plastic windows, blue or silver hubs, black tires, silver headlights. Value $75-85.
1. Yellow cab and rear, green cover.
2. Blue cab and rear, green cover.

4/77 BERLIET COVERED TRUCK TRAILER 103 mm 1960
Trailer, tin body, axle mounts/hitch, and green cover, silver hubs, black or white tires. Value $40-50.
1. Yellow body, green cover.

4/78 SAVIEM DUMP TRUCK 123 mm 1959
Dumper, cast cab, tipper, tailboard, and black chassis, clear plastic windows, blue hubs, black tires, silver and black grille and headlights. Value $75-85.
1. Red cab, blue tipper and tailboard.

4/80 SAVIEM DUMP TRUCK 124 mm 1960

Dumper, cast cab, tipper, tailboard, and black chassis, black tin tipping lever, clear plastic windows, silver hubs, black tires, black and silver grille, silver headlights. Same tipper as 3/80. Value $75-85.

    1. Green cab, yellow tipper.

4/81 BERLIET GARBAGE TRUCK 139 1964

Reissue of JRD #131, cast cab, tipping rear body, opening rear section, and black chassis, orange hubs, black tires, unpainted tin parts, wire tipping lever, red grille, front bumper and taillights, silver headlights. Value $90-100.

    1. Red cab, silver rear.

4/84 SAND BIN AND BUCKET CRANE 1963/64

No data.

7/1 CITROEN AMI-6 PRODUCTION LINE SET 1964

No data.

14/75 EIGHT-CAR PARKING LOT 1964

No data.

16/53 & 16/54 TRAFFIC LIGHTS

No data.

44/6 GIFT SET

Includes 3/32, 3/33, 3/34 and 3/36.

44/8 GIFT SET

Includes 3/81, 3/82 and 4/80.

MICRO-MINIATURES

HO scale diecast vehicles. Value $35-$50.

M1 SOMUA BUS 62 mm 1958

Single-deck bus, single casting, black tin base, unpainted wheels.

    1. Cream upper, green lower body.

M2 PEUGEOT 403 52 mm 1957

Sedan, single casting, unpainted wheels.

    1. Black body.

M3 RENAULT BOX VAN 50 mm 1957

Truck, cast cab-chassis and rear body, unpainted wheels.

    1. Light gray and red.

M4 RENAULT DUMP TRUCK 50 mm 1957

Dumper, cast cab-chassis and tipper, unpainted wheels.

    1. Green cab-chassis, silver tipper.

M5 RENAULT TANK TRUCK 48 mm 1957

Single casting, unpainted wheels.

    1. Red body, silver tank.

M6 RENAULT 1000 KG AMBULANCE 43 mm 1957

Vna-type ambulance, single casting, unpainted wheels, red cross decals.

    1. White body.

M7 RENAULT 1000 KG VAN 43 mm 1957

Van, single casting, unpainted wheels.

    1. Gray body.

M8 RENAULT DAUPHINE 52 mm 1958

Sedan, single casting, black tin base, unpainted wheels, silver bumpers and headlights.

    1. Dark red body.

M9 SIMCA ARIANE 52 mm 1959
Sedan, single casting, black tin base, unpainted wheels, silver grille, bumpers and headlights, red taillights.

    1. Pale yellow body.

M10   RENAULT 1000 KG ARMY AMBULANCE   43 mm 1959
Same casting and parts as M7, black tin base, white panels with red crosses.

    1. Olive body.

CLE

The firm of Cle takes its name from the first syllable of proprietor Clément Gaget's name, and since "clef" is the French word for "key," the firm's trade mark is its name plus the drawing of a key. Miniature car production seems to have begun in 1958, and the firm was still alive in the seventies when its old-time cars were used promotionally by an American gasoline company.

Cle models are made of plastic and range from 1/48 scale through 1/64 to 1/90, the last used for a small series of truck models. Many Cle models appear not to be numbered, which makes listing them a challenge. The series of old-timers is numbered, beginning with #201, and there was also a "Series of 25" models, some of which bear those numbers on their baseplates. As the numbers go at least to 27, it is obvious that the Series of 25 was expanded at some time. Many of these models have baseplates made in the same color as the car's body but sprayed silver at both ends for the sake of the integral bumpers.

More recent Cle products include small series of sports and racing cars, the latter interesting because it includes not only the familiar BRM, Ferrari, and Lotus of the late sixties, but also the front-engined Ferguson four-wheel-drive car. These models, like the earlier issues, are not of the highest quality, but neither are they entirely lacking in personality and interest, and I wish I knew more about them. As it is, I can only list those that I know to have numbers and then add the others that are known to me in alphabetical and, in the case of the last two series, chronological order.

As for their values, I do not believe any Cle model is worth more than ten dollars at most; a realistic average would be five dollars apiece.

Series of 25

1 PEUGEOT 203 91 mm 1/48 1958
Four-door sedan with plastic body, mostly silver base with bumpers, white spoked hubs, black tires.
    1. Pale green body.

2 CITROEN 11CV 98 mm 1/48 1958?

Four-door sedan with plastic body, partly silver base with bumpers, clear windows and headlights, gray hubs, white tires.
1. Pale gray body.

3 PEUGEOT 403 98 mm 1/48 1958
Four-door sedan with plastic body, partly silver base with bumpers, white spoked hubs, black tires.
1. Gray body.

6 SIMCA P60 86 mm 1/48 1960
Four-door sedan with plastic body, partly silver base with bumpers and grille, white spoked hubs, black tires.
1. Orange body.

11 RENAULT DAUPHINE 86 mm 1/48 1958?
Four-door sedan with plastic body, partly silver base with bumpers, white spoked hubs, black tires.
1. Red body.

12 RENAULT CARAVELLE COUPE 87 mm 1/48
Two-door coupe with plastic body, top, white chassis-interior with silver bumpers, white spoked hubs, black tires.
1. White body, red top.

13 RENAULT CARAVELLE CABRIOLET 87 mm 1/48
Two-door convertible with plastic body (as #12), folded top, white chassis-interior with silver bumpers, white spoked hubs, black tires.
1. White body, red top.

16 PANHARD DYNA 92 mm 1/48 1958
Four-door sedan with plastic body, partly silver base with bumpers and body panels, white spoked hubs, black tires.
1. Cream body.

18 CITROEN 1200 KG VAN 88 mm 1/48
Van with plastic body, matching base, chrome grille, white spoked hubs, black tires. There may be other versions besides:
1. White body and base, red roof light and crosses (ambulance).
2. Red body, base and ladder (fire truck).

20 FIAT 600 67 mm 1/48
Two-door minicar with plastic body, partly silver base with bumpers, black hubs, white tires.
1. Light green body.

21 PEUGEOT 403 BREAK 100 mm 1/48
Four-door wagon with plastic body and base including tow hook, black wheels.
1. Aqua body and base.

24 PEUGEOT 404 91 mm 1/48
Four-door sedan with plastic body, partly silver base with bumpers and grille, clear windows and headlights, white spoked hubs, black tires.
1. Probably exists in civilian form.
2. White body, red roof light and cross (ambulance).

25 CITROEN AMI 6 80 mm 1/48
Four-door sedan with plastic body, partly silver base with bumpers, white spoked hubs, black tires.
1. Dark cream body.

26 RENAULT R4L 76 mm 1/48
Four-door square back with plastic body, partly silver base with bumpers, gray grille, black hubs, white tires.
1. maroon body.

27 SIMCA 1000 79 mm 1/48

Four-door sedan with plastic body, partly silver base with bumpers, white spoked hubs, black tires.
    1. Orange body.

Other models, presumably from this series:

CITROEN 2CV 1/48 1958
No data.

CITROEN 2CV VAN 75 mm 1/48 1958
Light van with plastic body, partly silver base with bumpers, clear windows and headlights, gray antenna, black hubs, white tires; #115?.
    1. Gray body.

CITROEN 15-SIX 1/48 1958
No data

CITROEN DS 19 1/48 1958
No data.

PANHARD DYNA CONVERTIBLE 1/48 1958
No data.

PEUGEOT 404 CONVERTIBLE 93 mm 1/48
Convertible with plastic body, folded top, partly silver base with bumpers and grille, gray antenna, white spoked hubs, black tires.
    1. Tan body, light blue top.

PEUGEOT 404 COUPE 93 mm 1/48
Coupe with plastic body (as above), top, partly silver base with bumpers and grille, gray antenna, white spoked hubs, black tires.
    1. Tan body, gray top.

RENAULT FLORIDE CONVERTIBLE 1/48 1960
No data.

RENAULT FLORIDE HARDTOP 1/48 1960
No data.

RENAULT FLORIDE GRAND PAVOIS 1/48 1958
No data.

SIMCA OCEANE 1/48 1960
No data.

SIMCA PLEIN CIEL 1/48 1960
No data.

SIMCA P60 GRAND LARGE 1/48 1960
No data.

SIMCA 1300 89 mm 1/48
Four-door sedan with plastic body, partly silver base with bumpers and grille, gray antenna, white spoked hubs, black tires.
    1. Light green body.

The following models were made to 1/64 scale; as I have no data on them, I can only list them alphabetically:

Citroen 15-Six, 1958.
Citroen 2CV, 1958.
Citroen 2CV Van, 1958.
Citroen DS19, 1958.
Panhard Dyna, 1958.
Panhard Dyna Cabriolet, 1958.

Peugeot 203, 1958.
Peugeot 403, 1958.
Peugeot 403 Cabriolet, 1958.
Renault Floride Coupe, 1960.
Renault Floride Cabriolet, 1960.
Simca Oceane, 1960.
Simca Plein Ciel, 1960.
Simca P60, 1960.
Simca P60 Grand Large, 1960.

The following 1/90 scale model trucks are known to me:

BERLIET BOX VAN   87 mm   1/90
Long-chassis cab-over with plastic cab, rear body, silver gray chassis with bumpers and grille, black wheels.
    1. Light blue cab, green rear body.

BERLIET DUMP TRUCK   1/90
My records say I have it, but I can't find it.

BERLIET FLAT TRUCK   65 mm   1/90
Short-chassis cab-over with plastic cab, rear bed, tan chassis with bumpers and grille, black wheels. Has slots to carry box like models below. May have been issued only with a load.
    1. Red cab, yellow rear bed.

UNIC FLAT TRUCK WITH BOX   76 mm   1/90
Short-chassis conventional truck with plastic cab, rear bed, silver chassis, chrome lights, blue box, brown wheels.
    1. Pale blue cab, olive rear bed.

UNIC FLAT TRUCK WITH BOTTLES   76 mm   1/90
Short-chassis conventional truck with plastic cab, matching chassis, rear body, bronze load, silver grille and lights, gray wheels.
    1. Gray cab and chassis.

The following more recent models exist; their scale is approximately 1/40, definitely bigger than the 1/48 scale cars:

Sports Cars:
CHAPPARAL MARK III   100 mm
Open sports-racing car with plastic body, matching airfoil and base, yellow driver, aqua seat, tinted windshield, white hubs, black tires.
    1. Blue body, airfoil and base.

FERRARI 330P2   105 mm
Open sports-racing car with plastic body, matching base, orange driver, white seat, clear windshield, silver hubs, black tires.
    1. Red body and base.

FORD GT MARK II
No data.

MATRA-BRM 620   100 mm
Sports-racing coupe with plastic body, matching base, yellow driver, blue seat, clear windows, white hubs, black tires.
    1. Green body and base.

McLAREN-ELVA MARK 2   98 mm
Open sports-racing car with plastic body, matching base, light green driver, white seat, tinted windshield, white hubs, black tires.
    1. Red body and base.

PORSCHE CARRERA 6   101 mm
Sports-racing coupe with plastic body, matching base, green driver, yellow seat, tinted top, white hubs, black tires.

1. Blue body and base.

Racing Cars:
BRM 108 mm
Racing car with plastic body, light gray base, blue driver, clear windshield, gray spoked hubs, black tires.
    1. White body.

FERGUSON 102 mm
Racing car with plastic body, light gray base, white driver, clear windshield, gray spoked hubs, black tires.
    1. Red body.

FERRARI 109 mm
Racing car with plastic body, light gray base, red driver, clear windshield, gray spoked hubs, black tires.
    1. Blue body.

LOTUS 108 mm
Racing car with plastic body, light gray base, white driver, clear windshield, gray spoked hubs, black tires.
    1. Light orange body.
    2. Gray-blue body.

PORSCHE 1962
No data.

The 200 "La Belle Epoque" series of old-time cars was probably also made to 1/48 scale. Some of them also exist with cast-in "Prior" or "Huilor" lettering, apparently for promotional use.

201 SCOTTE 1892 STEAMER
No data. Presumably resembles the RAMI model.

202 PEUGEOT 1895 WITH ROOF 60 mm
Covered four-seater with plastic body, top, black seats, gold chassis, controls, lights, horn and spoked hubs, black tires.
    1. Red body, cream top.

203 PEUGEOT 1895 VIS-À-VIS 61 mm
Top-up four-seater with plastic body, top, red seats and tiller, gold grille, lights, crank and lever, black spoked wheels.
    1. Blue body, black top.

204 GAUTHIER-WEHRLÉ 1897 62 mm
Open-front coupe with plastic upper body, lower body-chassis, gold seat, lights, controls and steps, black spoked wheels.
    1. Aqua upper body, gray lower body-chassis.

205 RENAULT 1900 COUPE 62 mm
Closed two-seater with plastic body, chassis, black top, trunk and spoked wheels, gold radiator shell and lights.
    1. Green body, silver gray chassis.

206 DE DION-BOUTON 1900 VIS-À-VIS 55 mm
Open four-seater with plastic body, chassis, gold seats, lights and controls, silver or black spoked wheels.
    1. Yellow body, black chassis and wheels.
    2. Silver body, chassis and wheels.

207 DE DION-BOUTON 1900 DOCTOR'S COUPE 66 mm
Closed two-seater with plastic upper and lower body, gold lights, black chassis and spoked wheels.
    1. Light tan upper, red lower body.
    2. Brown upper, red lower body.

208 DELAHAYE 1901
Open four-seater with parasol; no other data.

209 GEORGES RICHARD 1902 TONNEAU 73 mm
Open four-seater with plastic body, chassis, white or cream seats, gold grille, lights, levers, and crank, black spoked wheels.

    1. Red body, black chassis.

210 PEUGEOT 1905 5CV 66 mm
Open two-seater with plastic body, chassis, cab, red seat, gold grille, lights, levers, and crank, silver or black spoked wheels.

    1. White body and chassis, gray cab, black wheels.
    2. Light gray body and chassis, silver cab and wheels.

211 SIZAIRE-NAUDIN 1906 RACING CAR 72 mm
Two-seat racer with plastic body, chassis, red seats, gold grille, springs, lights, and levers, black spoked wheels.

    1. White body and chassis.

212 LION-PEUGEOT 1908 79 mm
Open four-seater with plastic body, chassis, white seats, gold grille, lights, levers, horn, and spoked hubs, black tires.

    1. Red body, black chassis.
    2. Green body, black chassis.

213 HISPANO-SUIZA 1922 TORPEDO 90
Open-cab folding-top tourer with plastic body, black top, chassis, spare and spoked wheels, red seats, gold grille, bumpers, lights, and windshield frames.

    1. Maroon body.
    2. Blue body.

214 CITROEN 1923 B2 AMBULANCE 70 mm
Van with plastic body, black chassis, gold radiator shell, lights, horn, crank, windshield, and hubs, black tires, red cross and "Ambulance Municipale" labels.

    1. White body.

215 PANHARD-LEVASSOR 1926 LIMOUSINE 90 mm
Roofed-cab town car with plastic body, black top, chassis, tires and spares, gold radiator shell, lights, windshield, and hubs.

    1. Gray body.

216 ISOTTA-FRASCHINI 1926 TOWN SEDAN 87 mm
Open-cab town car with plastic body, black top, chassis, spoked wheels and spares, gold radiator shell, lights, windshield, and bumpers.

    1. Silver gray body.

217 BENTLEY 1927 TOURER 88 mm
Top-up tourer with plastic body, black top, chassis, spare and spoked wheels, red seats, gold grille-lights, windshield, horn, and levers.

    1. Blue body.
    2. Gray body.

218 MERCEDES SS 1928 90 mm
Open four-seat sports car with plastic body, black folded top, chassis, spares and tires, red seats, gold grille, lights, windshield, exhaust pipes, bumpers, and spoked hubs.

    1. Gray body.

219 MERCEDES SSK 1929 87 mm
Open sports four-seater with plastic body, chassis, red seats, gold grille, lights, windshield, dash, and exhaust pipes, black spoked wheels and spare.

    1. White body and chassis.
    2. Yellow body and chassis.

220 BENTLEY LE MANS 1929 87 mm
Open sports tourer with plastic body and chassis, gold grille, lights, folded windshield, and blower, black folded top-seats, spares and spoked wheels.

1. Red body and chassis.

221 PACKARD 1930 SPORT PHAETON   92 mm
Open four-seater with plastic body, red seats, gold grille, bumpers, lights, mirrors, windshields, black chassis, folded top, spares, and spoked wheels.
1. White body.

222 PACKARD 1930 ROADSTER   92 mm
Two-seat convertible with plastic body, red seats, gold grille, bumpers, lights, mirrors, and windshield, black top, chassis, spares and spoked wheels.
1. White body.

223 ROLLS-ROYCE 1931 PHANTOM 2   94 mm
Top-up convertible with plastic body, red seats, gold or silver grille, lights, bumpers, windshield, and running boards, black top, chassis, spares, and spoked wheels.
1. Maroon body.
2. Blue body.
3. Gray body.

224 MERCEDES 1928 SS TOURER
No data.

FRANCE JOUETS

France Jouets models, or F.J. for short, were produced by a firm of the same name in Marseille. The first 1/45 scale F.J. models came onto the market in 1959, with new models issued until 1967 and production continuing until 1969. During the seventies the dies were bought by Safir, who reissued a number of the models, sometimes in plastic.

The firm of France Jouets was a pioneer in the production of miniature vehicle components that could be used for more than one model. They made only six basic chassis: the 100 Berliet GAK truck, 200 Pacific heavy tractor, 300 GMC and 400 Dodge military trucks, 500-600 Jeep, and 700 Berliet Stradair, a few trailers, and a number of rear bodies that could be applied to two or more chassis. All the models represented either military, public service, or commercial vehicles. The major components are diecast, with plastic parts such as windows, interiors, and, in later years, wheel hubs, plus an occasional piece of sheet metal. Many models also include plastic drivers and other figures; those of soldiers are light olive, civilians blue. Some models may have been issued in more than one color, but I have no knowledge of any except a few military vehicles that exist in both olive and white. I have very little information on F.J. models beyond those I have in my collection, and can only list others I have seen mentioned elsewhere without being able to provide any data on them, though in some cases the rear body in question is obviously that known to exist, and described here, on a different chassis.

As for their values, so few of them come on the market–at least on this side of the ocean–that I can only say that the big 200 series semis are worth $100 or more–I have heard prices as high as $350–and that the average value of the other models is in the vicinity of $50 to $75.

For what it's worth, the firm also made a set of miniature World War I army rifles. But then, Solido made toy pistols!

101 BERLIET GAK TANK TRUCK 98 mm 1962
Cast cab, tank, black chassis, unpainted hubs, black tires, spare wheel, clear plastic windows, cream interior, grille, and front bumper, silver trim, two figures.
1. Red cab, dark yellow tank.

102 BERLIET GAK LUMBER TRUCK 1962

Same cab and chassis as above; rear body presumably that described in 300 series.

    1. No data.

103 BERLIET GAK COVERED TRUCK 96 mm 1962

Same cab and chassis as above, cast rear body, unpainted hubs, black tires, spare wheel, tin cover, clear plastic windows, cream interior, grille, and bumper, two figures, silver trim.

    1. Red cab, dark yellow rear body and cover, black chassis.

104 BERLIET GAK DUMP TRUCK 101 mm 1962

Same cab and chassis as above, cast tipper, unpainted hubs, white tires, spare wheel, clear plastic windows, cream interior, grille, bumpers, and trim, two figures.

    1. Light gray cab, dark yellow tipper, black chassis.

105 BERLIET GAK GROCERY TRUCK 96 mm 1962

Same cab and chassis as above, cast rear body, unpainted hubs, white tires, spare wheel, clear plastic windows, red blinds, cream interior, grille, bumper, and trim, two figures, red "Viandes" logo.

    1. Red cab, white rear body, black chassis.

106 BERLIET GAK STREET SWEEPER 115 mm 1962

Same cab and chassis as above, cast tank, unpainted hubs, white tires, spare wheel, tin rack with brush, clear plastic windows, cream interior, grille, bumpers, and trim, two figures, yellow and black "Balayeuse-Arroseuse" and emblem.

    1. Light gray cab, green tank, black chassis.

107 BERLIET GAK CEMENT MIXER 101 mm 1962

Same cab and chassis as above, cast rear body, mixer, chute, unpainted hubs, black tires, spare, clear plastic windows, cream interior, grille and bumpers, silver trim, two figures.

    1. Red cab, orange mixer, yellow rear and chute, black chassis.

108 BERLIET GAK CRANE TRUCK 96 mm 1964

Same cab and chassis as above, cast rear body and crane, unpainted hook and hubs, white tires, spare wheel, clear plastic windows, cream interior, silver grille, bumper, and trim, five figures, winch with line.

    1. Dark yellow cab, light gray rear and crane, black chassis.

109 BERLIET GAK GARBAGE TRUCK 108 mm 1964

Same cab and chassis as above, cast two-piece raising rear body, unpainted hubs, black tires, spare wheel, clear plastic windows, yellow interior, grille, and bumpers, silver trim, two figures, wire tipping lever.

    1. Light gray cab, silver rear body, black chassis.

110 BERLIET GAK OVERHEAD SERVICE TRUCK 112 mm 1964

Same cab and chassis as above, cast rear body, mount, arms and basket, unpainted hubs, black tires, spare wheel, clear plastic windows, cream interior, silver grille, bumper, and trim, two figures.

    1. Dark yellow cab, light gray rear and parts, black chassis.

111 BERLIET GAK FARM TRUCK 96 mm 1964

Same cab and chassis as above, cast rear bed and stakes, unpainted hubs, black tires, spare wheel, clear plastic windows, cream interior, silver grille, bumper, and trim, two figures.

    1. Dark yellow cab, green bed and stakes, black chassis.

112 BERLIET GAK PIPE TRUCK 96 mm 1964

Cast cutaway cab, rear body and black chassis, unpainted hubs, white tires, spare wheel, yellow sheet metal cab panel, cream interior, grille, and bumper, silver trim, one figure, metal pipes.

1. Dark yellow cab, green rear body.

113 BERLIET GAK GLASS TRUCK 96 mm 1964
Same cab and chassis as usual, cast rear bed, unpainted hubs, white tires, spare wheel, light gray tin rack, clear plastic windows, cream interior, grille, and bumper, silver trim, two figures.
1. Green cab, light gray rear and rack, black chassis.

114 BERLIET GAK CRANE TRUCK 96 mm 1964
Same cab and chassis as usual, cast rear body and crane, unpainted hook, unpainted or white plastic hubs, black tires, spare wheel, clear plastic windows, cream interior, silver grille, bumper, and trim, two figures, winch with line.
1. Dark yellow cab and crane, green rear, black chassis.

115 BERLIET GAK TOW TRUCK 112 mm 1964/65
Same cab and chassis as usual, cast rear body and bar, unpainted hubs, white tires, spare wheel, tin cover and hook, clear plastic windows, cream interior, grille, bumper, and trim, two figures.
1. Green cab, dark yellow rear, bar and cover, black chassis.

116 BERLIET GAK BUCKET TRUCK 96 mm 1965
Same cab and chassis as usual, cast bucket and arms, unpainted hubs, black tires, spare wheel, clear plastic windows, cream interior, silver grille, bumper, and trim, two figures.
1. Dark yellow cab, green bucket and arms, black chassis.

201 PACIFIC HEAVY CRANE TRUCK 143 mm 1967
Cast truck (cab unit of models below) parts, mount and crane, unpainted hook and hubs, black tires, steering spare wheel on roof, winch with line, "Convoi Exceptionel," roundel, checker and other decals.
1. Olive body, mount and crane.

202 PACIFIC PIPE CARRIER TRUCK 362 mm 1959
Cast cab and semi parts, unpainted hubs, black tires, steering spare wheel on roof, tin racks, silver cardboard pipe with roundels and "Pétroles du Sahara éléments de pipe line" decals.
1. Metallic light blue cab and semi.

203 PACIFIC ROCKET LAUNCHER TRUCK 362 mm 1959
Cast cab and semi parts as above, unpainted swiveling radar dish, launcher parts and hubs, black tires, steering spare wheel on roof, crank, white plastic rocket with "U.S. Army," roundel and checker decals.
1. Metallic light blue cab and semi.

204 PACIFIC TRANSFORMER CARRIER 362 mm 1965
Cast cab and semi parts as above, folding ramp, gray swiveling searchlight, unpainted transformer parts and hubs, black tires, steering spare wheel on roof, black and white plastic transformer parts, clear lens, winch, checker decals.
1. Dark yellow cab and semi.

205 PACIFIC CEMENT TRUCK 362 mm 1966
Cast cab and semi parts as above, light gray containers, yellow folding ramp, light gray searchlight, unpainted hubs, black tires, steering spare wheel on roof, black plastic parts, clear lens, "S.F.J.I." cement logo and checker decals.
1. Dark yellow cab and semi.

206 PACIFIC ATOMIC CANNON TRUCK 362 mm 1966/67
Cast cab and semi parts as above, adjustable barrel, swiveling AA guns, unpainted hubs, black tires, steering spare wheel on roof, roundel and checker decals.
1. Olive cab and semi.

207 ATOMIC CANNON
Stationary cannon of 206 and 208, not mounted on a truck.
    1. Presumably olive.

208 PACIFIC ATOMIC CANNON TRUCK 362 mm 1967
Identical to 206 except for cast searchlight with clear plastic lens instead of AA guns behind cab.
    1. Olive cab and semi.

301 GMC AMBULANCE TRUCK 114 mm 1959
Cast cab-chassis, rear body, white hubs, and tires, sheet metal rear cover and front base, red cross and "Ambulance" decals.
    1. White cab, rear body and cover.

302 GMC COVERED TRUCK 114 mm 1961
Cast cab-chassis, rear body and unpainted hubs, black tires, silver tin cover.
    1. Light gray cab, yellow rear body.

303 GMC ANTI-AIRCRAFT GUN TRUCK 114 mm 1959
Cast cab-chassis, rear body, mount, guns, and olive hubs, black tires, four plastic figures.
    1. Olive cab, rear body, mount and guns.

304 GMC LANCE-ROCKET TRUCK 114 mm 1959
Cast cab-chassis, rear body, mount, launchers, and olive hubs, black tires, four plastic figures.
    1. Olive cab, rear body, mount and launchers.

305 GMC ROCKET CARRIER TRUCK 117 mm 1965
Cast cab-chassis, rear body, mount, and launcher, white hubs and tires, silver gray plastic two-piece rocket, clear nose cone, three figures.

    1. White cab, rear body, mount and launchers.

306 GMC DUMP TRUCK WITH SHOVEL 132 mm 1961
Cast cab-chassis, tipper, shovel loader, light gray hubs, black tires.
    1. Light gray cab, dark yellow tipper and shovel.

Numbers not known:

GMC CRANE TRUCK 1961

GMC DUMP TRUCK 1961
See below.

GMC DUMP TRUCK AND TRAILER 200 mm 1961?
Cast cab-chassis, tipper, trailer body, and chassis, unpainted hubs, black tires.
    1. Red cab, dark yellow tipper and trailer.

GMC FIRE TRUCK 1961

GMC LUMBER TRUCK 114 mm 1959
Cast cab-chassis and rack, unpainted hubs, load of wood.
    1. Red cab, dark yellow rack.

GMC QUARRY DUMP TRUCK 1961

GMC RADAR TRUCK 114 mm 1959
Cast cab-chassis, rear body, mount, unpainted radar dish and hubs, black tires.
    1. Olive cab, rear body and mount.

GMC ROAD REPAIR TRUCK 1961

GMC SEARCHLIGHT TRUCK 114 mm 1959
Cast cab-chassis, rear body, mount, and searchlight, unpainted hubs, black tires, clear plastic lens.
    1. Olive cab, rear body, mount and searchlight.

GMC STREET SWEEPER 1961

GMC TANK TRUCK 119 mm 1961
Cast cab-chassis, tank, unpainted hubs, black tires.
    1. Green cab, dark yellow tank.

GMC TROOP CARRIER 1959

401 DODGE OPEN ARMY TRUCK 94 mm 1960
Cast body, olive sheet metal windshield frame and sideboards, silver gray plastic hubs, black tires.
    1. Olive body.

402 DODGE ARMY TROOP CARRIER 94 mm 1964
Same casting and parts as 401 with olive hubs, plus olive plastic figures.
    1. Olive body.

403 COVERED ARMY TRUCK 94 mm 196_
Same casting and parts as 401 plus tin cover, no other data.
    1. Olive body.

404 DODGE ANTI-AIRCRAFT TRUCK 94 mm 1960
Same casting and parts as 401 plus cast mount and AA guns, olive hubs and plastic figures.
    1. Olive body, mount and guns.

405 DODGE RADAR TRUCK 94 mm 1960

Same casting and parts as 401 with olive hubs and mount, unpainted radar dish, olive plastic figures. White version has white hubs and tires.
    1. Olive body and mount.
    2. White body and mount.

406 DODGE SEARCHLIGHT TRUCK 94 mm 1960
Same castings and parts as 405 but with cast searchlight and clear plastic lens instead of guns.
    1. Olive body, mount and searchlight.
    2. White body, mount and searchlight.

407 DODGE FIRE TRUCK 94 mm 1966
Cast body, mount, unpainted extending ladder and hubs, dark red windshield frame, black tires, blue plastic figures.
    1. Dark red body and mount.

408 DODGE LANCE-ROCKET TRUCK 94 mm 1966
Same casting and parts as 401 with gray hubs, plus cast mount, olive plastic launchers and figures.
    1. Olive body and mount.

409 DODGE AMBULANCE TRUCK 94 mm 196_
Cast body, white plastic cover, silver gray hubs, black tires; may have had red crosses.
    1. White body and cover.

410 DODGE ROCKET CARRIER
Presumably same body with rocket and mount as on 305.
    1. Olive or white body?

501 OPEN ARMY JEEP 80 mm 1961
Cast body, olive windshield frame, gray hubs, black tires, spare

wheel, olive figures, roundel decal.
1. Olive body.

502 COVERED ARMY JEEP 80 mm 1964
Same casting and parts as 501 plus green plastic cover on wire hoops.
1. Olive body.

503 ARMY JEEP WITH ANTI-AIRCRAFT GUNS 80 mm 1961
Same casting and parts as 501 plus olive cast mount and guns.
1. Olive body, mount and guns.

504 ARMY JEEP WITH LANCE-ROCKETS 80 mm 1961
Same casting and parts as 501 plus olive cast mount and plastic launchers.
1. Olive body and mount.

505 ARMY RADAR JEEP 80 mm 1961
Same casting and parts as 501 plus olive cast mount and unpainted radar dish.
1. Olive body and mount.

506 ARMY JEEP WITH SEARCHLIGHT 80 mm 1961
Same casting and parts as 501 plus olive cast mount and light, clear plastic lens.
1. Olive body, mount and light.

507 FIRE JEEP 80 mm 1961
Same casting and parts as 501 with red hubs, white tires, red windshield frame, plus red cast mount and unpainted extending ladder.
1. Red body and mount.

508 POLICE JEEP 80 mm 1965

Same casting and parts as 502 including green cover, with silver gray hubs and antenna, white tires, "Police" lettering.
1. Dark blue body.

601 JEEP AND ANTITANK GUN 160 mm 1961
Same Jeep as 501 plus cast gun, shield, chassis and olive hubs, black tires.
1. Olive Jeep and gun.

602 JEEP AND GENERATOR TRAILER 135 mm 196_
Same Jeep as 501 plus cast box trailer, olive hubs, black tires.
1. Olive Jeep and trailer.

603 JEEP AND OPEN TRAILER 144 mm 1961
Same Jeep as 501 plus cast open trailer, olive hubs, black tires.
1. Olive Jeep and trailer.

604 not known; may be one of models listed below.

605 ANTITANK GUN 84 mm 1961
Same gun as in 601, without Jeep.
1. Olive gun.

Numbers not known:

ANTI-AIRCRAFT GUN TRAILER 1960

LANCE-ROCKET TRAILER 65 mm 1960
Cast open trailer and mount, olive plastic launchers, unpainted hubs, black tires, wire tow hook.
1. Olive body and mount.

RADAR TRAILER 1960

SEARCHLIGHT TRAILER 65 mm 1960
Cast open trailer, mount, and searchlight, unpainted hubs, black tires, clear plastic lens, wire tow hook.
  1. Olive body, mount and light.

701 BERLIET STRADAIR DUMP TRUCK 105 mm 1967
Cast cab, tipper, opening tailgate, black chassis, clear plastic windows, cream interior, blue figures, light gray hubs, black tires, wire tipping lever.
  1. Dark red cab, dark yellow tipper.

702 BERLIET STRADAIR GROCERY TRUCK 105 mm 1967
Cast cab, rear body, black chassis, red plastic blinds, clear windows, cream interior, blue figures, light gray hubs, black tires.
  1. Red cab, white rear body.

703 BERLIET STRADAIR TOW TRUCK 121 mm 1967
Cast cab, rear body, bar, black chassis, yellow tin cover and hook, clear plastic windows, cream interior, blue figures, light gray hubs, black tires, "Service Dépannage" decals.
  1. Light green cab, dark yellow rear body.

704 BERLIET STRADAIR GLASS TRUCK 105 mm 1967
Cast cab, rear body, black chassis, light gray tin rack, clear plastic glass load and windows, cream interior, blue figures, light gray hubs, black tires.
  1. Light green cab, light gray rear body and rack.

705 not known

706 BERLIET STRADAIR STREET SWEEPER 115 mm 1967
Cast cab, rear body, black chassis, unpainted tin rack with brush, clear plastic windows, cream interior, blue figures, light gray hubs, black tires.
  1. Light gray cab, light green tank.

707 BERLIET STRADAIR GARBAGE TRUCK 1967
Same cab and chassis as above, presumably with rear body as 109.
  1. No data.

708 BERLIET STRADAIR COCA-COLA TRUCK 105 mm 1967
Cast cab, rear body, black chassis, red and black plastic cases, clear windows, cream interior, blue figures, light gray hubs, black tires, Coca-Cola logo.
  1. Dark yellow cab and rear body.

J. R. D.

Though I assume that the J stands for "Jouets" (toys), I cannot even guess what the R and the D stand for, unless the "R" is for its founder, M. Rabier. The firm of J.R.D. was founded in Montreuil in 1935 and produced plaster-and-flour toys in the late thirties. Only in 1958 did the firm begin to produce diecast miniature vehicles–at a time when it seems everybody else in France was doing the same. In terms of quality and subject matter, J.R.D. products much resembled those of their competitors, particularly C.I.J., and the two three-letter firms are remembered in the same breath by many of us as being two of a kind. When J.R.D. gave up miniature car production in 1962, it was C.I.J. that bought some of the dies and reissued them, often with only a new box or an adhesive tape label to show the new maker's name. When C.I.J. in turn ceased production, the story ended–or seemed to until the late eighties, when seven models reappeared, proclaimed as being made from the original dies, but selling for much higher prices. Not having seen the new reissues, I can only list them and relate them to the original models that they represent.

Like most models of the fifties, J.R.D. products consist of cast bodies and hubs, white or black tires, and sometimes clear plastic windows, plus sheet metal baseplates. The last models feature turned hubs, windows, detailed interiors and suspension, plus an occasional opening hood or trunk–apparently an attempt to catch up with the competition. Some models were issued in more than one color–I can only list what I know to exist–, but only one color version of other models exists. Almost all the models represent French vehicles, the first thirteen in numerical order being Citroens. There are two versions of the familiar 2CV car and van; the earlier casting can be recognized easily by its not-quite-square grille of horizontal bars with an oval Citroen chevron emblem in the middle, plus its longitudinal hood lines; the later type has an oval grille with superimposed chevron, and the hood has just two recessed channels.

Beyond that, we can only say that J.R.D. models are exactly the kind of miniatures that appeal to those of us who started to collect in the old days and have a soft spot in our hearts for the sort of models that take us back to our early years in the hobby. If you like models of the fifties without modern gimmicks or styling–models that rattle convincingly when you roll them across your desk–chances are you'll like J.R.D. models too.

Plaster and flour models:

BLUEBIRD SPEED RECORD CAR 1/43 1936

PEUGEOT 402 DARL'MART 1/43 1938

PEUGEOT 402 CONVERTIBLE 1/43 1938
Top up.

PEUGEOT 402 CONVERTIBLE 1/43 1938
Top down.

PEUGEOT 402 SEDAN 1/43 1938

Diecast models:

106 CITROEN 1200 KG POLICE VAN 100 mm 1/45 1962
Van with cast body, sliding side door, turned hubs, black tires, black sheet metal base, amber plastic dome light, silver gray Police sign with red and white lettering, white Police decals, silver grille and headlights. Value $60-75.
1. Black body, white lower body, nose and roof.

107 CITROEN 1200 KG RED CROSS VAN 100 MM 1/45 1958
Same castings and major parts as #106, white tires, red cross decals. The Esso van listed here as #113 has also been listed under this number. Value $75-85.
1. White body, red crosses.

108 CITROEN 2CV VAN: EDF 92 mm 1/45 1958
Light van with cast body, unpainted hubs, white tires, black sheet metal base, unpainted ladders on roof, black-on-yellow "EDF" diamond emblem decals, silver grille and headlights.
1. Gray body, first casting. Value $60-75.
2. Gray body, second casting.

109 CITROEN 2CV FIRE VAN 92 mm 1/45 1958
Same casting and parts as #108 including ladders, "SP" and emblem decals. Value $80-90.
1. Red body, first casting.
2. Red body, second casting.

110 CITROEN 2CV SEDAN 91 mm 1/45 1958
Four-door sedan with cast body, unpainted hubs, white tires, black sheet metal base, silver grille and headlights, red taillights. Value $60-75.
1. Dark gray body, ? roof, first casting.
2. Gray body, dark green roof, first casting.
3. Metallic blue body, light tan roof, second casting.

111 CITROEN 2CV VAN 92 mm 1/45 1958
Same casting and parts as #108, white tires, no ladders or logo. Value $60-70.
1. Gray body, first casting.
2. Bluish-gray body, second casting.
3. Yellow body, "PTT" logo, first casting.
4. Yellow body, "PTT" logo, second casting.

112 CITROEN 11CV SEDAN 102 mm 1/45 1958
Four-door sedan with cast body and headlights, unpainted cast or turned hubs, black or white tires, black sheet metal base, silver grille, louvers, lights and bumpers. Value $75-85.
1. Gray body, cast hubs.
2. Blue-gray body, ? hubs.

3. Black body, cast hubs.
4. Black body, turned hubs.

113 CITROEN 1200 KG VAN; ESSO 100 mm 1/45 1958

Same casting and parts as #106, white tires, red-white-blue "Esso Extra Motor Oil" decals. Value $85-95.
1. Silver gray body.
2. Silver gray body, no logo decals.

114 CITROEN P55 COVERED TRUCK 108 mm 1/45 1958

Covered truck with cast body, unpainted hubs, white tires, green sheet metal cover, black cab base, spare wheel, silver emblem and headlights. Value $60-70.
1. Orange body, green cover.
2. Yellow body, green cover.
3. Dark green body, green cover.

115 CITROEN P55 ARMY TRUCK & TRAILER 170 mm 1/45 1958

Same truck casting and parts as $114 with olive cover, cast two-wheel water tank trailer with sheet metal base and ladder, army decals. Value $75-85.
1. Olive truck and trailer.

116 CITROEN DS19 SEDAN 113 mm 1/45 1958

Four-door sedan with cast body, unpainted hubs, white tires, black sheet metal base, clear plastic windows, silver grille, bumpers and headlights, red taillights. Value $65-75.
1. Orange body, cream roof.
2. Yellow body, light green roof.
3. Light gray body, turquoise roof.
4. Gray body, black roof.

117 CITROEN 2CV ROAD SERVICE VAN 92 mm 1/45 1958

Same casting and parts as #111, black-white-red "Secours Routier Francais" decals. Value $75-85.
1. White body, first casting.
2. White body, second casting.

118 CITROEN 2CV VAN: AIR FRANCE 92 mm 1/45 1958

Same casting and parts as #111, blue and white "Air France" logo. Value $75-85.
1. Blue body, white upper rear body, first casting.
2. Blue body, white upper rear body, second casting.

119

Number not used, unless it was given to a "COMAP Robinetterie" promotional 2CV van.

120 BERLIET SEMI-TRAILER: KRONENBOURG 200 mm 1/45 1958

Semi with cast cab, semi, opening rear door, unpainted hubs, and rests, white tires, black sheet metal cab base and semi chassis, cream bumper, headlights and semi roof, white or red and white "Kronenbourg–Biere d'Alsace" logo. Value $150-175.
1. Red cab and semi, cream semi roof.

121 BERLIET SEMI-TRAILER TANKER: TOTAL 204 mm 1/45 1958

Tanker semi with cast cab, semi, unpainted spotlight, and hubs, white tires, black sheet metal cab base and trailer chassis, unpainted ladder, white bumper and lights, orange and blue "Total" logo. Value $150-165.
1. Orange-red cab and lower semi, white tank, blue tank top.

122 UNIC TANK TRUCK: ANTAR 142 mm 1/45 1958

Tanker with cast cab-chassis, tank and silver gray hubs, white tires, black sheet metal cab base, silver grille and headlights, white and black "Antar" logo. Value $125-135.

    1. Red cab and tank.

123 UNIC CAB, TRAILER & RAILROAD CAR 259 mm 1/45 1958

Truck with cast cab and flat trailer, cast freight car, unpainted hubs and railroad wheels, white tires, black sheet metal cab base, freight car roof, chassis and ladder, silver grille and headlights, red and white "Kronenbourg–Biere d'Alsace" logo. Value $175-200.

    1. Red and cream cab, red trailer, white freight car.

124 UNIC IZOARD CIRCUS TRAIN 375 mm 1/45 1958

Truck with same cab as #123, no trailer, two freight cars as #123, green sheet metal car roofs, cream "Cirque" logo on cab, red logo on cars. Value $175-200.

    1. Red and cream cab, cream cars.

125 BERLIET WEITZ CRANE TRUCK 180 mm 1/45 1959

Crane truck with cast body, crane, mount, unpainted controls, hook and hubs, black tires, black sheet metal base, clear plastic windows, silver grille and headlights, working winch and line. Value $120-135.

    1. Orange body, crane and mount.

Note: the red and yellow "Sablieres de la Loire" version is the CIJ reissue.

126 UNIC VAN: HAFA 192 mm 1/45 1959

Truck with cast cab, rear body, opening rear doors, and unpainted hubs, white tires, silver grille and headlights, orange-white-blue "Hafa" logo. Value $150-165.

    1. Orange-red and blue cab and body, blue chassis.

127 UNIC VAN: TRANSPORTS INTERNATIONAUX 192 mm 1/45 1959

Same castings and parts as #126, black tires, cream "Transports Internationaux" logo. Value $150-165.

    1. Green and orange cab and semi.

128 UNIC MILK TANK TRUCK 149 mm 1/45 1959

Truck with cast cab-chassis, rear bed, white tanks, unpainted hubs, white tires, black sheet metal cab base, unpainted ladder and catwalk, red and yellow "60 Hectos" on tanks. Value $140-150.

    1. Blue cab-chassis and bed, white tanks.

129 FRUEHAUF TRUCK TRAILER 150 mm 1/45 1959

Trailer with cast body, chassis, opening rear doors, and unpainted hubs, black tires, cream "Transports Internationaux" logo, matching #127 truck. Value $100-110.

    1. Green and orange trailer.

130 UNIC LIQUID TRANSPORTER 195 mm 1/45 1960

Truck with cast cab, rear body, 3 tanks, and unpainted hubs, black tires, black sheet metal cab base, red ladders, black plastic hose, yellow and maroon "60 Hectos" on tanks. Value $125-135.

    1. Silver and red cab, red rear body, silver tanks.

131 BERLIET GARBAGE TRUCK 138 mm 1/45 1960

Truck with cast cab, rear body, opening rear section, black chassis and unpainted hubs, black tires, clear plastic windows, red fenders, grille, and bumper, silver headlights, tipping lever. Value $125-135.

    1. Silver cab and rear body, red fenders.

132 BERLIET SEMI-TRAILER: ANTARGAZ   214 mm   1/45   1961

Open semi with cast cab, chassis, and semi-trailer, unpainted hubs, black tires, black and red plastic bottle load, clear windows, tan grille and bumper, silver headlights and trim, black stakes, red and black "Antargaz" logo. Value $140-150.

1. Red cab and semi, black chassis.

133 BERLIET FIRE TRUCK   125 mm   1/45   1961

Fire truck with cast cab, rear body, black chassis and unpainted hubs, black tires, unpainted sheet metal ladder, black plastic hose, silver gray reel, clear windows, 4 blue figures, tan bumper and grille, silver parts and lights. Value $150-165.

1. Red cab and rear body, black chassis.

134 BERLIET BOTTLE TRUCK   157 mm   1/45   1962

Truck with cast cab, rear body, black tailboard, unpainted hubs, black tires, green sheet metal cab base, black roof sign, tan plastic cases, clear windows, orange cloth cover, red and white "Préfontaines" logo, red bumper and grille, silver headlights.

1. Green cab and rear body. Value $140-150.

151 PEUGEOT 404 SEDAN   109 mm   1/45   1962

Four-door sedan with cast body, black sheet metal base, turned hubs, white tires, red plastic interior, clear windows, suspension, silver grille, bumpers and headlights, red taillights. Value $50-65.

1. Cream body.
2. Red body.
3. Light blue body.

152 CITROEN DS19 CABRIOLET   113 mm   1/45   1962

Convertible with cast body, black sheet metal chassis, turned hubs, white tires, clear plastic windshield, cream interior, silver grille, bumpers, and headlights, red taillights. Value $50-65.

1. Orange body.
2. Blue body.

153 MERCEDES-BENZ 220S SEDAN   119 mm   1/45   1962

Four-door sedan with cast body, black sheet metal base, turned hubs, white tires, suspension, clear plastic windows, gray interior, chrome grille and bumpers, silver headlights, red taillights. Value $50-65.

1. Metallic blue body.
2. Metallic brown body.
3. White and blue body.

154 CITROEN AMI 6   97 mm   1/45   1962

Four-door sedan with cast body, opening hood, matching chassis, turned hubs, white tires, suspension, clear plastic windows, cream interior, silver gray motor, wire front bumper, silver headlights and bumper, red taillights. Value $50-60.

1. Dusty blue body, pale blue roof.

155 SIMCA 1000 SEDAN   87 mm   1/45   1962

Four-door sedan with cast body, matching chassis, opening hood and trunk, turned hubs, white tires, suspension, clear plastic windows, red interior, silver grille, bumpers, and headlights, red taillights. Value $50-60.

1. Cream body.
2. Red body.
3. Orange body.
4. Light blue body.

156 JAGUAR E-TYPE COUPE   never issued

157 FIAT 2300 STATION WAGON   never issued

Eighties reissues

111 Citroen DS19: ex-116

112 Citroen DS19 Convertible: ex-152

211 Citroen 2CV Sedan: ex-110

221 Citroen 2CV Fire Van: ex-109

223 Citroen 2CV Van: ex-111

301 Citroen HY Van: ex-113

401 Citroen 11CV Sedan: ex-112

MINIALUXE

While Minialuxe is a fairly familiar brand, it is a very frustrating one to research. Some of its models are numbered–maybe they all are!–but it seems that nothing short of a miracle would reveal their complete numbering system. At least their 1/43 scale "Tacots" series of old-timers is numbered throughout, so we can start with them–but first a few notes on their structural history.

Minialuxe models have gone through several stages of development since the original models appeared in or before 1959. One authority cites 1959 as the earliest date of issue, but earlier dates, notably 1954, have been cited elsewhere. Those first models had one-piece bodies (sometimes with painted parts), plain black chassis with two longitudinal bars and small lettering, no windows, interiors, or suspension, silver-painted features such as grilles, bumpers, and lights, and colored hubs with tires, the latter usually white–or at times one-piece wheels. Tabs rising from the base held the axles.

A big step forward during the sixties brought clear plastic windows and headlights, separate colored components for the roofs of two-tone cars–that of the Citroen DS19 is inside the window casting, oddly enough–and chrome-plated parts such as bumpers. The wheel hubs were often, but not always, cream and tended to crack; they carried white or black tires, and their axles were held down by four slim bars, part of the black plastic chassis, which also served as springs, hence the "Suspension breveté" lettering on the base–and the base lettering in general was now easier to read. These suspension members were joined to the main part of the base toward the center but not at the ends, providing the flexibility that made them function as springs.

The obvious next step was the addition of an interior and a steering wheel, but at roughly the same time, opening hoods and trunks, detailed motors (at first integral with the body and painted silver, later chromed), and chromed hubs with black tires were introduced. This was about where things stood by 1968 or 1969.

In the seventies, solid chassis returned, now detailed; chromed hubs also grew more detailed, and the suspension was hidden inside the car, though it probably functioned somewhat as before. Toward the end, the amount of silvering decreased, bumpers and/or grilles were often left black, and motors cast integrally with the body were left in the body color, regardless of what it was. The quality of casting had improved considerably by this point, and parts fit together a lot better than before. Still in all, the cost-cutting measures just noted must have had some relation to the firm's financial stability, and though I can't prove it, I assume the firm faded out of existence, or at least out of miniature car production, somewhere in the mid-seventies. The last date I have found for the introduction of a new model is 1974. The firm rarely, if ever, produced great quantities of new models, but kept some venerable ones, such as the Formula I Mercedes-Benz and Gordini of the mid-fifties, in production for many years. As has been pointed out in the pages of the journal "Ma Collection," the Minialuxe models of such cars as the Delahaye coupe and the Hotchkiss-Gregoire have become popular among collectors because they represent cars rarely available in model form–and the four-door Panhard and Peugeot 404 convertibles are unique in that they represent cars that never really existed.

Minialuxe products include the aforementioned "Tacots," a series that extended to 34 models until the old Citroen 11 CV was resurrected and added to it in 1974, a small series of HO scale old-timers (six models announced, apparently only four produced), a number of passenger cars (16 of them in an S series extant around 1969), some chromed versions of them, a small C series of commercial vehicles (I can only verify two members of it), and an assortment of motorcycles, car-and-trailer sets, and the like. A series of 1/32 scale plastic vehicles also appeared in 1959, with a few light vans added to it during the sixties. Though these models are far from being finest-quality, priceless collectors' items, still they have a personality of their own and include some unusual vehicles.

Most, if not all, Minialuxe models were made in a variety of colors; I can only list what I know to exist. As for values, a few of the oldest cars may reach $50, but most Minialuxe models are probably worth $5 to $10 each.

Tacots

1/43 scale plastic old-timers, value $8-15 each

1 FORD MODEL T ROADSTER 1909 84 mm 1964
Three-seater, top up, with front and rear body, roof, seats, black chassis, gold grille, lights, etc., clear windshield, white spoked hubs, black tires.
    1. Yellow front and rear body, gray roof, light gray seats.
    2. Red-brown front and rear body, white roof, red seats.

2 PACKARD 1912 88 mm 1964
Town car, front and rear body, roof, seats, black chassis, gold radiator shell, lights, etc., black grille, clear windows, white spoked hubs, black tires.
    1. Red front and rear body, white roof and seats.
    2. Blue front and rear body, light gray roof and seats.

3 FORD MODEL T 1911 75 mm 1964
Two-seater, top down, with body, cab, seats, folded top, black chassis and grille, gold radiator shell, lights, etc., clear windshield, red spoked hubs, black tires.
    1. White body and seats, red cab, red and black top.
    2. Blue body and cab, yellow seats and top.

4 RENAULT PARIS-MADRID 1903 85 mm 1964
Two-seat racing car with hood, rear body, chassis, seats, and dash, gold radiators, lights, spoked hubs, black tires.
    1. Yellow hood and rear body, red chassis, seats, and dash.
    2. Blue hood and rear body, cream chassis, yellow seats and dash.

5 RENAULT LANDAU 1907 88 mm 1964
Roofed-closed car with front and rear body, top, red front seats, black

chassis, gold grille, lights, etc., clear windows, spoked hubs, black tires.

    1. Green front and rear body, black top, brown hubs.

    2. Gray front, light green rear body, dark green top, chrome hubs.

    3. ? front, yellow rear body, red top.

6 CITROEN B2 1925 87 mm 1964

Four-door sedan with body, roof, black chassis and grille, silver radiator shell, lights, and disc hubs, black tires, clear windows.

    1. Light gray body, tan roof.

    2. Light gray body, dark blue roof.

    3. Light gray body and roof.

7 RENAULT TAXI DE LA MARNE 1907 88 mm 1964

Open-cab taxi with front and rear body, front seats, black top and chassis, gold radiator, lights, etc., spoked hubs, black tires, spare tire.

    1. Red front and rear body, gray seats, red hubs.

    2. Yellow front and rear body, red seats, brown hubs.

8 PEUGEOT DOUBLE PHAETON 1906 96 mm 1964

Open four-seater with body and opening rear doors, seats, black chassis, gold grille, lights, etc., cream or white spoked hubs, black tires, spare tire.

    1. White body and doors, brown and blue seats.

    2. Red-brown body and doors, cream and red-brown seats.

    3. Red-brown body and doors, white and blue seats.

9 PEUGEOT TORPEDO 1906 98 mm 1964

Four-seater, top up, with same parts as 8 plus black top, with cream and red or blue seats, red or brown hubs.

    1. White body and doors, cream and red seats, red hubs.

    2. Red-brown body and doors, cream and blue seats, brown hubs.

10 RENAULT TRUCK 1910 96 mm 1964

Truck with front body, cab roof, rear body, red chassis and seats, gold grille, lights, etc., clear windows, cream spoked hubs, black tires, load of three brown wooden barrels.

    1. Gray front, black rear body and cab roof.

11 FORD MODEL T 1915 79 mm 1964

Two-seater, top up, with same parts as 3 plus black top.

    1. Red body and cab.

    2. Yellow body and cab.

12 FORD ROADSTER 1907 85 mm 1965

Open two-seater with same parts as 1 plus black folded top, red or cream seats, spare tire.

    1. White front and rear body, red seats.

    2. Red front and rear body, cream seats.

13 OLDSMOBILE CURVED DASH 1902 65 mm 1965

Four-seater with body, raised front top, red seats, floor, and dash, gold lights, etc., clear hubs, black tires.

    1. Black body and top.

14 PEUGEOT VICTORIA 1892 72 mm 1965

Four-seater with body, black raised rear top, seats, dash, and chassis, gold lights, etc., clear hubs, black tires.

    1. Red body.

15 AUTOCAR TONNEAU 1903 94 mm 1965

Roofed six-seater with body, opening rear door, seats, hampers, gold lights, etc., black top and chassis, clear windshield, spoked hubs, black tires.

    1. Red body, red-brown seats, yellow hampers, cream hubs.

    2. Maroon body, light gray seats, cream hampers, red hubs.

    3. Gray body, red-brown seats, yellow hampers, cream hubs.

16   PEUGEOT ROYAL VIS-À-VIS 1891   64 mm   1965
Four-seat vis-à-vis with body, chassis, raised rear top, red seats, gold lights, etc., clear hubs, black tires.
1. White body, chassis, and top.

17   PANHARD-LEVASSOR 1895   58 mm   1965
Coupe with upper and lower body, opening trunk, black chassis, roof, and seats, gold lights, etc., clear windows, red spoked hubs, black tires.
1. Gray upper and lower body and trunk.

18   PANHARD-LEVASSOR 1891   60 mm   1965
Open two-seater with body, opening hatch, black chassis and seats, gold lights, etc., red parasol and spoked hubs, black tires.
1. Yellow body and hatch.
2. Gray body and hatch.

19   PANHARD SKIFF LABOURDETTE 1914   110 mm   1965
Sports four-seater with body parts, black raised top, chassis, and grille, gold radiator shell, lights, etc., clear hubs, black tires, spare tire.
1. Yellow and black body.
2. Blue and tan body.

20   BALDA VIS-À-VIS 1895   64 mm   1966
Four-seat vis-à-vis with body, blue chassis and seats, white and bronze fringed top, gold lights, etc., white spoked hubs, black tires.
1. White body.

21   RENAULT GRANDE REMISE 1906   93 mm   1966
Partly closed car with body, chassis, light brown roof, seats, and folded rear top, gold radiators, lights, etc., clear windshield, spoked hubs, black tires.
1. Yellow body, black chassis, red front seat, gray hubs.

2. Black body and chassis, light brown front seat, clear hubs.

22   PEUGEOT QUADRICYCLE 1892   71 mm   1966
Open four-seater with body, black chassis, seats, and dash, gold lights, etc., clear hubs, black tires.
1. Blue body.

23   RENAULT ARMY TRUCK 1914   99 mm   1966
Covered truck with chassis, cab, rear cover, black seats, cab roof, rear body and radiator, gray spoked hubs, black tires, white-on-black "8 Artillerie" labels.
1. Light gray chassis, cab, and rear cover.

24   PANHARD 1892 COUPE   61 mm   1966
Four-seater, top up, with same body as 18, gray top, black chassis, and seats, silver lights, etc., spoked hubs, black tires.
1. Blue body, gray hubs.
2. Gray body, red hubs.

25   PEUGEOT VIS-À-VIS 1892   67 mm   1966
Roofed vis-à-vis with body, roof, yellow chassis and seats, gold lights, etc., clear hubs, black tires.
1. Black body and roof.

26   JAMIESON 1902   79 mm   1967
Open racing car with body, chassis, seat, opening rear panels, red seats, floor, and panels, gold and black parts, clear hubs, black tires.
1. Gray body, chassis, and seat.

27   PARK ROYAL LANDAU 1912   102 mm   1967
Motorized coach with body, cab, opening doors, black chassis, top, and seats, yellow spoked hubs, black tires.
1. Red-brown body, cab, and doors.

28 AUSTIN VAN 1911 95 mm 1967
Box van with body, chassis, seat, opening door, black cab and grille, gold radiator shell, lights, etc., brown spoked hubs, black tires, gold "Lawrence White & Co." logo.
    1. Red body, chassis, seat, and door.
    2. Dark blue body, chassis, and door, red and black seat.

29 LANCHESTER 1908 85 mm 1967
Town car with body, blue seats, black chassis, rear top, and dash, gold grille, lights etc., gray spoked hubs, black tires.
    1. Yellow body.

30 PANHARD ROI DES BELGES 1905 97 mm 1967
Touring car with body, chassis, top, seats, black grille, gold radiator shell, lights, etc., spoked hubs, black tires.
    1. Maroon body, chassis, and top, black seats, brown hubs.
    2. Black body, chassis, and top, maroon seats, red hubs.

31 DE DION-BOUTON LIMOUSINE 1912 117 mm 1967
Closed car with body, chassis, cab roof, grille, maroon seats, gold radiator shell, lights, etc., red spoked hubs, black tires.
    1. Black body, chassis, roof, and grille.

32 LORRAINE-DIETRICH TORPEDO 1905 106 mm 1967
Open tourer with body, chassis, black folded top, seats, and grille, gold radiator shell, lights, etc., brown spoked hubs, black tires.
    1. Dark blue body and chassis.

33 BERLIET OPEN TRUCK 1913 1968/69?
No data. Was it ever issued?

34 PEUGEOT DOUBLE PHAETON 1906 92 mm 1968
Touring car with body, opening doors, seats, black chassis and two raised tops, gold grille, lights, etc., spoked hubs, black tires, spare tire.
    1. White body and doors, red seats, gray hubs.
    2. Blue body and doors, red-brown seats, brown hubs.

35 CITROEN 11CV 1974
May have been reissue of earlier car; see below.

101 DELAUNAY-BELLEVILLE 1911 57 mm 1968
Double-bodied closed car with body, black chassis, seats, and grille, gold radiator shell and lights, clear windows, red spoked hubs, black tires.
    1. Rust red body.

102 MULLER 1913 64 mm 1968
Double-ended steamer with central cab, black chassis and hoods, gold grilles, brown spoked wheels.
    1. Yellow cab.

103 CLÉMENT-BAYARD 1912 50 mm 1968
Closed car with upper and lower body, hood, dark blue chassis, gold radiator and lights, tinted windows, brown spoked hubs, black tires.
    1. Light gray body and hood.

104 HILLS LOCOMOTIVE 1839 65 mm 1968
Open steamer with main body, yellow and black body parts, black chassis and stack, red-brown seats, brown spoked wheels.
    1. Yellow main body.

105 ISOTTA-FRASCHINI
Apparently not issued.

106 BUGATTI ROYALE
Apparently not issued.

Modern vehicles, 1/43 scale plastic; value $5-10 unless otherwise noted; numbered models first:

C-1 BERLIET STRADAIR TANKER SEMI 1969
No data.

C-2 BERLIET PARIS BUS 257 mm 1969
Single deck bus with body parts, opening doors, brown interior, clear windows, tinted headlights, red taillights, chrome grille, labels. Value $15-20.
    1. White upper body, green lower body, roof, and doors.

S-1 SIATA-FIAT 1500 TS 98 mm 1967
Coupe with body, opening hood, chassis, interior, clear windows, clear or tinted headlights, silver motor, chrome grille and bumpers. Value $10-15.
    1. Maroon body and hood, red chassis, white interior.
    2. Blue body and hood, black chassis and interior.

S-2 BMW 1500 106 mm 1967
Four-door sedan with body, black chassis and interior, clear windows, yellow headlights, red taillights, chrome grille and bumpers. Value $10-15.
    1. Red body.
    2. Blue body.

S-3 SIMCA 1300 97 mm 1964
Four-door sedan with body, opening hood, black chassis, +/- interior, clear windows and headlights, red taillights, silver motor. Value $8-12.
    1. Light gray body and hood, tan interior.
    2. Dark gray body and hood, no interior.

S-4 FORD CONSUL 105 mm 1963
Four-door sedan with body, opening hood, black interior and chassis, clear windows and headlights, silver motor, chrome grille and bumpers. Value $8-12.
    1. Yellow-orange body.

S-5 PEUGEOT 204 93 mm 1969
Four-door sedan with body, opening hood, black chassis and interior, clear windows and headlights, red taillights, chrome motor, grille, and bumpers. Value $8-12.
    1. White body.
    2. Dark green body.
    3. Light blue body.

S-6 FIAT 124 92 mm 1969
Four-door sedan with body, opening hood and trunk, black chassis and interior, clear windows, chrome motor, grille, headlights, and bumpers.
    1. Green body.

S-7 SIMCA 1100 1968?
No data.

S-8 VOLVO 144 105 mm 1968
Four-door sedan with body, opening hood and trunk, black chassis, tan interior, clear windows and headlights, yellow taillights, chrome motor, grille, and bumpers.
    1. Red body, hood, and trunk.

S-9 CITROEN AMI 6 BREAK 92 mm 1962
Wagon with body, opening hood and hatch, black chassis, red interior, clear windows, tinted headlights, silver motor, grille, and bumpers.

1. Gray body.

S-10   RENAULT 16TS   98 mm   1968

Four-door hatchback with body, opening hood and hatch, interior, black chassis, clear windows, tinted headlights, red taillights, chrome motor, grille, and bumpers.
1. Maroon body, hood, and hatch, brown interior.
2. Dark blue body, hood, and hatch, black interior.

S-11   CITROEN DYANE   90 mm   1972 or before

Four-door hatchback with body, opening hood and hatch, black chassis, red interior, clear windows, chrome motor, grille, bumpers, and headlights.
1. Pale blue body, hood, and hatch.

S-12   PORSCHE 911S TARGA CABRIOLET   98 mm   1968

Sports car with body, opening hood, black chassis and interior, clear windows and headlights, chrome bumpers.
1. Red body.
2. Turquoise body.

S-13   RENAULT R10 MAJOR   94 mm   1968

Four-door sedan with body, opening front and rear hoods, black chassis, tan interior, clear windows and headlights, chrome motor and bumpers.
1. Cream body and hoods.
2. Dark green body and hoods.

S-14   MATRA DJET 6   95 mm   1968

Sports coupe with body, opening hatch, interior, black chassis, clear windows and headlights, red taillights, chrome bumpers, spare wheel.
1. Dark green body, tan interior.
2. Blue body and hatch, black interior.

S-15   JAGUAR E-TYPE ROADSTER   100 mm   1968

Details presumably like next model minus hardtop.
1. No data.

S-16   JAGUAR E-TYPE COUPE   100 mm   1968

Sports coupe with body, opening hood, chassis, tan interior, clear windows, tinted headlights, chrome motor and bumpers.
1. White body.

Unnumbered 1/43 scale plastic models, listed alphabetically.
Value $5-10 unless otherwise noted.

ALPINE-RENAULT A310   94 mm   1973

Fastback coupe with body, opening hood, black chassis and interior, clear windows and headlights.
1. Yellow body.

BMW   196_

No data; may be S-2 BMW 1500.

BMW 1500 WITH SKIS   106 mm   1967 or later

S-2 model plus skis and racks.
1. Light blue body and hood.

CITROEN AMI 6   92 mm   1962

Four-door sedan with body, roof, black chassis, clear windows and headlights, chrome grille and bumper.
1. Red body, cream roof.

CITROEN CX 2000   106 mm   1971

Four-door fastback with body, opening hood, black chassis and interior, clear windows, silver motor, chrome bumper and lights.

1. Dark tan body and hood.

CITROEN DS19   107 mm   1959
Four-door sedan with body, roof, black chassis, clear windows, chrome bumper. Value $8-12.
1. Green body, white roof.

CITROEN DS19 CONVERTIBLE   107 mm?   1959?
No data.

CITROEN DS19 TAXI   107 mm   196_
DS 19 sedan with white plastic roof sign, red "Taxi" lettering and antenna.
1. Black body, red roof.

CITROEN DS21   110 mm   1970
No data, but see next model.

CITROEN DS21 POLICE CAR   110 mm   1970
Sedan with plastic body, silver roof, clear windows and headlights, blue dome light, white antenna, silver bumpers and hubs, black tires, white-on-black "Police" labels.
1. Black body.

CITROEN DS21 PRESS CAR   110 mm   1970?
No data.

CITROEN DYANE MEHARI   84 mm   1970
Two-seat Jeep-type vehicle with body, hood, black chassis, windshield frame, and seats, clear windshield and headlights, brown steering wheel, spare wheel.
1. Red body and hood.

CITROEN 11CV TRACTION AVANT   106 mm   1959
Four-door sedan with body, chassis, red interior, clear windows, silver headlights, grille, and bumpers. Value $10-15.
1. Black body.

CITROEN GS   94 mm   1972
Four-door fastback with body, opening hood, black chassis and interior, clear windows, chrome motor, lights, and bumpers.
1. Dark turquoise body and hood.

CITROEN SM   113 mm   1971
Two-door hatchback with body, opening hood and hatch, and chassis, black interior, clear windows, chrome motor, headlights, and bumpers, red taillights.
1. Dark turquoise body, chassis, hood, and hatch.

CITROEN SM POLICE CAR   113 mm   1971
Same basic model as above, no other data.

DELAHAYE 235 COUPE   1956
No data. Value $25 plus.

FERRARI FORMULA I   88 mm   1972
Racing car with body, chassis, white airfoils, chrome or black motor, black seat, racing number.
1. Red body and chassis, chrome motor.
2. Red body and chassis, black motor.

FIAT 124 DRIVING SCHOOL CAR   92 mm   1969
Same basic model as S-6, no other data.

FIAT 124 WITH LUGGAGE RACK   92 mm   1969
Same basic model as S-6, no other data.

FORD ANGLIA   89 mm   1964
Two-door sedan with body, black chassis, clear windows and head-lights, chrome grille and bumpers. Value $8-12.
    1. Red body.

FORD GT MARK IV   99 mm   1970
Sports-racing coupe with body, chassis, black interior, clear windows and headlights, silver motor, racing number.
    1. White body, yellow chassis.
    2. Yellow-orange body, red chassis.

FORD TAUNUS 17M   102 mm   1963
Two-door sedan with body, black chassis, clear windows and head-lights, chrome grille and bumper. Value $8-12.
    1. Blue body.

FORD VEDETTE   1959
No data.

FORDSON TRACTOR   196_
No data.

GORDINI FORMULA I   93 mm   1961?
Racing car with body, chassis, yellow dash, clear windshield, white steering wheel, chrome grille, black racing number. Value $10-15.
    1. Red body and chassis.
    2. Blue body and chassis.
    3. Chrome body and chassis.

HOTCHKISS-GREGOIRE   105 mm   1956?
Four-door sedan with body, black chassis, white headlights, silver grille and bumpers. Value $40-50.
    1. Gray body.

HOTCHKISS-GREGOIRE WITH LUGGAGE RACK   105 mm   1958?
Same basic model as above; no other data.

JAGUAR D-TYPE   90 mm   1959
Sports-racing car with body, chassis, cream dash and steering wheel, clear windshield and headlights, chrome grille. Value $10-15.
    1. Red body and chassis.
    2. Green body and chassis.
    3. Chrome body and chassis.

MATRA DJET 6 POLICE CAR   95 mm   1972
Same basic model as S-14, no other data.

MATRA MS80 FORMULA I   96 mm   1972
Racing car with body, airfoil, black suspension, chrome motor and exhaust pipes, clear windshield, racing number.
    1. Blue body.

MERCEDES-BENZ 300SLR
No data. Does it exist?

MERCEDES-BENZ W196 FORMULA I   97 mm   1959
Racing car with body, chassis, cream dash and steering wheel, silver grille, clear windshield, black racing number. Value $10-15.
    1. Yellow body and chassis.
    2. Red body and chassis.
    3. Blue body and chassis.
    4. Chrome body and chassis.

PANHARD PL17   101 mm   1962
Four-door sedan with body, roof, black chassis, clear windows and headlights, silver bumpers. Value $10-15.

1. Cream body, red roof.

PANHARD PL17 CABRIOLET   101 mm   1962
Same parts as above minus roof, plus interior; may have silver gray chassis. Value $10-15.
1. Light blue body, cream interior.
2. Red body and interior.

PEUGEOT 203   1956
No data.

PEUGEOT 203 TAXI   1957
No data.

PEUGEOT 203 BREAK   103 mm   1957
Four-door wagon with body, black chassis, white headlights, silver grille and bumpers. Value $10-15.
1. Gray body.

PEUGEOT 403   109 mm   1959
Four-door sedan with body, black chassis, clear windows and headlights, silver grille and bumpers. Value $8-12.
1. Aqua body.

PEUGEOT 404   105 mm   1962
Four-door sedan with body, black chassis, clear windows and headlights, silver grille and bumpers. Value $8-12.
1. Dark blue body.
2. Chrome body.

PEUGEOT 404 CABRIOLET   1962
No data.

PEUGEOT 504   103 mm   1972
Four-door sedan with body, opening hood and trunk, black chassis and interior, clear windows, chrome motor, grille, and bumpers, tinted headlights.
1. White body, hood, and trunk.
2. Orange-tan body, hood, and trunk.
3. Light blue body, hood, and trunk.

PEUGEOT 504 POLICE CAR   103 mm   1972
Same basic model as above; no other data.

PEUGEOT 604   109 mm   197_
Four-door sedan with body, opening hood, black chassis, grille, and bumpers, orange interior, clear windows and headlights, red taillights.
1. Red body and hood.

PEUGEOT 604 WITH LUGGAGE RACK   109 mm   197_
Same basic model as above plus black rack, yellow and brown luggage. Week-End II Set.
1. Red body and hood.

RENAULT DAUPHINE   1959
No data.

RENAULT FLORIDE CABRIOLET   196_
No data.

RENAULT FLORIDE COUPE   99 mm   1961
Two-door coupe with body, roof, black chassis, clear windows and headlights, chrome bumper and rear grille. Value $10-15.
1. Blue body and roof.
2. Chrome body and roof.

RENAULT FRÉGATE AMIRAL   1956
No data.

RENAULT ONDINE   92 mm   1961
Four-door sedan with body, black chassis, clear windows and headlights, chrome bumpers; later issues have black interior.
    1. Ivory body. Value $8-12.

RENAULT ONDINE POLICE CAR   92 mm   1961
Same basic model as above plus amber dome light, light gray antenna, black and white "Police" labels. Value $8-12.
    1. Black and white body.

RENAULT 5   81 mm   1972
Three-door hatchback with body, opening hood and hatch, black chassis and interior, clear windows, silver motor, gray grille and bumpers, red taillights.
    1. Red body, hood, and hatch.
    2. Yellow body, hood, and hatch.
    3. Dark blue body, grille, and hatch.

RENAULT 17TS   96 mm   1972
Two-door hatchback with body, opening hood and hatch, black chassis, grille, and interior, clear windows, chrome motor and headlights, red taillights.
    1. Red body, hood, and hatch.
    2. Tan body, hood, and hatch.

RENAULT 30TS   106 mm   1975
Four-door hatchback with body, opening hood and hatch, black chassis, interior, and grille, clear windows, chrome bumpers.
    1. Red body, hood, and hatch.
    2. Blue body, hood, and hatch.

SIMCA ARIANE   1960
No data.

SIMCA 9 ARONDE   104 mm   1957
Four-door sedan with body, black chassis, silver grille, bumpers, headlights, and trim, red top and taillights.
    1. Tan body, red painted top. Value $8-12.

SIMCA MARLY AMBULANCE   196_
No data.

SIMCA OCEANE   99 mm   1959
Two-door convertible with body, black chassis, clear windows and headlights, silver grille and bumpers. Value $10-15.
    1. Red body.

SIMCA PLEIN CIEL   99 mm   1959
Coupe with body, black chassis, clear windows and headlights, silver grille and bumpers. Value $8-12.
    1. Ivory body.

SIMCA VERSAILLES   1959
No data.

SIMCA 1000   96 mm   1962
Four-door sedan with body, black chassis, clear windows and headlights, silver grille and headlights, red taillights.
    1. Ivory body.
    2. Tangerine red-orange body.

SIMCA 1000 POLICE CAR   96 mm   1963
Same basic model as above plus amber dome light, gray antenna, black and white "Police" labels.

1. Black and white body.

SIMCA 1100 SPECIAL 90 mm 1970

Four-door hatchback with body, opening hood and hatch, black chassis and interior, clear windows, chrome motor, grille and bumpers, red taillights.
1. Blue body, hood, and hatch.

VESPA 2CV 70 mm 1959

Two-door minicar with body, black chassis, silver grille and bumpers, chrome headlights. Value $8-12.
1. Maroon body.

VOLKSWAGEN K-70 103 mm 1973

Four-door sedan with body, opening hood and trunk, black chassis and interior, clear windows and headlights, silver motor, chrome bumpers, red taillights.
1. Dark turquoise body, hood, and trunk.

The following sets were available in the sixties:

Bicycle Racers (set of five)
Car and animal trailer
Car and open trailer
Citroen DS19 and police motorcycles
Citroen DS21 and caravan trailer
Citroen DS21 and open trailer
Menagerie set
Police motorcycles (set of two)
Road roller and site hut wagon
Week-End I: car and canoe on trailer: trailer illustrated.
Week-End II: car with luggage rack

Commercial vehicles:
BERLIET GAK LUMBER TRUCK 196_
No data.

BERLIET STRADAIR SEMI-TRAILER TRUCK 1968
No data.

MINIBUS 116 mm 196_

Light bus with body, cream interior, clear windows, black chassis, chrome roof rack, ladder, grille, and bumpers, yellow headlights, labels. Value $10-15.
1. Red body.
2. Blue body.

MOVING VAN 1968
No data.

SOMUA LYONNAIS BUS 196_
No data.

SOMUA PARIS BUS 220 mm 1959

Single deck bus with upper and lower body, opening green and cream doors, cream grille, red interior, clear windows and headlights, labels. Value $15-20.
1. Green lower, cream upper body.

Motorcycles:
FIRE DEPARTMENT MOTORCYCLE 196_
No data.

MILITARY POLICE MOTORCYCLE 196_
No data.

POLICE MOTORCYCLE 196_
Presumably similar to next model minus sidecar.

POLICE MOTORCYCLE AND SIDECAR 78 mm 196_
Bodies, gray handlebars, antennas, and stand, two black and white figures, chrome spoked hubs, white tires.
   1. Black bodies.

RALLY MOTORCYCLE 196_
No data.

RALLY MOTORCYCLE AND SIDECAR 196_
No data.

Minialuxe 1/32 scale plastic models:
Citroen 11CV Sedan, 1959.
Citroen DS19 Convertible, 1959.
Citroen 1200 KG Ambulance Van, 1959.
Citroen 1200 KG Autoroute Van, 196_.
Citroen 1200 KG Fire Truck, 1959.
Citroen 1200 KG Pickup Truck, 1959.
Citroen 1200 KG Police Van, 1959.

Ford Vedette, 1959.
Go-Kart, 1964.
Hotchkiss-Gregoire, 1959.
Peugeot 403, black body, 1959.
Renault Dauphine, 1959.
Renault Floride, 1959.
Renault Frégate, 1959.
Renault 1000 KG Van, 1959.
Renault 1000 KG Electric Service Van, 196_.
Renault 1000 KG Mail Van, 196_.
Renault 1000 KG Police Van, dark blue body, white roof and chassis, 196_.
Renault 1000 KG Police Van and Motorcycles, 196_.
Renault 1000 KG Taxi Van, light orange body and roof, 196_.
Simca Aronde, 1959.
Simca Beaulieu, 1959.
Simca Marly, 1959.
Simca Oceane, 1959.
Simca Plein Ciel, 1959.
Somua Bus, 1959.
Somua Paris-Nice Coach, 1959.

NOREV

The firm of Norev first came on the market late in 1953. The trade name was that of its owner, M. Veron, spelled backward, and the firm was located in Villeurbanne, a suburb of Lyon in southeastern France. The first Norev models were made of plastic to 1/43 scale and featured brightly colored bodies, red plastic hubs with white tires, silver grilles and bumpers, silver or tinted headlights, plastic antennas and the like. They had plain tinplate (or in a few cases plastic) chassis (baseplates), usually black, sometimes gold, and sometimes including a raised drive train, and with longitudinal lettering, and their windows were simply open spaces. They were eye-catching, reasonably priced toys that were also accurate models of real cars, and they were a success from the start.

Their catalog numbers, though, underwent numerous changes in the fifties, and little information on the subject has been published until recently. In fact, no Norev catalog seems to have used numbers at all until 1963! I am indebted to Dr. Paolo Rampini for much of my data on the original numbers, but some of my questions still remained unanswered until I obtained a copy of the October, 1990 special issue of "Argus de la Miniature," which includes a thorough listing of all Norev models to date–and all Norev models reissued by other firms. This excellent volume includes much more data on variations than can–or should–be offered here, and I highly recommend it to anyone who likes Norev. Hearty thanks to Andre-Jacques Chailloux for sending it to me!

During the fifties few features were changed; the red hubs and white tires were usually replaced by silver hubs and black tires, but other than these, the models remained as they had been before. By 1962, though, clear plastic windows, suspension, and plastic chassis with transverse lettering, and often with catalog numbers, had appeared. Many chassis included rounded axle bulges, though some lacked them and also lacked suspension; later types had flat surfaces meeting at angles instead of rounded bulges. Later in the sixties, features such as fingertip steering and whitewall tires were added to some models, and either colored plastic hubs or more realistic patterned silver types were used. Some early hubs and tires had reacted unfavorably, and it is not uncommon to find early Norev models with misshapen plastic hubs, but this problem seems to have been solved by the early sixties.

In 1957 the 1/43 models were joined by the 500 series of similar models in 1/87 scale, including some of the same cars that had been issued in 1/43 scale, but the series also included several interesting trucks never produced in 1/43 scale. So the Norev lines remained until 1970, when the first 1/43 scale diecast metal models appeared. They formed three series, with 600, 700 and 800 numbers, the first digit indicating the price in francs. What with inflation, the 600 series did not last long. At about the same time, some metal 500 series models were also made.

The old 500 series was on its way out by then, to be replaced by 1975 by a new 500 series, this one composed of 1/43 scale plastic trucks, car-and-trailer sets and the like. No subsequent 1/87 scale models were made, but in the late seventies a number of 1/66 scale Schuco diecast models appeared in France under the Norev name, still bearing their 800 series Schuco numbers. By 1982 the survivors among them had been renumbered as part of a 400 series of "Matchbox-size" models, which still appears to be in production. A new 600 series of vehicle-and-trailer sets based on the 400 models also appeared.

Despite the emphasis on diecast metal models, Norev has continued to produce some plastic vehicles as well, and in 1981 a 300 series appeared, these being reissues of earlier models with nothing changed but their baseplates—now textured plastic—and their catalog numbers. In most cases the 300 series number was based on the model's earlier number; for example, 3 became 303, 207 became 307, 117 became 317, etc. Most of them seem to have been dropped after 1984, though a few are still in production.

During the eighties, too, the 1/43 scale diecast models went through sme number changes. Some models were downgraded from 800 to 700 status, while some 700 and 800 models simply were given new numbers. This can be confusing in some cases, and we can only hope that the individual listings will show what became what.

Beyond that, the nineties seem to be bringing more changes in Norev numbering, but since we have to stop somewhere to get into print, we'll stop at 1989 and realize that, since Norev is in good health and now part of a firm that also includes Majorette and Solido, there will probably be more to tell of this time-honored firm for many years to come. There is, in fact, a new numbering system currently in use, with four-digit numbers, but we won't try to include it; the aforementioned "Argus de la Miniature" volume includes information on it, and time will tell what is added to it in the future.

From the start, many Norev models have been offered in a variety of colors, and the list below will be far from complete, as I can list only what I know to exist–and I am indebted to the "Argus" listing for much of the data included here. Any additions are very welcome. To save space in the listings, the chassis types will be listed as follows for those models and series where different chassis types are found:

1-: Tinplate, longitudinal lettering, no features.
1+: Tinplate, longitudinal lettering, drive train.
2: Plastic, longitudinal lettering, no features.
3-: Plastic, transverse lettering, no features.
3+: Plastic, transverse lettering, axle bulges, suspension.
4: Plastic, transverse lettering, steering, suspension.
5: Plastic, transverse lettering, flat surfaces, suspension.
6: Plastic, transverse lettering, including fenders.
7. Plastic, transverse lettering, textured surfaces.

More thorough details of chassis, wheels, and other components can be found in the "Argus de la Miniature" volume.

Plastic 1/43 Series

1 SIMCA ARONDE 9   92 mm   1/43   1953-1956>#5

Four-door sedan with plastic body, gold or black 1+ chassis, silver antenna, grille, and bumpers, clear headlights, orange taillights, red hubs, white tires. There are three versions: the 1951 model, the 1954 type, and the 1956 Élysée. Value $45-55.
1. 1951 type, light blue and gray body, gold chassis
2. 1951 type, light blue and gray body, gold chassis.
3. 1951 type, tan body, gold chassis.
4. 1951 type, gray body, gold chassis.
5. 1954 type, tan body, black chassis.
6. 1954 type, ivory body, friction motor, gold chassis.
7. 1954 type, blue-gray body, friction motor, gold chassis.
8. 1954 type, gray body, friction motor, black chassis.
9. 1956 type, light green body, black chassis.
10. 1956 type, dull blue body, black chassis.
11. 1956 type, gray body, friction motor, black chassis.

1 OPEL REKORD L-1700   100 mm   1/43   1965-1969

Two-door sedan with plastic body, opening hood, doors, and trunk, black 3+ chassis, number, gray interior, clear windows and headlights, silver grille and bumpers, red taillights, silver hubs, black tires. Value $10-15.
1. Ivory body.
2. Light green body.
3. Light blue body.

2 FORD VEDETTE 54   104 mm   1/43   1953-1959

Four-door sedan with plastic body, 1+ chassis, silver grille, bumpers, antenna, and taillights, clear headlights, red hubs, black tires. Value $30-40.
1. Red and tan body, gold chassis.

2. Maroon and tan body, gold chassis.
3. Green and tan body, gold chassis.
4. Dark green and gray body, gold chassis.
5. Dark blue-green body, gold chassis.
6. Tan body, gold chassis.
7. Light gray body, gold chassis.
8. Yellow body, black chassis.
9. Light blue body, black chassis.
10. Gray body, black chassis.
11. Maroon body, friction motor, black chassis.

2 CITROEN AMI 6 BREAK   88 mm   1/43   1965-1980

Wagon with plastic body, opening hood and hatch, black 3+ chassis, number, gray interior, clear windows and headlights, silver motor and bumpers, red taillights, silver hubs, black tires. Value $12-16.
1. Yellow body.
2. Blue body.

3 CITROEN 15CV 6   113 mm   1/43   1954-1959

4-door sedan with plastic body, black 1- chassis, silver grille, bumpers, headlights, and antenna, red or black hubs, white tires.
Value $50-60.
1. Black body, red hubs.
2. Gray body, black hubs.
3. Gray body, friction motor.
4. Black body, friction motor.

3 RENAULT 16/16TX   96 mm   1/43   1965-1980

4-door sedan with plastic body, opening hood and hatch, black 3+ chassis, gray interior, clear windows, silver motor, grille, headlights, and bumper, red taillights, silver hubs, black tires. Modified to 16TX in 1975. $6-12.
1. Ivory body.

2. Dark blue body.
3. Red body, 16TX.
4. Blue body, 16TX.

4 PANHARD DYNA 102 mm 1/43 1954-1960
4-door sedan with plastic body, black 1- chassis, clear headlights, silver grille, bumpers, and antenna, red or black hubs, white tires. Modified 1956. Value $35-45.
1. Yellow body, ? hubs.
2. Dark gray body, red hubs.
3. Light gray body, black hubs, friction motor.

4 PANHARD PL17 BREAK 104 mm 1/43 1965-1971
Wagon with plastic body and opening hatch, black 3+ chassis, gray interior, clear windows, tinted headlights, red taillights, silver bumpers and hubs, black tires. Value $25-35.
1. White body.
2. Orange body.
3. Light olive body.
4. Light blue body.

5 RENAULT 4CV 83 mm 1/43 1955-?>#17
4-door sedan with plastic body, black 1- chassis tinted headlights, silver bumpers and antenna, red hubs, white tires.
1. Pale green body. Value $35-45.
2. Turquoise body.
3. Blue body.
4. Pale tan body.
5. Pale gray-brown body.

5 SIMCA ARONDE 9 ÉLYSÉE 92 mm 1/43 1956-1962?
4-door sedan with plastic body, black or gold 1+ chassis, silver grille, bumpers, and antenna, clear headlights, orange taillights, red hubs,

white tires. Presumably same model as last type #1.
1. Aqua body, black chassis. Value $30-40.
2. Dark blue-gray body, gold chassis.

5 PANHARD DYNA WITH SKIS 102 mm 1/43 ca. 1956?
Doubtful numbering. See #22.

5 PEUGEOT 204 89 mm 1/43 1965-1980
4-door sedan with plastic body, opening hood, trunk, and roof panel, black 3+ chassis, mottled interior, clear windows, silver motor, grille, bumper, and headlights, red taillights, silver hubs, black tires. Value $5-10.
1. Ivory body.
2. Light blue body.
3. Blue body.

6 SIMCA VERSAILLES 103 mm 1/43 1955-1959
4-door sedan with plastic body, second-color roof, black 1- chassis, clear windows and headlights, silver grille and bumpers, red taillights and hubs, white tires. Value $35-45.
1. Cream body, red roof.
2. Cream body, orange roof.
3. Cream body, green roof.
4. Cream body, light blue roof.
5. Red body, cream roof.
6. Red body, aqua roof.
7. Unknown single colors including roof.
8. Cream body, light blue roof, friction motor.

6 PEUGEOT 201 1930 91 mm 1/43 1966-1971
4-door sedan with plastic body, black 6 chassis and roof panel, light gray interior and hubs, clear windows, silver grille, bumper, and headlights, red taillights, black tires. Value $15-25.

1. Red body.
2. Turquoise body.
3. Dark blue body.
4. Light gray body.

7 SIMCA TRIANON 101 mm 1/43 1955-1958
4-door sedan with plastic body, black 1- chassis, clear windows, silver grille, bumpers, and antenna, orange taillights, red hubs, white tires. Value $30-40.
1. Dark green body.
2. Blue body.
3. Navy blue body.
4. Tan body.
5. Gray body.
6. Black body.

7 PEUGEOT J7 VAN 108 mm 1/43 1967-1973
Van with plastic body, sliding and opening doors, light gray interior, black 3+ chassis, clear windows, tinted headlights, red taillights, silver grille and bumpers, gray hubs, black tires. Value $20-30.
1. Orange body, "Airflam" logo.
2. Red body, "Cereal" logo.
3. ? body, "Chalet Ideal" logo.
4. Yellow body, "Hertz" logo.
5. Gray body, "Larousse" logo.
6. Navy blue body, "Levitan" logo.
7. ? body, "Petrole Hahn Bleu" logo.

8 PEUGEOT 203 101 mm 1/43 1955-1958>#14
4-door sedan with plastic body, black 1- chassis, silver grille, bumpers, and antenna, clear headlights, red hubs, white tires. Value $35-45.
1. Red body.
2. Orange body.

3. Yellow body.
4. Green body.
5. Light blue body.
6. Medium gray body.
7. Dark blue-gray body.
8. Gray body, friction motor.

8 PEUGEOT 172R 1927 78 mm 1/43 1967-1971
Touring car with plastic body, black 6 chassis and raised top, white interior, clear windows, silver radiator and headlights, black grille, maroon hubs, black tires, spare. Value $15-20.
1. Yellow body.
2. Maroon body.
3. Light blue body.

9 PEUGEOT 403 101 mm 1/43 1955-1958>#15
4-door sedan with plastic body, black 1- chassis, other details presumably as #15 but with red hubs, white tires. Value $30-40.
1. Green body.
2. Gray body.
3. Green body, friction motor.
4. Navy blue body, friction motor.

9 RENAULT R10 94 mm 1/43 1966-1977?
4-door sedan with plastic body, opening hoods, black 3+ chassis, mottled interior, clear windows, tinted headlights, red taillights, silver motor, bumpers, and hubs, black tires. Value $10-15.
1. Ivory body.
2. Red body.
3. Dark blue body.

10 CITROEN DS19 110 mm 1/43 1956-1960>#48
4-door sedan with plastic body, roof, interior, black chassis, red hubs,

black tires. Value $35-45.
1. White body, orange-red roof.
2. White body, green roof.
3. Yellow body, orange roof.
4. Yellow body, mauve roof.
5. Yellow body, lilac roof.
6. Light blue body, mauve roof.
7. Light blue body, gray roof.
8. Light blue body, black roof.
9. Navy blue body, light blue roof.
10. Black body, white roof.
11. Black body, red roof.
12. Black body, yellow roof.
13. Black body, light green roof.
14. Light green body, gray roof, friction motor.
15. Black body, white roof, friction motor.
16. Black body, yellow roof, friction motor.

10 RENAULT JUVAQUATRE 86 mm 1/43 1966-1970
4-door sedan with plastic body, fenders, and opening trunk, black 3+ chassis, gray interior, clear windows, tinted headlights, red taillights, silver grille, bumpers, and hubs, black tires, spare. Value $15-25.
1. Yellow body.
2. Blue body.
3. Gray body.
4. Black body.

11 RENAULT FRÉGATE GRAND PAVOIS 107 mm 1/43 1956
4-door sedan with plastic body, black 1- chassis, clear headlights, red taillights, silver bumper, antenna, and grille, red hubs, white tires. Value $30-40.

1. Tan and brick red body.
2. Black and yellow body.
3. ? body, friction motor.

11 RENAULT FRÉGATE AMIRAL 107 mm 1/43 1956-1959>#23
Details basically as #11 above; single-color body. Value $30-40.
1. Light blue body.
2. Tan body.
3. Green body, friction motor.

11 ALFA ROMEO GIULIETTA SPRINT 91 mm 1/43 1958-1968
Sport coupe with plastic body, black 3- chassis, clear windows, silver grille, bumpers, and headlights, red taillights, silver hubs, black tires. Value $20-30.
1. Red body.
2. Maroon body.
3. Light orange body.
4. Yellow body (may be same as light orange).
5. Green body.
6. Olive green body.
7. Light blue body.

12 MERCEDES-BENZ GRAND PRIX 97 mm 1/43 1956-1958>#13
Details as #13 below, but may have had red hubs, white tires. Value $35-45.
1. Silver body.
2. Gray body.
3. Red body.
4. Blue body.

12 MASERATI 200-S 94 mm 1/43 #20>1959-1968

Sports-racing car with plastic body, black 3- chassis, yellow dash and number, clear windshield and headlights, silver grille, exhaust, and hubs, black tires. Value $20-25.

1. Red body.
2. Green body.
3. Blue body.

13 RENAULT DAUPHINE 88 mm 1/43 1956-1960?

4-door sedan with plastic body, black 3- chassis, clear windows, tinted headlights, silver bumper, red taillights and hubs, white tires. Value $30-40.

1. Red body.
2. Orange body.
3. Light green body.
4. Olive body (may be same as light green).
5. Dark blue body.

13   MERCEDES-BENZ GRAND PRIX   97 mm   1/43 #12>1959?-1968

Formula I car with plastic body, black 3- chassis, red dash and number, silver grille and hubs, black tires. Value $30-40.

1. Red body.
2. Green body.
3. Blue body.
4. Blue body, "Zerex Special" logo.

14 FORD VEDETTE AMBULANCE 104 mm 1/43 1957-1959

4-door sedan with plastic body (based on #2), black 1+ chassis, red and white roof sign and side panels, silver siren, grille, bumper, antenna, and taillights, clear headlights, red hubs, white tires. Value $35-45.

1. Cream body.
2. Red body.

14 PEUGEOT 203 101 mm 1/43 #8>1957?-1963

4-door sedan with plastic body (as #8), black 1- chassis, clear headlights, silver grille and bumpers, red or black hubs, white tires, no antenna. Value $25-30.

1. Yellow body, red hubs.
2. Gray body, black hubs.
3. Dark blue-gray body.

14 RENAULT 8 GORDINI 90 mm 1/43 1968-1974

4-door sedan with plastic body, black 3+ chassis, mottled interior, clear windows, silver bumpers, tinted headlights, red taillights, silver hubs, black tires, blue and white stripe/racing number labels. Value $8-15.

1. Blue body.
2. Dark blue body.

14 RENAULT 8 90 mm 1/43 1975

Details as above but minus rally stripes and numbers. Value $8-12.

1. White body.

15 CITROEN 15 POLICE CAR 113 mm 1/43 1957-1959

4-door sedan with plastic body (as #3), black 1- chassis, white and red roof sign and side panels, silver grille, headlights, bumpers, and antenna, red hubs, white tires. Value $55-65.

1. Black body.
2. Black body, friction motor.
3. Red body (not police car?).
4. Red body, friction motor.

15 PEUGEOT 403 101 mm 1/43 #9>1959-1968
4-door sedan with plastic body (as #9), black 1- chassis, silver grille and bumper, tinted headlights, red taillights, silver hubs, black tires. Value $30-35.
  1. Pale olive body.
  2. Green body.
  3. Light gray body.
  4. Blue-gray body.

16 CITROEN 2CV VAN 83 mm 1/43 1957-1960>#26
Light van with plastic body without opening rear doors, black 3- (or earlier?) chassis, silver grille and headlights, clear windows, gray hubs, black tires. Earlier types minus windows and with different chassis, hubs, etc. may exist. Value $30-40.
  1. Light gray body, no logo.
  2. Pale blue body, "Ames Vaillantes" logo.
  3. ? body, "Armor Rubans" logo.
  4. ? body, "Calor" logo.
  4. Red body, "Coeurs Vaillants" logo.
  5. White body, "Fleury Michon" logo.
  6. ? body, "Fripounet et Marizette" logo.
  7. Yellow body, "Kodak" logo.
  8. ? body, "Laden" logo.
  9. ? body, "Lavix" logo.
  10. Red body, "Perlin et Pinpin" logo.
  11. Green body, "Perlin et Pinpin" logo.
  12. Blue body, "Perlin et Pinpin" logo.
  13. Dark blue body, "La Pie qui chante" logo.
  14. Gray body, "Teinture Ideala" logo.
  15. Dark green body, "Teppaz" logo.
  16. Gray body, "Herford" logo.

16 PORSCHE CARRERA 91 mm 1/43 #21>1959-1968
Sport coupe with plastic body (as #21), black 3- chassis, clear windows, silver bumpers and hubs, black tires. Value $25-35.
  1. Orange body.
  2. Light green body.
  3. Light blue body.
  4. Light gray body.

17 JAGUAR 2.4 105 mm 1/43 1957-1958>#24
4-door sedan with plastic body, basically as #24 though perhaps with some earlier details. Value $25-30.
  1. White body.
  2. Maroon body.
  3. Light blue body.

17 RENAULT 4CV 83 mm 1/43 #5>1959-1968
4-door sedan with plastic body (as #5), black 1- chassis, tinted headlights, silver bumpers, red or silver hubs, white or black tires, no antenna. Value $25-30.
  1. Light green body, red hubs, white tires.
  2. Dark green body, red hubs, white tires.
  3. Light blue body, silver hubs, black tires.

18 SIMCA PLEIN CIEL 97 mm 1/43 1957-1958>#33
Coupe with plastic body, basically as #33 though perhaps with some earlier details. Value $25-30.
  1. White body, red roof.
  2. Turquoise body, black roof.
  3. Black body, white roof.

18 VESPA 400 65 mm 1/43 1958-1968
Minicar with plastic body, black 3+ chassis, clear windows, silver bumpers and headlights, red taillights, gray hubs, black tires. Value $20-25.

1. White body.
2. Pink body.
3. Yellow body.
4. Light green body.
5. Dull blue body.

18 MONTEVERDI 375L 107 mm 1/43 1971-1977?

Sport coupe with plastic body, opening hood, doors, and trunk, black 5 chassis and interior, clear windows, silver motor, grille, and bumpers, red taillights. Value $8-12.
1. Dark yellow body.
2. Blue-black body.

19 SIMCA OCEANE 99 mm 1/43 1957-1959>#32

Convertible with plastic body, basically as #32 though perhaps with earlier details. Value $25-30.
1. White body, black interior.
2. Maroon body, ? interior.

19 JAGUAR MARK X 118 mm 1/43 1965-1971

4-door sedan with plastic body, black 5 chassis, red interior and taillights, silver grille, bumpers, and hubs, black tires. Value $20-25.
1. White body (may be same as light gray).
2. Light gray body.
3. Black body.

20 MASERATI 200-S 94 mm 1/43 1957-1958>#12

Sports-racing car with plastic body, other details presumably as #12. Value $20-25.
1. Red body.
2. Green body.

20 FIAT 500 JARDINIERE 72 mm 1/43 1965-1969

Mini-wagon with plastic body, black 3+ chassis, light gray interior, clear windows and headlights, silver bumpers and hubs, black tires. Value $10-15.
1. Orange-red body.
2. Aqua body.

21 PORSCHE CARRERA 1500 91 mm 1/43 1957-1962>#16

Basically as #16 but may have some earlier features. Value $30-35.
1. Light blue body.
2. Olive green body.

21 PEUGEOT 203 WITH SKIS 101 mm 1/43 1957-1958

#5/14 with plastic skis and rack. Value $40-45.
1. Dark blue-gray body, gray racks, red and blue skis.

21 SIMCA ARIANE MIRAMAS 100 mm 1/43 1959-1964

4-door sedan with plastic body, black 1- chassis, silver grille and bumpers, clear headlights, red taillights and hubs, black tires. Value $35-40.
1. White body.
2. Turquoise body.
3. Light blue body.
4. Gray body.

21 MERCEDES-BENZ 250SE 112 mm 1/43 1966-1977

4-door sedan with plastic body, opening hood and trunk, black 3+ chassis, gray interior, clear windows and headlights, red taillights, silver motor, grille, bumpers, and hubs, black tires. Value $10-15.
1. Red body.
2. Pale olive body.
3. Turquoise body.
4. Light blue body.
5. Gray body.

22 PANHARD DYNA WITH SKIS 102 mm 1/43 1957-1959

#4 with plastic skis and rack. Value $40-45.
1. Red body, gray racks, red and blue skis.
2. Orange body, no other data.
3. Yellow body, no other data.
4. Maroon body, no other data.
5. Gray body and racks, presumably red and blue skis.

22 LANCIA AURELIA GT 99 mm 1/43 1958>#25

Basically as #25 but may have some earlier features. Value $25-30.
1. Red body.
2. Pale blue body.
3. Mauve body.

22 SIMCA P60 ARONDE 98 mm 1/43 1959-1965

4-door sedan with plastic body, black 3- chassis, clear windows and headlights, orange taillights, silver grille, bumpers, and hubs, black tires. $20-25.
1. Dark red body.
2. Yellow body.
3. Light green body.
4. Turquoise body.
5. Light blue body.
6. Light gray body.

22 VOLKSWAGEN 1600TL 95 mm 1966-1969

2-door fastback with plastic body, opening hood and doors, black 3+ chassis, mottled interior, clear windows and headlights, red taillights, silver bumpers and hubs, black tires. Value $10-15.
1. Red body.
2. Dark aqua body.
3. Light blue body.

22 CHRYSLER 180 103 mm 1/43 1971-1980

4-door sedan with plastic body, opening hood, 4 doors and trunk, black 3+ chassis, maroon interior, clear windows, red taillights, silver motor, grille, bumpers, headlights, and hubs, black tires. Value $8-12.
1. Ivory body.
2. Red body.
3. Light blue body.
4. Light gray body.

23 RENAULT FRÉGATE GRAND PAVOIS 108 mm 1/43 #11>1959-1964

4-door sedan with plastic body, second-color roof, black 1- chassis, clear headlights, orange taillights, silver grille and bumpers, red hubs, white tires. Probably exists with later hubs.
Value $35-40.
1. Brick red body, tan roof.
2. Maroon body, gray roof.
3. Aqua body, blue roof.
4. Aqua body, black roof.

23 SIMCA 8 1200 1937 91 mm 1/43 1966-1970

4-door sedan with plastic body, fenders, opening trunk, gray interior, clear windows, silver grille, bumpers, headlights, and hubs, black taillights and tires. Value $20-25.
1. Maroon body.
2. Orange body.
3. Blue body.
4. Pale tan body.
5. Gray body.

24 JAGUAR 2.4 LITRE 105 mm 1/43 1959-1966

4-door sedan with plastic body, black 3+ chassis, clear windows, red taillights, silver grille, bumpers, headlights, and hubs, black tires. Value $25-30.

1. Maroon body.

24   SIMCA 5 1936   71 mm   1/43   1967-1971

Coupe with plastic body, opening hood, doors, and spare cover, black 3+ chassis, light gray interior, clear windows, silver grille, headlights, and hubs, black tires. Value $20-25.
1. Orange body.
2. Dark blue body.
3. Light gray body.

25   LANCIA AURELIA GT   99 mm   1/43   #22>1959-1965

2-door fastback with plastic body, black 3- chassis, clear windows, orange taillights, silver grille, bumpers, headlights, and hubs, black tires. Value $25-30.
1. Maroon body.
2. Green body.
3. Blue body.
4. Light gray body.

25   PEUGEOT J7 BUS   108 mm   1/43   1968-1973...

Minibus with plastic body, opening doors, black 3+ chassis, tan or mottled interior, clear windows, tinted headlights, silver grille and bumpers, gray hubs, black tires. Value $20-25.
1. Pale yellow body.
2. Light green body.
3. Blue body.
4. Light gray body.

26   CITROEN 2CV VAN   83 mm   1/43   1961-1980

Light van with plastic body, opening rear doors, black 3+ chassis, clear windows, silver grille and headlights, gray hubs, black tires. Value $20-40
1. Yellow body, Amora logo.
2. Many promotional versions.

27   CITROEN 2CV AZ   84 mm   1/43   1960-1968

4-door sedan with plastic body, light gray roof and hubs, black 3+ chassis, clear windows, silver grille, headlights, and bumpers, black tires. Value $20-25.
1. Maroon body.
2. Salmon body.
3. Olive body.
4. Light blue body.

27   CITROEN SM COUPE   110 mm   1/43   1971-1980

2-door coupe with plastic body, opening hood, doors, and hatch, black 3+ chassis, gray interior, clear windows and headlights, red taillights, silver motor, bumpers, and hubs, black tires. Value $6-12.
1. Red body.
2. Dark green body.

28   PEUGEOT 404 BREAK   104 mm   1/43   1964-1980

Wagon with plastic body, opening hatch, black 3+ chassis, gray interior, clear windows, tinted headlights, red taillights, silver grille, bumpers, and hubs, black tires. Value $5-10.
1. Dark orange body.
2. Maroon body.
3. Light blue body.

29   PANHARD PL17   105 mm   1/43   1960-1963

4-door sedan with plastic body, black 3+ chassis, clear windows and headlights, red taillights, silver bumpers and hubs, black tires. Value $10-15.
1. Orange body.
2. Yellow body.
3. Lilac body.
4. Gray body.

29 CITROEN 11A 1937 99 mm 1/43 1968-1972
4-door sedan with plastic body, opening trunk, black 3+ chassis, mottled interior, clear windows, red taillights, silver grille, headlights, and bumpers, gray hubs, black tires. Value $20-25.
1. Blue body.
2. Dark blue body.
3. Gray body.
4. Black body.

30 SIMCA 1300 96 mm 1/43 1963-1968
4-door sedan with plastic body, black 3+ chassis, mottled interior, clear windows, red taillights, silver grille, headlights, bumper, and hubs, black tires. Value $8-12.
1. Ivory body.
2. Turquoise body.

31 DAF VARIOMATIC 84 mm 1/43 1965-1968
2-door sedan with plastic body, opening trunk, black 3+ chassis, mottled interior, red taillights, silver grille, bumpers, and hubs, black tires. Value $8-12.
1. Ivory body.
2. Light aqua body.

32 SIMCA OCEANE 99 mm 1/43 1959-1964
Convertible with plastic body, second-color interior and folded top, black 3+ chassis, clear windows and headlights, red taillights, silver grille, bumpers, and hubs, black tires. Value $20-25.
1. Maroon body, gray interior.
2. Aqua green body, black interior.
3. Light blue body, ? interior.

32 PEUGEOT 204 BREAK 90 mm 1/43 1966-1980
Wagon with plastic body, opening hood, black 3+ chassis, gray interior, clear windows, red taillights, silver motor, grille, headlights, bumpers, and hubs, black tires. Value $5-10.
1. White body.
2. Red body.
3. Light blue body.

33 SIMCA PLEIN CIEL 97 mm 1/43 1959-1966
Coupe with plastic body, black roof and 3+ chassis, clear windows and headlights, red and silver taillights, silver grille, bumpers, antenna, and hubs, black tires. Value $25-30.
1. Orange-red body, black roof.

33 ROLLS-ROYCE SILVER SHADOW 115 mm 1/43 1967-1972
4-door sedan with plastic body, opening hood and trunk, black 5 chassis, gray interior, clear windows and headlights, red taillights, silver motor, grille, bumpers, and hubs, black tires. Value $15-20.
1. White body.
2. Dark green body.
3. Blue body.
4. Dark blue body.
5. Tan body.
6. Light gray body.
7. Dark gray body.
8. Black body.

34 FORD VEDETTE WRECKER 107/125 mm 1/43 1960-1972
Tow truck with plastic body, black 3+ chassis, gray boom, mount, crank, and tow hook, clear windows, tinted headlights, silver or gray rear spotlight, silver "Garage de Paris" logo, grille, bumpers, and hubs, black tires. Value $25-30.
1. Light orange body.

2. Blue body.
3. Dark blue-green body.

35 SIMCA VERSAILLES 103 mm 1/43 #6>1959-1963
4-door sedan with plastic body, second-color roof, black 1- chassis, clear windows and headlights, silver grille and bumpers, red or black hubs, white tires. Value #30-35.
1. Turquoise body, cream roof.
2. Green body, black roof.
3. Blue body, black roof.
4. Yellow body, black roof, in kit form.

35 CITROEN ROSALIE 1934 98 mm 1/43 1967-1971
4-door sedan with plastic body, black 6 chassis and opening trunk, mottled interior, clear windows, silver grille, headlights, bumpers, and hubs, black tires, spare. Value $20-25.
1. Yellow body, black chassis and fenders.
2. Brown body, black chassis and fenders.
3. Gray body, black chassis and fenders.

36 FIAT 1100-D 87 mm 1/43 1964-1968...
4-door sedan with plastic body, black 3+ chassis, mottled interior, clear windows and headlights, red taillights, silver grille, bumpers, and hubs, black tires. Value $10-15.
1. Pale aqua body.
2. Green body.
3. Blue body.
4. Light gray body.

37 DKW JUNIOR 91 mm 1/43 1964-1968
2-door sedan with plastic body, black 3+ chassis, mottled interior, clear windows and headlights, red taillights, silver grille, bumpers, and hubs, black tires. Value $10-15.

1. Light green body.
2. Light blue body.

38 FIAT 2300 BERLINE 102 mm 1/43 1964-1969
4-door sedan with plastic body, black 3+ chassis, mottled interior, clear windows, red taillights, silver grille, headlights, bumpers, and hubs, black tires. Value $10-15.
1. Red body.
2. Light blue body.
3. Metallic gray-green body.

39 SIMCA BEAULIEU 110 mm 1/43 1958-1963
4-door sedan with plastic body, interior, black 5 chassis, roof and trim, clear windows, red taillights, silver grille, bumpers, antennas, and hubs, black tires. Value $25-30.
1. Red body, white roof.
2. Yellow body, black roof.
3. Green body, black roof.
4. Blue body, white roof.
5. Two-tone blue body.
6. Three-tone blue body.

39 PANHARD 35CV 1927 89 mm 1/43 1967-1971
4-door sedan with plastic body and removable hood, black 6 chassis, radiator, and opening trunk, clear windows, silver motor, radiator, lights, and spoked hubs, black tires, spare. Value $20-25.
1. Red body, pale gray interior, black chassis and fenders.
2. Yellow body, ? interior, black chassis and fenders.
3. Light green body, ? interior, black chassis and fenders.
4. Green body, ? interior, black chassis and fenders.
5. Blue body, ? interior, black chassis and fenders.
6. Dark gray body, red interior, black chassis and fenders.

40 SIMCA CHAMBORD 110 mm 1/43 1959-1966

4-door sedan with plastic body, second-color roof, sides and interior, black 5 chassis, clear windows and headlights, red taillights, silver grille, bumpers, antennas, and hubs, black or whitewall tires. Value $20-25.

1. White body, red roof and sides.
2. Cream body, dark red roof and sides.
3. Lilac body, yellow roof and sides?
4. Gray body, black roof and sides.

40 CITROEN ID19 AMBULANCE 116 mm 1/43 1967-1980

Wagon with plastic body and interior, opening hood, hatch, and tailgate, black 3+ chassis, clear windows, blue dome light, tinted headlights, red taillights, silver motor, bumper, and hubs, black tires, spare. Value $10-15.

1. White body, red interior.
2. Red body, ? interior.
3. Blue body, ? interior.
4. Light gray body, dark gray interior.

41 SIMCA MARLY AMBULANCE 108 mm 1/43 1960-1973...

Wagon with plastic body, black 3+ chassis, red, white or green tailgate and trim, flags, and siren, clear windows and headlights, orange taillights, white stretcher, silver grille, bumpers, and hubs, black tires. Value $25-30.

1. White body, red or green trim.
2. Red body, white trim.
3. Orange body, white trim.
4. Light green body, red or white trim.

42 RENAULT ESTAFETTE VAN 94 mm 1/43 1961-1973...

Light van with plastic body, opening rear doors, black 3+ chassis, mottled interior, clear windows, tinted headlights, silver grille, bumpers, and hubs, black tires. Value $20-30.

1. White body, "Cusenier-Freezor" logo.
2. Blue body, "Cusenier-Freezor" logo.
3. Gray body, "Cusenier-Freezor" logo.
4. Ivory body, "Fleury-Michon" logo.
5. Green body, "Marchal" logo.
6. Blue body, "Marchal" logo.
7. White body, "Melli" etc. logo.
8. White body, "Michelin" logo.
9. Yellow body, "Pain" label.
10. Blue body, "Pain" logo.
11. Yellow body, "Pampryl" logo.
12. ? body, "Serigraphie Trapinex" etc. (Tour de France) logo.

43 FORD TAUNUS 17M 101 mm 1/43 1962-1969?

4-door sedan with plastic body, black 3+ chassis, mottled interior, clear windows and headlights, red taillights, silver grille, bumpers, and hubs, black tires. Value $10-15.

1. Ivory body.
2. Dull green body.
3. Blue body.
4. Dark gray body.

44 VOLVO P-1800 98 mm 1/43 1962-1969

Coupe with plastic body, black 3+ chassis, mottled interior, clear windows, tinted headlights, red taillights, silver grille, bumpers, and hubs, black tires. Value $10-15.

1. Ivory body.
2. Yellow body.
3. Green body.

45 FIAT 1500 90 mm 1/43 1962-1969?

4-door sedan with plastic body, black 3+ chassis, brown interior, clear windows, red taillights, silver grille, headlights, bumpers, and hubs, black tires. Value $8-12.
1. Pale aqua body.
2. Light gray body.

46 CITROEN 5CV 1922 72 mm 1/43 1958-1971
Old-time convertible with plastic body, black chassis and interior, light gray 3- base, dash, windshield frame and folded top, cream radiator and headlights, red hubs, black tires, spare. Value $20-25.
1. Red body.
2. Light yellow body.
3. Turquoise body.

47 CHRYSLER NEW YORKER 127 mm 1/43 1959-1966
Convertible with plastic body, black 3+ chassis and interior, light gray dash and folded top, clear windshield, red taillights, silver grille, headlights, bumpers and hubs, black tires. Value $25-35.
1. Salmon body.
2. Dark yellow body.
3. Aqua body.
4. Blue body.

47 SIMCA 1501 100 mm 1/43 1967-1971
4-door sedan with plastic body, opening hood and trunk, black 3+ chassis, mottled interior, clear windows, red taillights, silver motor, grille, headlights, bumpers, and hubs, black tires. Value $8-12.
1. Dull green body.

48 CITROEN DS19 1960 108 mm 1/43 1961-1962
4-door sedan with plastic body, roof, and black 2 chassis, clear windows, silver bumpers and headlights, red taillights and hubs, white tires, no antenna. Value $25-35.

1. Ivory body, orange roof.
2. Ivory body, green roof.
3. Ivory body, blue roof.
4. Ivory body, black roof.
5. Light green body, darker green roof.
6. Light blue body, black roof.
7. Gray body, orange-red roof.
8. Black body, red roof.

48 CITROEN DS19 1963 110 mm 1/43 1963-1971
4-door sedan with plastic body, interior, second-color roof, black 4 chassis, clear windows, red taillights, silver headlights and bumpers, black tires. Value $20-25.
1. White body, light blue roof.
2. Red body, gray roof.
3. Red body, black roof.
4. Dark orange body, gray roof.
5. Light green body, darker green roof.
6. Gray-green body, black roof.
7. Dark green body, black roof.
8. Blue body, white roof.
9. Blue body, black roof.
10. Gray body, yellow roof.
11. Black body, yellow roof.
12. Police car version in 1971?

49 MERCEDES-BENZ 220SE 110 mm 1/43 1961-1971
4-door sedan with plastic body, black 4 chassis, gray interior, clear windows and headlights, red taillights, silver grille, bumpers, and hubs, black tires. Value $10-15.
1. Dark orange body.
2. Maroon body.
3. Light green body.

50 RENAULT ONDINE   87 mm? 1/43 1961-1962
Probably similar to #50 Dauphine. Value $20-25.
    1. Orange body.
    2. Light blue body.

50 RENAULT DAUPHINE   87 mm 1/43 1963-1969
4-door sedan with plastic body, black 4 chassis, tan interior, clear windows, red taillights, silver bumpers, headlights, and hubs, black tires. Value $15-20.
    1. White body.
    2. Green body.
    3. Light blue body.

51 PEUGEOT 404   101 mm 1/43 1961-1979
4-door sedan with plastic body, black 4 chassis, tan interior, clear windows, red taillights, silver grille, bumper, headlights, and hubs, black tires. Value $8-12.
    1. White body.
    2. Orange body.
    3. Yellow body.
    4. Turquoise body.
    5. Light blue body.
    6. Blue body.
    7. Navy blue body.

52 RENAULT FLORIDE 4   95 mm 1/43 1961-1969
Coupe with plastic body, black 4 chassis, mottled interior, clear windows, silver bumpers, headlights, and whitewall hubs, black tires. Value $15-25.
    1. White body.
    2. Orange body.
    3. Light green body.
    4. Light blue body.
    5. Lilac body.

53 RENAULT 4L   83 mm 1/43 1961-1980
4-door sedan with plastic body, opening rear door, black 3+ chassis, mottled interior, clear windows, tinted headlights, red taillights, silver grille, bumper, and hubs, black tires. Value $8-12.
    1. Turquoise body.
    2. Light blue body.
    3. Blue body.
    4. Dark brown body?
    5. Light gray body.

54 CITROEN AMI 6   89 mm 1/43 1962-1979
4-door sedan with plastic body, black 3+ chassis, gray interior, clear windows and headlights, silver bumpers and hubs, black tires. Value $10-15.
    1. White body.
    2. Orange body.
    3. Light green body.
    4. Blue body.

55 RENAULT ESTAFETTE BUS   95 mm 1/43 1961-1973...
Minibus with plastic body, opening rear doors, black 3+ chassis, brown interior, clear windows, tinted headlights, red taillights, silver grille, bumpers, and hubs, black tires. Value $10-15.
    1. Yellow body.

56 CITROEN 2CV AZ-LUXE   85 mm 1/43 1961-1975?
4-door sedan with plastic body, dark gray roof and interior, black 3+ chassis, clear windows, silver grille, headlights, bumpers, and hubs, black tires. Value $8-12.
    1. Dark red body.
    2. Yellow body.
    3. Light gray body.

56 CITROEN 2CV6 85 mm 1/43 1978-1980
Same basic model as #56 above. No other data. Value $5-10.

57 SIMCA 1000 85 mm 1/43 1962-1980
4-door sedan with plastic body, black chassis, mottled interior, clear windows, tinted headlights, red taillights, silver grille, bumpers, and hubs, black tires. Updated in 1969. Value $5-10.
   1. White body, first type.
   2. Turquoise body, first type.
   3. Yellow body, second type.
   4. Green body, second type.

57 SIMCA 1000 RALLY 85 mm 1/43 1971-?
Rally version of same basic model as #57 above. Value $10-15.
   1. Orange-red body, black hood.

58 LANCIA FLAMINIA 110 mm 1/43 1964-1968
4-door sedan with plastic body, black 3+ chassis, gray interior, clear windows, red taillights, silver grille, headlights, bumpers, and hubs, black tires. Value $10-15.
   1. Green body.
   2. Blue body.
   3. Light gray body.

59 ALPINE A110 COUPE 88 mm 1/43 1967-1980
Coupe with plastic body, opening hood and trunk, black 3+ chassis, gray interior, red taillights, silver grille, bumpers, and hubs, black tires. Value $5-10.
   1. Red body.
   2. Maroon body.
   3. Green body.
   4. Blue body.

59A ALPINE A110 POLICE CAR 88 mm 1/43 1970-1976...
Police version of #59, with red dome light, "Gendarmerie" labels. Value $8-12.
   1. Dark blue body.

60 BMW 700LS 88 mm 1/43 1965-1971
2-door with plastic body, black 3+ chassis, gray interior, clear windows, silver headlights, bumpers, and hubs, black tires. Value $8-12.
   1. Red body.

61 FIAT 600 74 mm 1/43 1962-1969
Minicar with plastic body, black 3+ chassis, silver headlights, bumpers, and hubs, black tires. Value $8-12.
   1. Ivory body.
   2. Red body.
   3. Orange body.
   4. Yellow body.

62 VOLKSWAGEN 1200 113 93 mm 1/43 1962-1965
2-door with plastic body, black 3+ chassis without #62, mottled interior, clear windows and headlights, red taillights, silver bumpers and hubs, black tires. Value $8-12.
   1. Brick red body.
   2. Olive green body.

62 VOLKSWAGEN 1300 93 mm 1/43 1965-1980
Same basic model as #62 above, with #62 on chassis. Value $8-12.
   1. Red body.
   2. Orange body.
   3. Yellow body.
   4. Light gray body.

63   VOLKSWAGEN 1500   97 mm   1/43   1962-1969
2-door with plastic body, black 3+ chassis, brown interior, clear windows, red taillights, silver headlights, bumpers, and hubs, black tires. Value $8-12.
   1. Pale blue body.
   2. Light gray body.

64   OPEL KAPITÄN   112 mm   1/43   1962-1969
4-door sedan with plastic body, black 3+ chassis, gray interior, clear windows, red taillights, silver grille, headlights, bumpers, and hubs, black whitewall tires. Value $10-15.
   1. Light olive body.
   2. Blue body.
   3. Dark blue body.

65   RENAULT R4 VAN   83 mm   1/43   1963-1980
Light van with plastic body, opening doors, black 3+ chassis and interior, red taillights, silver grille, headlights, bumpers, and hubs, black tires, Hoover logo labels. Value $20-30.
   1. Gray body.
   2. See Argus for promotional versions.

66   FIAT 1500 CABRIOLET   93 mm   1/43   1965-1971
Convertible with plastic body, opening hood, doors and trunk, black 3+ chassis, interior and folded top, clear windows, red taillights, silver and black motor, silver grille, headlights, bumpers, and hubs, black tires. Value $10-15.
   1. White body.
   2. Orange body.
   3. Light yellow body.
   4. Green body.
   5. Light blue body.

67   FORD ANGLIA SEDAN   87 mm   1963-1969
2-door with plastic body, black 3+ chassis, gray interior, clear windows, red taillights, chrome grille, headlights, bumpers and hubs, black tires. Value $8-12.
   1. Ivory body.
   2. Orange body.
   3. Green body.
   4. Light blue body.
   5. Navy blue body.

68   RENAULT R8   90 mm   1/43   1962-1969
4-door sedan with plastic body, black 3+ chassis, brown interior, clear windows, tinted headlights, red taillights, silver bumpers and hubs, black tires. Value $8-15.
   1. Orange body.
   2. Light blue body.

68   RENAULT R8 GORDINI   90 mm   1/43   1968>#14
Details as #68 above plus blue and white stripe and racing number labels. Value $5-10.
   1. Dark blue body.

69   CORVAIR MONZA   103 mm   1/43   1963-1971
2-door sedan with plastic body, black 3+ chassis, mottled interior, clear windows, red taillights, silver headlights, bumpers, and hubs, black tires. Value $25-30.
   1. White body.
   2. Red body.
   3. Yellow body.
   4. Blue body.

70   BMW 2002   102 mm   1/43   1969-1973...
4-door sedan with plastic body, opening hood, 4 doors, and trunk, black 3+ chassis, light gray interior, clear windows, red taillights,

silver grille, headlights, bumpers, and hubs, black tires. Value $10-15.
1. White body.
2. Red body.
3. Orange body.

71   PEUGEOT 404 COUPE   103 mm   1/43   1963-1971

Coupe with plastic body, opening doors, black 3+ chassis, light blue interior, clear windows, tinted headlights, red taillights, silver grille, bumpers, and hubs, black tires. Value $10-15.
1. Ivory body.
2. Red body.
3. Light blue body.
4. Dark blue body.

72   PANHARD 24CT COUPE   98 mm   1/43   1/43   1963-1971

Coupe with plastic body, opening doors, black 5 chassis, gray interior, clear windows and headlights, red taillights, silver bumpers and hubs, black tires. Value $10-15.
1. Yellow body.
2. Green body.
3. Blue body.

73   SIMCA 1000 COUPE   90 mm   1/43   1963-1971

Coupe with plastic body, opening doors, black 3+ chassis, brown interior, clear windows, silver grille, headlights, bumpers, and tires. Value $8-12.
1. White body.
2. Red body.
3. Yellow body.
4. Light blue body.

74   FORD CONSUL 315   98 mm   1/43   1963-1968

4-door sedan with plastic body, black 3+ chassis, gray interior, clear windows, silver grille, headlights, bumpers, and hubs, black tires.

Value $8-12.
1. White body.
2. Red body.
3. Green body.
4. Pale blue body.

75   MORRIS 850 MINI-MINOR   70 mm   1/43   1963-1972

Minicar with plastic body and interior, black 3+ chassis, clear windows, tinted headlights, silver grille, bumpers, and hubs, black tires. Value $10-20.
1. Cream body, ? interior.
2. Red body, mottled interior.
3. Dark orange body, orange interior.
4. Green body, ? interior.
5. Metallic blue body, ? interior.

76   PANHARD PL17   106 mm   1/43   1963-1969

4-door sedan with plastic body, black 3+ chassis, gray interior, clear windows, tinted headlights, red taillights, silver bumpers and hubs, black tires. Modified in 1964? Value $10-15.
1. Ivory body.
2. Olive green body.

77   FORD TAUNUS 12M   97 mm   1/43   1963-1971

2-door sedan with plastic body, opening doors, black 3+ chassis, tan interior, clear windows, red taillights, silver grille, headlights, bumpers, and hubs, black tires. Value $8-12.
1. White body.
2. Red body.
3. Orange body.
4. Green body.
5. Dark blue body.
6. Dark gray body.

78 RENAULT NN1 TOURER 1928 89 mm 1/43 1969-1971
Tourer with plastic body, opening hood, matching hubs, black top, windshield, and 6 chassis, red interior, silver motor, headlights, and bumpers, black tires, spare. Value $15-20.
  1. Red body.
  2. Yellow body.
  3. Pale blue body.

79 SIMCA 1500 107 mm 1/43 1963-1969?
4-door sedan with plastic body, black 3+ chassis, gray interior, clear windows, red taillights, silver grille, headlights, bumpers, and hubs, black tires. Value $8-12.
  1. Orange body.
  2. Light blue body.
  3. Gray body.

80 FIAT 2300 COUPE 106 mm 1/43 1965-1969
Coupe with plastic body, opening doors, black 5 chassis, blue interior, clear windows, red taillights, silver grille, headlights, bumpers, and hubs, black tires. Value $8-12.
  1. White body.
  2. Green body.
  3. Light gray body.

81 CITROEN 1200 KG VAN 97 mm 1/43 1959-1973...
Van with plastic body, matching hubs, opening and sliding doors, black 5 chassis, clear windows, silver grille, headlights, and bumpers, black tires, blue & red "Pile Wonder" logo labels (two sides different). Value $20-30.
  1. Blue body.
  2. See Argus for promotional versions.

82 CITROEN 3CV VAN 85 mm 1/43 1965-1972
Light van with plastic body, opening doors, black 3+ chassis, mottled

interior, clear windows, silver grille, headlights, and bumpers, gray hubs, black tires. Value $20-30.
  1. Red body.
  2. Orange body.
  3. Light green body.
  4. Light blue body.
  5. Blue body.
  6. Red body, "Dalami" logo.

83 MORRIS 1100 85 mm 1/43 1965-1968
4-door sedan with plastic body, black 3+ chassis, gray interior, clear opening windows, red taillights, silver grille, headlights, bumpers, and hubs, black tires. Value $8-12.
  1. Dull green body.
  2. Gray body.

84 FORD CORTINA 97 mm 1/43 1964-1968...
2-door sedan with plastic body, opening doors, black 3+ chassis, brown interior, clear windows, tinted headlights, silver grille, bumpers, and hubs, black tires. Value $8-12.
  1. White body.
  2. Red body.
  3. Orange body.
  4. Yellow body.

85 PANHARD 24BT 105 mm 1/43 1964-1971
2-door sedan with plastic body, opening hood, doors, and trunk, black 5 chassis, brown interior, clear windows and headlights, silver motor, bumpers, and hubs, black tires. Value $10-15.
  1. Orange body.

86 SIMCA 1500 BREAK 97 mm 1/43 1967-1969...
Wagon with plastic body, opening hatch, matching interior, black 3+ chassis, clear windows, red taillights, silver grille, headlights, bump-

ers, and hubs, black tires. Value $10-15.
1. Red body.
2. Aqua body.
3. Light blue body.
4. Blue body.

87 CITROEN ID19 BREAK 115 mm 1965-1973...

Wagon with plastic body, opening hood, hatch, and tailgate, black 3+ chassis, brown interior, clear windows, tinted headlights, red taillights, silver motor, bumpers, and spoked hubs, black tires. Value $10-15.
1. Green body.

88 CITROEN ID19 CABRIOLET 111 mm 1/43 1965-1972

Convertible with plastic body, opening doors and trunk, contrasting interior, black 3+ chassis, clear windows, tinted headlights, red taillights, silver bumpers and hubs, black tires. Value $20-25.
1. Ivory body, red interior.
2. Red body, black interior.
3. Orange body, ? interior.
4. Yellow body, ? interior.
5. Green body, ? interior.
6. Light blue body, ? interior.
7. Blue body, ? interior.
8. Light gray body, ? interior.
9. Gray body, ? interior.

88 CITROEN ID21 CABRIOLET 111 mm? 1/43 1966?

Model #88 above may have been updated in 1966. No other data.

89 AUSTIN 1100 85 mm 1/43 1965-1968

4-door sedan with plastic body, black 3+ chassis, gray interior, clear opening windows, red taillights, silver grille, headlights, bumpers, and hubs, black tires. Value $8-12.

1. White body.
2. Aqua body.
3. Light olive body.

89 PEUGEOT 304 94 mm 1/43 1970-1980

4-door sedan with plastic body, opening hood, 4 doors, and trunk, black 3+ chassis, red interior and taillights, clear windows, silver motor, grille, headlights, bumpers, and hubs, black tires. Value $8-12.
1. Ivory body.
2. Red body.
3. Turquoise body.

90 MG 1100 85 mm 1/43 1965-1969

4-door sedan with plastic body, black 3+ chassis, gray interior, clear opening windows, red taillights, silver grille, headlights, bumpers, and hubs, black tires. Value $10-15.
1. Orange body.
2. Green body.
3. Blue body.
4. Light gray body.

91 SIMCA CHAMBORD & HENON CARAVAN 254 mm 1/43 1959-1968

#40 car pulling caravan with white body and chassis, gray interior, clear opening windows, red taillights, silver hubs, black tires. Value $20-25.
1. Standard car colors, white trailer.

92 CHRYSLER NEW YORKER & BOAT TRAILER 240 mm 1/43 1959-1969

#47 car pulling gray trailer with black wheels, carrying Rocca outboard boat with ivory hull, red deck, pale blue interior and motor. Boat may exist in other colors. Value $35-45.
1. Standard car colors, boat and trailer as above.

92 FIAT DINO & BOAT TRAILER ? mm 1/43 1970-1977
#163 car pulling trailer with boat as above. Value $10-15.
  1. Standard car colors.

92 SIMCA 1308 GT & BOAT TRAILER ? mm 1/43 1978-1978
#223/323 car pulling trailer with boat as above. Value $10-15.
  1. Standard car colors.

93 PEUGEOT 404 & DIGUE CARAVAN 220 mm 1/43 1962-1969
#51 car pulling trailer with white body, black chassis, blue interior, clear windows, silver hubs, black tires. Value $10-15.
  1. Standard car colors, white trailer.

93 CHEVROLET CORVAIR & DIGUE CARAVAN ? mm 1/43 1969
#69 car pulling trailer with boat as above. Value $35-45.
  1. Standard car colors.

93 PEUGEOT 504 & DIGUE CARAVAN ? mm 1/43 1969-1976
#160/360 car pulling trailer with boat as above. Value $10-15.
  1. Standard car colors.

94 RENAULT ESTAFETTE BUS 95 mm 1/43 1963-
#55 bus in police, fire, or ambulance livery. Value $30-40.
  1. White body, "Ambulance" logo.
  2. Red body, "Pompiers" logo.
  3. Blue body, "Police" logo.

94 SIMCA 1100 & VOILIER BOAT TRAILER 220 mm 1/43 1968-1969
#151 car pulling white trailer with black wheels, carrying boat with red or blue hull, white deck and sail. Value $10-15.
  1. Standard car colors, boat with red hull.
  2. Standard car colors, boat with blue hull.

94 SIMCA 1100S & VOILIER BOAT TRAILER 220 mm 1/43 1970-1982
Revised #151/351 (Talbot 1100) car, other details as above. Value $10-15.
  1. Standard car colors.

95 BERLIET AUTO TRANSPORTER 375 mm 1/43 1958-1981
Semi with plastic cab, semi parts, clear windows, tinted headlights, yellow hubs, black tires, spare wheels. Value $15-20.
  1. Red cab and semi.
  2. Red cab, blue semi.
  3. Yellow cab, blue semi.

96 BERLIET AUTO TRANSPORTER & 5 CARS 375 mm 1/43 1958-1977
#95 transporter with five cars. Value $50-75.
  1. Standard transporter and car colors.

97 BERLIET LADDER TRUCK 174/222 mm 1/43 1967-1990
Fire truck with plastic cab and body, light red ladder, clear windows, silver headlights, light gray mount, interior, and hubs, black chassis and tires. Value $10-15.
  1. Red cab and body.

98 SAVIEM BUS 254 mm 1/43 1969-1986>#1601-1606
Bus with plastic lower body, cream upper body, light gray interior, light gray or lower body color opening doors, clear windows, tinted headlights, red taillights, silver grille and hubs, black tires, black and white route sign. Value $10-15.

1. Red lower body, Lyon decals.
2. Green lower body, Paris decals.
3. Blue lower body, Marseille decals.
4. See Argus for promotional models.

99 LANCIA FLAMINIA & HENON CARAVAN ? mm 1/43 1969
#58 car pulling white #91 caravan. Value $10-15.
1. Standard car colors, white caravan.

99 MERCEDES-BENZ 250SE & HENON CARAVAN ? mm 1/43 1970-1978
#21 car pulling white #91 caravan. Value $10-15.
1. Standard car colors, white caravan.

100 SAVIEM CATTLE TRUCK 133 mm 1/43 1966-1983
Cattle truck with plastic cab, opening doors, rear body, opening tailgate, light gray interior and hubs, clear windows, tinted round or rectangular headlights, black chassis, front bumper, and tires. Value $15-20.
1. Red cab, light gray body.
2. Blue cab, light gray body.
3. Blue cab and body.

101 SAVIEM GARBAGE TRUCK 148 mm 1/43 1967-1983
Truck with plastic cab, opening doors, rear body, opening rear section, light gray interior and hubs, clear windows, tinted round or rectangular headlights, red taillights, black chassis, front bumper, and tires. Value $15-20.
1. Yellow cab, gray body.

102 SAVIEM MILK TANK TRUCK 130 mm 1/43 1967-1983
Tank truck with plastic cab, opening doors, rear body, tank, light gray interior, rear bed, and hubs, white cap, silver gray cans, clear windows, tinted round or rectangular headlights, red taillights, black chassis, front bumper, and tires. Value $15-20.
1. Blue cab, rear body and tank.

103 BMW 2000 & HORSE TRAILER 220 mm 1/43 1970-1971
#70 car pulling trailer with dull blue body, light gray chassis and cover, red sulky, clear spoked wheels, blue and white driver, black horse, cream hubs, black tires. Value $25-30.
1. Standard car colors, trailer as above.

104 PEUGEOT 504 & MATRA F.II 227 mm 1/43 1970-1971
#160 car pulling silver gray trailer with #138 Matra Formula II car. Value $15-20.
1. Standard car and racer colors.

105 RENAULT TRACTOR & CATTLE TRAILER 190 mm 1/43 1970-1982
#117/317 tractor pulling 4-wheel trailer with plastic body, light gray tailgate and hubs, black tires, white cattle. Value $15-20.
1. Standard tractor colors, red and white trailer.

106 RENAULT TRACTOR & CARGO TRAILER 190 mm 1/43 1970-1982
#117/317 tractor pulling trailer with plastic body, gray stakes, black chassis, fast wheels, load of stalks. Value $15-20.
1. Yellow tractor, blue trailer.
2. Orange tractor, green trailer.

107 LAND ROVER PICKUP & TRAILER ? mm 1/43 1970-
#153 Safari pickup pulling trailer. Value $25-30. No other data.

**108   MERCEDES-BENZ 250SE & PORSCHE   220 mm   1/43
1975-**
#21 car pulling silver gray 2-wheel trailer with #149 Porsche Carrera
6, racing number labels. Value $20-25.
  1. Standard car colors.

109   FIAT DINO & FERRARI GTB   227 mm   1/43   1971
#163 car pulling silver gray 2-wheel trailer with #142 Ferrari GTB.
Value $20-25.
  1. Standard car colors.

**110   CHEVROLET CORVAIR AND CD   ? mm   1/43   1971-
1976**
#69 car pulling trailer with #161 CD Le Mans car. Value $35-45.
  1. Standard car colors.

**110   MERCEDES-BENZ & PORSCHE   ? mm   1/43   1976-
1977?**
#21 car pulling trailer with #159 Porsche Carrera 6. Value $20-25.
  1. Standard car colors.

**111   CONTINENTAL CD-8 BULLDOZER   123 mm   1/43
1959-1979**
Dozer with plastic body, chassis, blade, yellow cab, motor, and stack,
gray arms and controls, dark gray hubs, silver gray tracks, silver blade
edge, red "Continental." Value $10-15.
  1. Red body, chassis and blade.

112   POWER SHOVEL   175 mm   1/43   1959-1980
Excavator with plastic cabin, clear windows, black floor and chassis,
silver gray arms, shovel, and tracks, gray hubs. Value $10-15.
  1. Maroon cabin.
  2. Orange cabin.
  3. Yellow cabin.

4. Green cabin.
5. Light gray cabin, green parts.
6. Blue cabin, red parts.

113   BERLIET DUMP TRUCK   180 mm   1/43   1960-1980
Dumper with plastic cab-chassis, tipper, black inner chassis, clear
windows, tinted headlights, gray controls, light gray hubs, black tires.
Value $10-15.
  1. Red cab, rose tipper.
  2. Yellow cab, orange tipper.
  3. Green cab, light gray tipper.

**114   BERLIET EXCAVATOR TRUCK   208 mm   1/43   1959-
1980**
Truck with plastic cab-chassis, cabin, light gray arms, shovel and
hubs, clear windows, tinted headlights, black floor, inner chassis, and
tires. Value $15-20.
  1. Dark green cab, red cabin.
  2. Olive green cab, orange cabin.
  3. Light blue cab, orange cabin.

**115   BERLIET-TITAN LOW LOADER   364 mm   1/43   1959-
1963**
Truck with plastic cab and low loader trailer. Value $15-20.
  1. Orange cab, gray 16-wheel trailer.

**115   BERLIET-TITAN & POWER SHOVEL?   364 mm   1/43
1976-1980**
Either updated version of above with 8-wheel trailer, or earlier #115
truck with #112 power shovel. No other data.

116   BERLIET BUCKET TRUCK   175 mm   1/43   1962-1980
Truck with plastic cab-chassis, rear body, dark gray bucket, gray
frame, clear windows, tinted headlights, light gray hubs, black inner

chassis and tires. Value $15-20.
1. Red cab, light gray body.
2. Orange cab, light gray body.
3. Blue cab, light gray body.

117 RENAULT R-86 TRACTOR 80 mm 1/43 ca. 1971-1977
Farm tractor with plastic body, matching hubs, gray and red driver, gray motor, silver parts, black tires. Value $5-10.
1. Red body.
2. Orange body.
3. Yellow body.
4. Green body.

118 LAND ROVER WRECKER & POLICE TRAILER ? mm 1/43 1971-
#154 Land Rover pulling flat trailer, "Zone Bleue" logo. Value $25-30.
1. Blue wrecker, gray trailer.

119 TROTTERS AND SULKIES ? mm 1/43 1971-
Five horses and sulkies as used on #103. Value $10-15. No other data.

120 ARMY LAND ROVER & TRAILER 144 mm 1/43 1971-1977
Open Land Rover and ammunition trailer with plastic bodies, opening doors, gray-green AA gun, windshield frame, and trailer hitch, tan men, silver gray chassis, grille, and load, tinted headlights, red taillights, gray hubs, black tires. Value $25-30.
1. Dark olive green bodies.

121 ARMY LAND ROVER & MACHINE GUN ? mm 1/43 1971-
Land Rover as #120 with machine gun and soldiers. Value $25-30.
1. Dark olive green body.

122 ARMY LAND ROVER & ROCKET TRAILER ? mm 1/43 1972-1977
Land Rover as #120 with 2-wheel trailer. Value $25-30.
1. Dark olive green body.

123 ARMY LAND ROVER WITH ROCKETS ? mm 1/43 1972-1977
Land Rover as #120 with 4-wheel trailer, radar screen, yellow and red rocket. Value $25-30.
1. Dark olive green body, gray trailer.

124 MERCEDES-BENZ LP2223 TRUCK 160 mm 1/43 1973-1984
Open truck with plastic cab, opening doors, rear body, tailgate, interior, clear windows, silver grille and headlights, gray hubs, black chassis and tires, later fast wheels. Value $10-15.
1. Yellow cab, red body.

125 MERCEDES-BENZ TRUCK & TRAILER 295 mm 1/43 1973-1980
Covered truck and trailer with plastic cab, opening doors, rear body, and trailer, orange interior and opening tailgates, clear windows, silver grille and headlights, gray covers and hubs, black tires. Value $20-25.
1. Blue cab, orange bodies.

126 MERCEDES-BENZ CEMENT TRUCK 165 mm 1/43 1973-1980
Truck with plastic cab, opening doors, interior, orange rear frame, gray barrel, clear windows, gray hubs, black chassis and tires, or fast wheels, orange and white stripe labels, red "Richier." Value $10-15.
1. Red cab.

127 RICHIER ROAD GRADER 185 mm 1/43 1973-1980
Grader with plastic body, chassis, clear windows, white parts, silver gray plow, ripper, and hubs, black tires, silver painted motor, red "Richier" lettering. Value $40-50.
  1. Orange body.

128 RICHIER C785 ROAD ROLLER 125 mm 1/43 1973-1980
Tire roller with plastic body, cab, silver gray engine cover, front wheel mount, grille, and hubs, clear windows, white driver, black tires and lettering. Value $10-15.
  1. Red body, yellow cab.
  2. Orange body, yellow cab.

129 PEUGEOT J7 ROAD SERVICE VAN 107 mm 1/43 1972-1979
Light van with varying "Autoroute" logo. Value $10-20.
  1. Orange body.

130 PANHARD M3 VTT ? mm 1/43 (1975)
Never issued.

131 SAVIEM CHERRY PICKER 150 mm 1/43 1973-1988
Truck with plastic cab, opening doors, rear body, arms, and basket, clear windows and headlights, black chassis, interior, jacks, and tires, gray hubs, or fast wheels, orange and white stripe labels. Value $10-15.
  1. Yellow cab and body, orange arms and basket, Sifev logo.
  2. Blue cab and body, light gray arms and basket, Norev logo.

132 SAVIEM MOVING VAN 138 mm 1/43 1973-1988
Same van as #133, with "Livraisons Norev" logo. Value $8-12.
  1. Yellow and red.
  2. Yellow, red and white.

133 SAVIEM RACING CAR TRANSPORTER 138 mm 1/43 197_-1980
Van with plastic cab, opening doors, upper body, white lower body and opening rear doors, clear windows and headlights, black chassis, interior, and tires, gray hubs, or fast wheels. Value $10-15.
  1. Dark medium blue cab and upper body, black "Norev" and black-on-yellow "Jimmy Mieusset" on upper, tan and white "Cites du Rhone Racing Team" on lower body.
  2. Dark medium blue cab and upper body, revised logo with smaller "Jimmy Mieusset" ahead of "Norev" on upper, black and yellow "Cellier des Dauphins" logo on lower body.
  3. Light medium blue cab and upper body, logo as type 2, fast wheels.

137 CITROEN MEHARI 78 mm 1/43 1970-1980
Covered open car with plastic body, opening hood, top, black chassis and interior, clear windows, silver motor, headlights, and hubs, black tires. Value $5-10.
  1. White body, blue top.
  2. Red body, black top.
  3. Yellow body, black top.

138 MATRA FORMULA II 90 1/43 1970-1971
Racer with plastic body and chassis, clear windshield, red driver, silver mirrors, exhaust, suspension, gearbox, and hubs, black tires, racing number labels. Value $8-12.
  1. White body and chassis.
  2. Red body and chassis.
  3. Yellow body and chassis.
  4. Green body and chassis.
  5. Blue body and chassis.

139 CITROEN AMI 8 90 mm 1/43 1970-1979
4-door sedan with plastic body, opening hood, 4 doors and trunk,

black 3+ chassis, gray interior, clear windows, red taillights, silver motor, grille, headlights, bumpers, and hubs, black tires. Value $8-12.

    1. Ivory body.
    2. Blue body.
    3. Tan body.

140 RENAULT 12 100 mm 1/43 1969-1980

4-door sedan with plastic body, opening hood, 4 doors and trunk, black 3+ chassis, gray interior, clear windows, red taillights, silver motor, grille, headlights, bumpers, and hubs, black tires. Value $5-10.

    1. Blue body, original version without stripes.
    2. Light gray body, without stripes.
    3. Blue body, blue and white Gordini stripe labels.

141 PORSCHE 911 TARGA 97 mm 1/43 1970-1979

Coupe with plastic body, opening hoods and doors, black 3+ chassis and interior, clear windows, red taillights, silver motor, headlights, rear light bar, bumpers, and hubs, black tires. Value $8-12.

    1. White body.
    2. Red body.
    3. Blue body.

142 FERRARI 275GTB 98 mm 1/43 1970-1977?

Coupe with plastic body, opening hood, doors, and trunk, black 3+ chassis and interior, clear windows, red taillights, silver motor, grille, headlights, bumpers, and hubs, black tires. Value $10-15.

    1. Red body.
    2. Yellow body.
    3. Dark blue body.

143 MATRA 530A 95 mm 1/43 1970-1979

Coupe with plastic body, opening hood, headlight covers, doors, and trunk, black 5 chassis and interior, clear windows, silver motor, headlights, bumpers, and hubs, black tires. Value $10-15.

    1. Ivory body.
    2. Orange body.
    3. Light blue body.

144 TRIUMPH TR5 91 mm 1/43 1969-1973

Sports car with plastic body, opening hood, doors, and trunk, black 3+ chassis, interior, and raised top, clear windows, silver motor, grille, headlights, bumpers, and hubs, black tires. Value $10-15.

    1. White body.
    2. Red body.
    3. Yellow body.
    4. Dark blue body.

145 LANCIA FLAVIA 103 mm 1/43 1968-1971

4-door sedan with plastic body, opening hood and trunk, black 3-chassis, gray interior, clear windows, tinted headlights, red taillights, silver motor, grille, bumpers, and hubs, black tires. Value $10-15.

    1. Blue body.
    2. Light gray body.

146 FIAT 525 1928 109 mm 1/43 1967-1971

4-door sedan with plastic body, black 6 chassis, gray interior, clear windows, silver grille, headlights, bumpers, and spoked hubs, black tires, two spares. Value $15-20.

    1. Red body.
    2. Blue body.
    3. Light gray body.
    4. Dark gray body.

147 PEUGEOT 204 COUPE 84 mm 1/43 1968-1971

Coupe with plastic body, opening hood, doors, and roof hatch, black 3+ chassis, gray interior, clear windows, red taillights, silver motor, grille, headlights, bumpers, and hubs, black tires. Value $10-15.

    1. Ivory body.

2. Red body.
3. Green body.
4. Light blue body.

148 FIAT 124 91 mm 1/43 1968-1977?
4-door sedan with plastic body, opening hood and trunk, black 3+ chassis, brown interior, clear windows, red taillights, silver motor, grille, headlights, bumpers, and hubs, black tires. Value $8-12.
1. Turquoise body.
2. Dark blue body.

149 PORSCHE CARRERA 6 92 mm 1/43 1969-1981
Sports-racing coupe with plastic body, second-color chassis, opening hood and doors, black interior, clear windows and headlights, red taillights, silver motor, rear panel, and hubs, black tires, racing numbers. Value $10-15.
1. White body, red chassis.
2. White body, green chassis.
3. White body, blue chassis.
4. Yellow body, orange chassis.
5. Green body, light green chassis.
6. Black body, orange chassis.

150 MERCEDES SSK 1928 102 mm 1/43 1968-1972
Sports car with plastic body, opening doors, black 6 chassis, interior, raised top, windshield frame, and hood strap, clear windows, silver grille, headlights, horns, exhaust, and spoked hubs, black tires, spare. Value $15-20.
1. Red body.
2. Light yellow body.
3. Turquoise body.

151 SIMCA 1100/1100S 88 mm 1/43 1967-1980
4-door sedan with plastic body, opening hood and hatch, black 3+ chassis, gray interior, clear windows, red taillights, silver motor, grille, headlights, bumpers, and hubs, black tires. Modified to 1100S in 1970. Value $5-10.
1. Light gray body (1100).
2. Orange body (1100S).

152 LAND ROVER POLICE CAR 83 mm 1/43 1969-1979
Closed car with plastic body, opening hood and doors, interior, black 3+ chassis and winch, tinted headlights, red dome and taillights, gray antenna and hubs, silver grille and bumper, black tires, spare. Value $10-15.
1. Dark blue body, gray interior.
2. Light gray body, light blue interior.

153 LAND ROVER SAFARI PICKUP 83 mm 1/43 1968-1973
Pickup truck with plastic body, opening hood and doors, interior, black 3+ chassis and winch, clear windows, tinted headlights, red taillights, silver motor, grille, and bumpers, gray hubs, black tires. Value $10-15.
1. Maroon body, tan ? interior.
2. Blue body, ? interior.
3. Gray body, aqua interior.

154 LAND ROVER WRECKER 86 mm 1/43 1969-1973
Pickup with plastic body, opening hood and doors, interior, black 3+ chassis and winch, gray boom and hook, roof rack and hubs, clear windows, tinted headlights, red taillights, silver motor, grille, and bumpers, black tires. Value $10-15.
1. Red body, gray interior.
2. Yellow body, ? interior.
3. Blue body, ? interior.
4. Tan body, ? interior.
5. Dark olive green body, ? interior: army model.

155   LAND ROVER EXPEDITION CAR   83 mm   1/43   1968-1973

Closed car with plastic body, opening hood and doors, interior, black 3+ chassis and winch, gray roof rack and hubs, clear windows, tinted headlights, red taillights, silver motor, grille, and bumpers, black tires, spare. Value $10-15.

   1. Tan body, aqua interior.
   2. Dark olive green body, ? interior: army model.

156   JAGUAR E-TYPE COUPE   101 mm   1/43   1968-1973

Sport coupe with plastic body, chassis, opening hood and doors, interior, clear windows, silver motor, headlights, bumpers, and spoked hubs, black tires. Value $10-15.

   1. White body and chassis, ? interior.
   2. Red body and chassis, black interior.
   3. Yellow body and chassis, ? interior.
   4. Green body and chassis, ? interior.
   5. Blue body and chassis, ? interior.
   6. Black body and chassis, red interior.

157   CITROEN DYANE   88 mm   1/43   1968-1980

4-door hatchback with plastic body, opening hood and hatch, black 3+ chassis, clear windows, red taillights, silver motor, grille, headlights, bumpers, and hubs, black tires or fast wheels. Value $8-12.

   1. White body.
   2. Orange body.
   3. Pale blue body.

158   CITROEN DS21   112 mm   1/43   1969-1979

4-door sedan with plastic body, opening hood, 4 doors, and trunk, black 3+ chassis and interior, clear windows, red taillights, silver motor, headlights, bumpers, and hubs, black tires or fast wheels. Value $10-15.

   1. Ivory body.
   2. Turquoise body.
   3. Blue body.

158P   CITROEN DS21 POLICE CAR   112 mm   1/43   1969-?

Same car as #158 plus red dome light, white-on-black "Police" or "Gendarmerie" labels. Value $15-25.

   1. White body, black hood, doors, and trunk, "Police" logo.
   2. Blue body, "Gendarmerie" logo.

159   PEUGEOT 404 VAN   103 mm   1/43   1969-1973...

Covered pickup with plastic body, opening hood and doors, light gray cover, cream interior, tinted headlights, red taillights, silver motor, grille, bumpers, and hubs, black tires. Value $15-20.

   1. Dark blue body.
   2. Dark green body, gray or black cover, army version.

160   PEUGEOT 504   102 mm   1/43   1969-1980

4-door sedan with plastic body, opening hood, 4 doors and trunk, black 3+ chassis, gray interior, clear windows, red taillights, silver motor, grille, headlights, bumpers, and hubs, black tires or fast wheels. Value $8-12.

   1. Maroon body.
   2. Yellow body.
   3. Light blue body.
   4. Blue body.

161   C.D. 24 LE MANS   101 mm   1/43   1969-1973...

Sports-racing coupe with plastic body, red hood, opening doors and engine cover, black 5 chassis and interior, clear windows, silver motor, headlights, and hubs, black tires, racing numbers. Value $10-15.

   1. White body.

162 RENAULT R6 88 mm 1/43 1969-1980
4-door hatchback with plastic body, opening hood, 4 doors, and hatch, and interior, black 3+ chassis, clear windows, silver grille, headlights, bumpers, and hubs, black tires or fast wheels. Value $5-10.
1. Red body, white interior.
2. Yellow body, red interior.
3. Olive green body, ? interior.
4. Tan body, ? interior.

163 FIAT DINO COUPE 102 mm 1/43 1969-1979
Fastback with plastic body, opening hood, doors, and trunk, black 3+ chassis, red interior and taillights, clear windows, silver motor, grille, headlights, bumpers, and hubs, black tires. Value $8-12.
1. Red body.
2. Pale blue-gray body.

167 RENAULT 15TS 97 mm 1/43 1971-1980
Fastback with plastic body, opening hood and doors, black 7 chassis, gray interior, clear windows, red taillights, silver motor, grille, headlights, bumpers, and hubs, black tires or fast wheels. Value $5-10.
1. Orange body.
2. Yellow body.
3. Blue body.

168 RENAULT 17TS 96 mm 1/43 1972-1980
2-door sedan with plastic body, opening hood and doors, black 7 chassis and taillights, gray interior, clear windows, silver motor, grille, headlights, bumper, and hubs, black tires or fast wheels. Value $5-10.
1. Dark orange body.

169 CITROEN GS 94 mm 1/43 1972-1980
4-door sedan with plastic body, opening hood and 4 doors, black 7 chassis, gray interior, clear windows, red taillights, silver motor, grille, headlights, bumpers, and hubs, black tires or fast wheels. Value $5-10.
1. White body.
2. Yellow body.

170 MASERATI GHIBLI 103 mm 1/43 1971-1980
Sport coupe with plastic body, opening hood and doors, black 7 chassis, gray interior, clear windows, red taillights, silver motor, grille, bumpers, and hubs, black tires or fast wheels. Value $8-12.
1. Dark green body.
[end of Norev.C file, #170]

171 ALPINE A220 106 mm 1/43 1971-1978
Sports-racing coupe with plastic body, opening doors and hoods, black 7 chassis and interior, clear windows and headlights, silver motor and hubs, black tires or fast wheels, racing numbers. Value $5-10.
1. Orange body.
2. Yellow body.
3. Blue body.

172 MERCEDES-BENZ C-111 101 mm 1/43 1972-1980
Sport coupe with plastic body, opening hoods, black 7 chassis, interior, and rear grille, clear windows, silver grille and hubs, black tires or fast wheels. Value $5-10.
1. Yellow body.

173 LIGIER JS2 95 mm 1/43 1971-1980
Sport coupe with plastic body, opening doors, 7 chassis, grille, and interior, clear windows and headlights, red taillights, silver hubs, black tires or fast wheels. Value $5-10.

1. Light orange body, black chassis.
2. Yellow body, green chassis?
3. Light green body, black chassis.
4. Blue body, black chassis

174 LIGIER JS3   81 mm   1/43   1972-1980

Sports-racing car with plastic body, chassis, black interior, clear windows, silver motor, roll bar, and hubs, black tires or fast wheels, racing numbers and other decals. Value $5-10.
1. Dark green body, light green chassis.

175 MERCEDES-BENZ 350SL   100 mm   1/43   1971-1979

Coupe with plastic body, opening hood and doors, black chassis, gray interior, clear windows, red taillights, silver motor, grille, headlights, bumpers, and hubs, black tires or fast wheels. Value $5-10.
1. Dull olive body.

176 ALPINE A310   94 mm   1/43   1972-1980

Sport coupe with plastic body, opening hood and doors, black 7 chassis and interior, clear windows and headlights, red taillights, silver hubs, black tires or fast wheels. Value $5-10.
1. Yellow body.
2. Blue body.

177 OPEL 1900GT   94 mm   1/43   1972-1980

Sport coupe with plastic body, opening hood and doors, black 7 chassis, white interior, clear windows, silver motor, bumpers, and hubs, black tires or fast wheels. Value $5-10.
1. Red body.
2. Dark green body.

178 RENAULT 5TL   79 mm   1/43   1972-1980

2-door sedan with plastic body, opening doors, silver gray 7 chassis, black roof panel, interior, and grille, clear windows and headlights, silver hubs, black tires or fast wheels. Value $5-10.
1. Light green body.
2. Blue body.

179 ALFA ROMEO MONTREAL   95 mm   1/43   1972-1980

Sport coupe with plastic body, opening doors, black 7 chassis, gray interior, clear windows, red taillights, silver grille, headlights, bumpers, and hubs, black tires or fast wheels. Value $8-12.
1. Light orange body.
2. Red body.

180 PORSCHE 917   110 mm   1/43   1972-1979

Sports-racing coupe with plastic body, opening rear hood, black 7 chassis and interior, clear windows and headlights, silver motor and hubs, black tires or fast wheels. Value $5-10.
1. Red body.
2. Yellow body.

181 ALFA ROMEO 33   101 mm   1/43   1973-1980

Sports-racing coupe with plastic body, opening hoods and doors, black 7 chassis and interior, clear windows and headlights, red taillights, silver motor, fast wheels. Value $5-10.
1. Dark orange body.
2. Light green body.
3. Blue body.

182 BERTONE CAMARGUE GS   94 mm   1/43   1972-1980

Sport coupe with plastic body, opening doors, black 5 chassis and interior, clear windows and headlights, red taillights, fast wheels. Value $5-10.
1. Red body.
2. Blue body.

183   LANCIA STRATOS   85 mm   1972-1979
Sports-racing coupe with plastic body, opening doors, black 7 chassis and interior, clear windows, red taillights, fast wheels. Value $5-10.
  1. Red body.
  2. Yellow body.

184   PORSCHE CARRERA RSR   93 mm   1/43   1974-1980
Sports-racing coupe with plastic body, opening doors, black 5 chassis and interior, clear windows and headlights, silver hubs, black tires or fast wheels, racing numbers and other decals. Value $5-10.
  1. Ivory body.

186   FERRARI DINO 246GTS   97 mm   1/43   1973-1980
Sport coupe with plastic body, opening doors, black roof and 5 chassis, light gray interior, clear windows and headlights, red taillights, silver bumpers, fast wheels. Value $5-10.
  1. Red body.
  2. Yellow body.
  3. Green body.

187   CITROEN SM PRÉSIDENTIELLE   ? mm   1/43   1976-1980
Plastic version of #838. Fast wheels. Value $5-10.
  1. Metallic gray body, black top.

188   PEUGEOT 104   83 mm   1/43   1973-1980
4-door hatchback with plastic body, 4 opening doors, black 7 chassis and grille, gray interior, clear windows, silver headlights and bumpers, fast wheels. Value $5-10.
  1. White body.
  2. Orange body.
  3. Blue body.

  4. Tan body.

189   MATRA SIMCA BAGHEERA   90 mm   1/43   1973-1980
Sport coupe with plastic body, opening doors, interior, black 7 chassis and grille, clear windows and opening hatch, silver lights, fast wheels. Value $5-10.
  1. Yellow body, gray interior.
  2. Orange body, black interior.
  3. Green body, ? interior.

190   CITROEN AMI 8 WITH LUGGAGE RACK   90 mm   1/43 1976-1977
Based on #139. Value $5-10.
  1. Blue body.

190   RENAULT R6 WITH LUGGAGE RACK   88 mm   1/43/// 1978-1979
Based on #162. Value $5-10.
  1. ? body.

190   RENAULT 14TL WITH LUGGAGE RACK   91 mm   1/43 1979-
4-door sedan (#227/327) with plastic body, opening hood, silver gray 5 chassis and luggage, red rack, black interior and grille, clear windows and headlights, fast wheels. Value $5-10.
  1. Pale gray body.

191   CHEVRON B23   83 mm   1/43   1973-1980
Sports-racing car with plastic body, opening rear hood, black chassis, interior and roll bar, clear windows and headlights, silver motor, fast wheels, racing number decals. Value $5-10.
  1. Blue body, "Norev" and "Cotes du Rhone" logo.
  2. Blue body, without logo.

192 FERRARI 312P 92 mm 1/43 1973-1980
Sports-racing car with plastic body, opening doors, black chassis, interior, roll bar, grille, and airfoil, clear windows and headlights, silver motor and hubs, black tires, or fast wheels, racing numbers and other decals. Value $5-10.
   1. Red body.

193 FIAT X1/9 89 mm 1/43 1973-1980
Sport coupe with plastic body, opening doors, black 5 chassis, interior, bumpers, and opening rear panel, clear windows, fast wheels. Value $5-10.
   1. Red body.
   2. Light orange body.
   3. Lime green body.
   4. Dark blue body.

194 MONICA 1973 ? mm 1/43 (1974)
Not issued.

195 DE TOMASO PANTERA 96 mm 1/43 1974-1980
Sport coupe with plastic body, black 5 chassis, interior, motor, and opening hoods, clear windows, silver hubs, black tires or fast wheels, racing numbers. Value $5-10.
   1. Red body.
   2. Yellow body.
   3. Blue body.

196 MATRA-SIMCA 670B SHORT 93 mm 1/43 1973-1980
Sports-racing car with plastic body, opening doors and rear hood, white airfoil and cowling, black chassis, interior, and roll bar, clear headlights, silver motor and hubs, black tires or fast wheels, racing numbers and other decals. Value $5-10.
   1. Blue body.

197 MATRA-SIMCA 670B LONG 105 mm 1/43 1973-1980
Sports-racing car with components as #196 but longer body. As of 1970, issued with Gitanes logo. Either wheel type. Value $5-10.
   1. Blue body, racing number 4.
   2. Blue body, racing number 5, Gitanes decals.

198 ALPINE A440 90 mm 1/43 1975-1980
Sports-racing car with plastic body, opening doors, black 5, gray interior, white airfoil, silver hubs, black tires or fast wheels, racing number and other decals. Value $5-10.
   1. Blue body.

199 MERCEDES-BENZ TRUCK WITH CRANE 190 mm 1/43 1971-1980
Open truck with plastic cab, opening doors, interior, crane mount, arms, grabs, rear body, black chassis and parts, clear windows, silver grille and headlights, gray hubs, black tires or fast wheels. Value $10-15.
   1. Red cab and crane, light gray rear body.
   2. Light orange cab and crane, light gray rear body.

200 CAR WITH SKI RACK var. mm 1/43 1974-1976?
#162 Renault R6, #189 Matra-Simca Bagheera, or #323 Talbot 1510 with plastic ski rack and skis. Value $5-10.
   1. Renault R6, olive green body.
   2. Matra Bagheera, light gray body.
   3. Talbot 1510, yellow body.

201 LOLA T-294 93 mm 1974-1979
Sports-racing car with plastic body, opening doors, black chassis and interior, silver airfoil, roll bar, motor, and headlights, fast wheels. Value $5-10.
   1. Light gray body.

202 DRIVING SCHOOL CAR var. mm 1/43 1973-1976

Various cars with red-on-white "Auto-Ecole" roof sign and door labels. Value $5-15.

1. #57 Simca 1000, red body; 1973.
2. #9 Renault 10, ? body; 1974.
3. #162 Renault 6, green body; 1974-1976.
4. #178 Renault 5, green body; 1976.

203 CAR WITH BOAT AND TRAILER var. mm 1/43 1974-1978

#22 Chrysler 180 or #223 Simca 1308 with white boat on roof, pulling gray two-wheel box trailer. Value $5-10.

1. #22 Chrysler 180, ? body; 1974-1977.
2. #223 Simca 1308, ? body; 1978.

204 RACING CAR TRANSPORTER 138 mm 1/43 1974-1981

Same van as #133, with #191 Chevron B23. Value $8-12.

1. Standard colors.

205 TAXI var. mm 1/43 1973-1977

Various cars with white and red "Taxi Radio" sign, white antenna, yellow and black door labels. Value $5-10.

1. #49 Mercedes-Benz 220SE, ? body; 1973.
2. #22 Chrysler 180, ? body; 1975.
3. #3 Renault 16TX, light blue body; 1975-76.

206 FERRARI 512 ? mm 1/43 (1975)

Not issued.

207 CITROEN CX 2200 107 mm 1/43 1974-1980

4-door sedan with plastic body, opening doors, black 3+ chassis, interior, and grille, clear windows, silver headlights and bumpers, fast wheels. Value $5-10.

1. Turquoise body.
2. Light gray body.

208 CITROEN SM PRÉSIDENTIELLE & CYCLES 1/43 ca. 1976

#187 Citroen and two #230 police motorcycles. Value $8-12.

1. Standard colors.

209 PEUGEOT POLICE VAN AND CYCLES 1/43 ca. 1976

#245 police van and two #230 police motorcycles. Value $8-12.

1. Standard colors (blue van, "Police" logo).

210 PEUGEOT FIRE AMBULANCE & LIFEBOAT 220 mm 1/43 1986-1988

"Accident SOS set" of #252 Peugeot fire dept. ambulance with tow hook, light gray two-wheel trailer with black wheels, and white boat with silver gray motor and oars. Value $8-12.

1. Red van body.

211 TOUR DE FRANCE AMBULANCE var. mm 1/43 1975-1983

#40 Citroen ID19 or #252 Peugeot J7 ambulance with "Ambulance Norev" labels, plus three Tour de France bicyclists. Value $8-12.

1. #40 Citroen ID19, off-white body; 1975.
2. #252 Peugeot J7, red (or white?) body; 1976.

212 TOUR DE FRANCE PRESS CAR 103 mm 1/43 1975-1977...

#160 Peugeot 504 with white-on-red "Presse Norev" labels, plus three Tour de France bicyclists. Value $8-12.

1. Orange body.

213 RENAULT 5LS ? mm 1/43 (1975)
Not issued.

214 PEUGEOT 504 POLICE CAR 102 mm 1/43 1976-1980
#160 car with white opening hood, 4 doors, and trunk, black 7 chassis and interior, red dome light, light gray antenna, white-on-black "Police" labels. Value $5-10.
    1. Black body.

215 FIAT X1/9 ABARTH 89 mm 1/43 1975-1980
#193 car with green roof panel, black rear panel with air scoop, racing number, Abarth emblem. Value $4-8.
    1. Red body.

216 RENAULT 17 RALLY 99 mm 1/43 1975-1980
#168 Renault 17 with white roof panel, black racing number and Elf logo, mottled interior, 7 chassis, fast wheels. Value $5-10.
    1. Yellow-orange body.

217 RENAULT 5 RALLY 82 mm 1/43 1975-1978
#178 Renault 5 with white hood panel, black racing number and Elf logo, black interior, silver gray 7 chassis, fast wheels. Value $5-10.
    1. Yellow-orange body, white doors, black roof panel.

218 ALPINE A310 RALLY 94 mm 1/43 1975-1980
#176 Alpine with racing number and Elf logo. Value $5-10.
    1. Blue body.

219 RENAULT 30TS ? mm 1/43 1976-1980
4-door sedan; no other data. Value $5-10.
1, Red body.
    2. Tan body.

220 SAVIEM FIRE TANK TRUCK 127 mm 1/43 1976-1984
Tanker with plastic cab, opening doors, rear body, tank, black chassis and interior, clear windows, blue dome light, driver and 3 fireman figures, gray hubs, black tires or fast wheels. "Sapeurs Pompiers" labels. Value $10-15.
    1. Red cab, body and tank.

221 PEUGEOT 604 ? mm 1/43 1977-1980
4-door sedan; no other data. Value $5-10.
    1. Red body.

222 PEUGEOT 504 SAFARI 102 mm 1/43 1977-1980
4-door sedan (#160) with plastic body, opening hood, 4 doors and trunk, black 7 chassis, interior, and equipment on roof, clear windows, silver grille, headlights, and bumpers, fast wheels, "East African Safari" labels. Value $5-10.
    1. Light gray body.

223 SIMCA 1308GT 96 mm 1/43 1977-1980
4-door sedan with plastic body, opening doors, silver gray 5 chassis, black interior and grille, clear windows and headlights, fast wheels. Value $5-10.
    1. Light green body.

224 OFFICIAL CAR AND MOTORCYCLES ? mm 1/43 1977
#221 Peugeot 604 plus two #230 motorcycles. Value $10-15.
    1. Standard colors?

225 POLICE CAR AND MOTORCYCLES ? mm 1/43 1977
#214 Peugeot 504 police car and two #230 police motorcycles. Value $10-15.
    1. Standard colors (black and white car).

226 "TOUR CYCLISTE" SET ? mm 1/43 1977
#212 Peugeot press car, three cyclists, and perhaps one #230 police motorcycle. Value $10-15.
    1. Standard colors (orange car).

227 RENAULT 14 ? mm 1/43 1978-1980
Sedan with fast wheels. Value $5-10. No other data.
    1. Red body.

228 RENAULT 20TL 103 mm 1/43 1978-1980
4-door hatchback with plastic body, opening doors, black 5 chassis, interior, hatch panel, and grille, clear windows, silver bumper and headlights, fast wheels. Value $5-10.
    1. Orange body.

229 CAR & CARAVAN TRAILER ? mm 1/43 1978
#221 Peugeot 604 plus generic caravan trailer. Value $8-12.
    1. Standard car colors, blue and white caravan.

230 BMW 750 POLICE MOTORCYCLE 68 mm 1/32 1978-
Cycle with plastic body, silver wheels, front fender, handlebars, motor, and exhaust, black seat, tires, and driver with white helmet, gloves, and belt. Value $4-8.
    1. White body.

231 CAR & MOTORCYCLE TRAILER ? mm 1/43 1978
#219 Renault 30TS and #230 motorcycle on gray 2-wheel trailer. "Bol D'Or" set. Value $8-12.
    1. Standard colors?

233 PEUGEOT J7 MAIL TRUCK 107 mm 1/43 1978-
Light van with plastic body, sliding and opening doors, gray 3+ chassis and grille, dark gray interior, clear windows, amber headlights, fast wheels, "PTT" emblem labels, plus #230 motorcycle. Value $10-15.
    1. Yellow body.

235 PEUGEOT BUS & BOAT TRAILER ? mm 1/43 1978
#249 Peugeot J7 bus, trailer, and two kayaks. Value $10-15.
    1. Gray trailer, yellow kayaks.

236 PEUGEOT BUS & MATRA BAGHEERA WITH SKIS ? mm 1/43 1978
#248 Peugeot J7 bus, #200 Matra Bagheera on 2-wheel trailer. Value $10-15.
Standard colors?

237 RENAULT POLICE VAN & MOTORCYCLES ? mm 1/43 1978
#250 Renault police van and one (or two?) #230 police motorcycle(s). Value $10-15.
    1. Standard colors.

238 CITROEN POLICE VAN & MOTORCYCLES ? mm 1/43 1978
#247 Citroen police van and one (or two?) #230 police motorcycle(s). Value $20-25.
    1. Standard colors.

239 ALPINE A310 POLICE CAR 95 mm 1/43 1978-1980
#176 car with red dome light, light gray antenna, "Gendarmerie" labels. Value $5-10.
    1. Blue body.

240 RENAULT 5 DOCTOR'S CAR 80 mm 1/43 1978-1980
#178 car with blue dome light, light gray antenna, "SOS Medecin" labels. Value $8-12.
   1. White body.

241 RENAULT R4 FIRE VAN 82 mm 1/43 1978-1980
Minivan with plastic body, opening doors, silver gray 3+ chassis and grille, blue dome lights, charcoal interior, clear windows, amber headlights, light gray antenna, driver figure, fast wheels, "Sapeurs Pompiers" labels. Value $8-12.
   1. Red body.

242 RENAULT R4 POLICE VAN 82 mm 1/43 1978-1980
Same van as #241 in police livery. Value $8-12.
   1. Blue body.

243 RENAULT R4 MAIL VAN 82 mm 1/43 1978-1980
Same van as #241 in postal livery. Value $10-15.
   1. Yellow body.
   2. Yellow body, "Wartburg" logo (promo).

245 PEUGEOT J7 POLICE VAN 107 mm 1/43 1978-1988
Light van with plastic body, sliding and opening doors, silver gray 3+ chassis and grille, black interior, clear windows, red dome light, light gray antenna, silver headlights, fast wheels, "Police" and window bar labels. Value $8-12.
   1. Dark blue body.

246 RENAULT ESTAFETTE SCHOOL BUS 95 mm 1/43 1978-1984
Minibus with plastic body, opening rear doors, silver gray 7 chassis, grille, and taillights, black interior, clear windows, silver headlights, fast wheels, "Transport d'Enfants" labels. Value $8-12.

   1. Red body.
   2. Blue body.

247 CITROEN 1200 KG POLICE VAN 99 mm 1/43 1978-1980
Van with plastic body, sliding and opening doors, silver gray chassis, grille, and headlights, clear windows, red dome light, gray antenna, fast wheels, "Police" labels. Value $10-15.
   1. Light gray body.

248 PEUGEOT J7 BUS WITH SKIS 107 mm 1/43 1978-1984
Minibus with plastic body, opening rear doors, silver gray 3+ chassis, grille, and interior, clear windows, amber headlights, +/- red skis, fast wheels, "Courchevel" labels. Value $8-12.
   1. Cream body, skis.
   2. Red body, no skis.
   3. Green body, skis.

249 PEUGEOT J7 BUS WITH KAYAK 107 mm 1/43 1978-1980
Also exists without kayak. Value $8-12.
   1. Blue body.

250 RENAULT ESTAFETTE POLICE VAN 95 mm 1/43 1978-1984
Van with "Gendarmerie" logo. Value $8-12.
   1. Blue body.

251 PEUGEOT J7 ROAD SERVICE VAN 107 mm 1/43 1980-1984
Light van (as #245) with red dome light, gray antenna, "Autoroute" labels. Value $8-12.
   1. Orange body.

252 PEUGEOT J7 FIRE AMBULANCE 107 mm 1/43 1978-1988
Light van (as #245) with blue dome light, gray antenna, red cross and "SOS Accident" labels. Value $8-12.
1. White body.
2. Red body.

253 PEUGEOT J7 MAIL VAN 107 mm 1/43 1978-1984
Light van (as #245) in PTT postal livery. Value $8-12.
1. Yellow body.

254 RENAULT ESTAFETTE VAN 95 mm 1/43 1978-1984
Light van with plastic body, opening rear doors, silver gray 7 chassis, grille, and taillights, clear windows, black interior, amber headlights, fast wheels, "Livraison Norev" logo. Value $8-12.
1. Cream body.
2. Red body.
3. Cream body, "Conforama" logo (promo).

255 ALPINE A110 POLICE CAR 88 mm 1/43 1978-1980
Same model as #59A. Value $5-10.
1. Blue body.

256 CITROEN DS21 POLICE CAR 112 mm 1/43 1978-1980
Same model as #158P. Value $8-12.
1. Blue and white body.

257 MERCEDES-BENZ AMBULANCE ? mm 1/43 1978-1983
Presumably plastic version of #874. Value $8-12.
1. White body.

300 Series: Reissues of Earlier Models
Value of each model: $4-8.

301 TALBOT 1510 WITH SKI RACK ? mm 1/43 1982-
Reissue of #200. No other data.

302 RENAULT 5 DRIVING SCHOOL CAR 80 mm 1/43 1982-
Reissue of #202. No other data.

303 RENAULT 16TX 96 mm 1/43 1981-1982
Reissue of #3. No other data.

305 CITROEN CX TAXI 107 mm 1/43 1982-
Revision of #207 with "Taxi Radio" logo. No other data.

307 CITROEN CX 107 mm 1/43 1981-1983
Reissue of #207. No other data.

314 PEUGEOT 504 POLICE CAR 103 mm 1/43 1981-1984
Reissue of #214. No other data.

315 PEUGEOT 204 89 mm 1/43 1981-1984
Reissue of #5. No other data.

317 RENAULT R86 FARM TRACTOR 80 mm 1/43 1981-1988
Reissue of #117.
1. Orange body and hubs.
2. Blue body and hubs.

318 ALPINE A310 RALLY 94 mm 1/43 1981-1983
Reissue of #218. No other data.

319 RENAULT 30TS ? mm 1/43 1981-1983
Reissue of #219. No other data.

321 PEUGEOT 604 ? mm 1/43 1981-1984
Reissue of #221. No other data.

322 PEUGEOT 504 SAFARI 103 mm 1/43 1981-1983
Reissue of #222. No other data.

323 TALBOT 1510 100 mm 1/43 1981-1983
Reissue of ? No other data.

326 CITROEN 2CV VAN 83 mm 1/43 1981-1984
Reissue of #26.
    1. Orange body, silver gray chassis, fast wheels.

327 RENAULT R14 ? mm 1/43 1981-1983
Reissue of #227. No other data.

328 RENAULT R20 103 mm 1/43 1981-1983
Reissue of #228. No other data.

332 PEUGEOT 204 BREAK 92 mm 1/43 1981-1984
Reissue of #32.
    1. Brick red body, black chassis, fast wheels.

337 CITROEN MEHARI 81 mm 1/43 1981-1984
Reissue of #137.
    1. Green body, black top, interior, and chassis, fast wheels.

339 ALPINE A310 POLICE 95 mm 1/43 1981-1983
Reissue of #239. No other data.

340 RENAULT R5 DOCTOR'S CAR 80 mm 1/43 1981-1984
Reissue of #240. No other data.

341 RENAULT R4 FIRE VAN 82 mm 1/43 1981-1989
Reissue of #241.
    1. Red body, silver gray chassis, fast wheels.

342 RENAULT R4 POLICE VAN 82 mm 1/43 1981-1984
Reissue of #242. No other data.

343 RENAULT R4 MAIL VAN 82 mm 1/43 1981-1984
Reissue of #243. No other data.

344 CITROEN ID19 AMBULANCE 115 mm 1/43 1981-1983
Reissue of #40.
    1. White body, black chassis, clear dome light, tinted windows, red interior, fast wheels, no labels.
    2. As above except red dome light, clear windows, red "Ambulance Norev" labels.

350 RENAULT R12 100 mm 1/43 1981-1984
Reissue of #140. No other data.

351 TALBOT 1100 88 mm 1/43 1981-1983
Reissue of #151. No other data.

353 RENAULT R4L 83 mm 1/43 1981-1984
Reissue of #53. No other data.

356 CITROEN 2CV6 89 mm 1/43 1981-1984
Reissue of #56.
    1. Yellow body, silver gray interior and chassis, fast wheels.

357 CITROEN DYANE 88 mm 1/43 1981-1984
Reissue of #157. No other data.

358 SIMCA 1000 85 mm 1/43 1981-1982
Reissue of #57. No other data.

360 PEUGEOT 504 102 mm 1/43 1981-1983
Reissue of #160. No other data.

361 RENAULT R6 88 mm 1/43 1981-1984
Reissue of #162. No other data.

362 VOLKSWAGEN 1300 93 mm 1/43 1981-1984
Reissue of #62.
    1. Pale tan body, black interior and chassis, fast wheels.

368 RENAULT 17TS 96 mm 1/43 1981-1982
Reissue of #168. No other data.

369 CITROEN GS 94 mm 1/43 1981-1984
Reissue of #169. No other data.

376 ALPINE A310 94 mm 1/43 1981-1983
Reissue of #176. No other data.

378 RENAULT 5TL 79 mm 1/43 1981-1983
Reissue of #178. No other data.

382 BERTONE CAMARGUE 94 mm 1/43 1981-1989
Reissue of #182. No other data.

384 PORSCHE CARRERA RSR 93 mm 1/43 1981-1989
Reissue of #184. No other data.

387 CITROEN SM PRESIDENTIELLE ? mm 1/43 1981-1982
Reissue of #187. No other data.

388 PEUGEOT 104 83 mm 1/43 1981-1983
Reissue of #188. No other data.

389 PEUGEOT 304 96 mm 1/43 1981-1986
Reissue of #89.
    1. Pale tan body, black interior and chassis, fast wheels.

391 MATRA SIMCA BAGHEERA 90 mm 1/43 1981-1982
Reissue of #189. No other data.

395 DE TOMASO PANTERA 96 mm 1/43 1981-1985
Reissue of #195. No other data.

398 ALPINE A440 90 mm 1/43 1981-1983
Reissue of #198. No other data.

450 PORSCHE CARRERA 6 92 mm 1/43 1984
Reissue of #149. No other data.

451 JAGUAR E-TYPE 101 mm 1/43 1984
Reissue of #156. No other data.

MINI-JET SERIES

1/66 scale diecast models. Value of each model $3-5.

400 CITROEN BX 77 mm 1/66 year?
4-door sedan with cast body, silver chassis, orange plastic interior, clear windows and headlights, fast wheels. See also #451.
    1. Red body.

401 LIGIER JS2 68 mm 1/66 1975-

2-door hatchback coupe with cast body, opening front doors, chassis-interior-headlights, clear or tinted plastic windows, fast wheels, #306887 on base.
1. Metallic red body.
2. Dark yellow body.
3. Metallic blue body.
4. Purple body.

402 MATRA BAGHEERA 60 mm 1/66 1975-

2-door hatchback coupe with cast body, opening front doors, chassis-interior, clear or tinted plastic windows, fast wheels, #301878 on base.
1. Metallic dark red body.
2. Copper body.
3. Yellow body.
4. Metallic green body.
5. Blue body.

404 CITROEN GS 68 mm 1/66 1975-1984

4-door sedan with cast body, opening doors, chassis-interior, clear or tinted plastic windows, fast wheels, #301882 on base.
1. Red body.
2. Yellow body.
3. Metallic green body.

405 PEUGEOT 504 68 mm 1/66 1975-1984

4-door sedan with cast body, chassis, black plastic interior, clear or tinted windows, fast wheels, #301884 on base.
1. Red body.
2. Metallic green body.
3. Blue body.

406 CITROEN CX 69 mm 1/66 1975-1983

4-door sedan with cast body, opening front doors, chassis-interior, clear or tinted windows, fast wheels, #301891 on base.
1. Red body.
2. Dark red body.
3. Yellow body.
4. Metallic green body.
5. Purple body.

407 RENAULT 12 69 mm 1/66 1975-1984

4-door sedan with plastic body, opening front doors, chassis, black plastic interior, clear or tinted windows, fast wheels, #301886 on base.
1. Tangerine body.
2. Maroon body.
3. Metallic maroon body.
4. Yellow body.
5. Metallic green body.
6. Metallic blue body.
7. Blue body.

408 CITROEN DYANE 70 mm 1/66 1976-1984

4-door sedan with cast body, +/- opening doors, chassis- interior-headlights, clear or tinted plastic windows, fast wheels, #301885 on base.
1. Light red body, without opening doors.
2. Red body, with opening doors.
3. Orange body.
4. Yellow body.
5. Metallic green body.
6. Silver gray body.

409 RENAULT 4L 61 mm 1/66 1976-1984

5-door wagon with cast body, opening rear door, chassis-interior, clear plastic windows, fast wheels, #301894 on base.

1. Red body.
2. Copper body.
3. Yellow body.
4. Metallic green body.
5. Metallic blue body.

410 MERCEDES-BENZ AMBULANCE 69 mm 1/66 1976-1984

Ambulance with cast body, chassis, black plastic interior, blue dome light, tinted windows, fast wheels, red cross labels, #318977 on base; originally #977.

1. White body.
2. Pale gray body.

411 MASERATI BOOMERANG 67 mm 1/66 1976-1984

Sports coupe with cast body, chassis-interior, tinted plastic windows, fast wheels, #306975 on base; originally #975.

1. Red body.
2. Orange body.
3. Metallic blue body.
4. Purple body.

412 BERTONE TRAPEZE 60 mm 1/66 1976-

Coupe with cast body, chassis, red plastic interior-stripe-grille-bumpers, tinted windows, fast wheels, #306976 on base.

1. White body and chassis.
2. Yellow body and chassis.
3. Blue body and chassis.

413 RENAULT 30TS 68 mm 1/66 1976-

4-door hatchback with cast body, opening hatch, chassis, black plastic interior, clear windows, fast wheels, #301895 on base.

1. Red body.

414 PEUGEOT 604 69 mm 1/66 1976-1984

4-door sedan with cast body, chassis, black plastic interior, tinted windows, fast wheels, #301896 on base; originally #896.

1. Red body.
2. Yellow body
3. Metallic green body.
4. Metallic brown body.
4. Silver gray body.

415 SIMCA 1308GT/TALBOT 1500SX 64 mm 1/66 1978-1984

4-door sedan with cast body, chassis, black plastic interior, tinted windows, fast wheels. Updated to Talbot in 1982.

1. Red body.
2. Metallic blue body.

416 BMW 633 CSI 68 mm 1/66 1978-1984

2-door coupe with cast body, chassis, black plastic interior, tinted windows, fast wheels.

1. Light orange body.
2. Metallic green body.
3. Blue body.

417 FIAT 1315 69 mm 1/66 1978-

4-door sedan with cast body, chassis, black plastic interior, tinted windows, fast wheels.

1. Maroon body.
2. Metallic gold body.
3. Silver gray body.

418 PORSCHE TURBO ? mm 1/66 1978-
No data.

419 RENAULT 14 69 mm 1/66 1978-1984
4-door sedan with cast body, chassis, black plastic interior, tinted windows, fast wheels.
    1. Maroon body.
    2. Metallic gold body.

420 PEUGEOT 305SR 68 mm 1/66 1978-1984
4-door sedan with cast body, chassis, black plastic interior, tinted windows, fast wheels.
    1. Cream body.
    2. Light orange body.
    3. Light green body.

421 SIMCA/TALBOT HORIZON 69 mm 1/66 1978-1984
4-door sedan with cast body, chassis, black plastic interior, tinted windows, fast wheels. Updated to Talbot in 1982.
    1. Light orange body.
    2. Metallic green body.

422 RENAULT 18GTS 69 mm 1/66 1982-1984
4-door sedan with cast body, chassis, black plastic interior, tinted windows, fast wheels.
    1. Metallic green body.
    2. Metallic blue body.

423 VOLVO 264 71 mm 1/66 1982-1984
4-door sedan with cast body, chassis, black plastic interior, tinted windows, fast wheels.
    1. Metallic blue body.
    2. Silver gray body.

424 FORD MUSTANG 75 mm 1/66 1982-1984
Coupe with cast body, chassis, gray plastic interior, tinted windows, fast wheels.
    1. Orange body.
    2. Silver gray body.

425 MERCEDES-BENZ 280SE 71 mm 1/66 1982-1984
4-door sedan with cast body, chassis, black plastic interior, tinted windows, fast wheels.
    1. Light orange body.
    2. Silver gray body.

428 CITROEN VISA 72 mm 1/66 1982-1984
4-door sedan with cast body, chassis, black plastic interior, tinted windows, fast wheels.
    1. Red body.
    2. Maroon body.

429 VW GOLF 70 mm 1/66 1982-1984
2-door hatchback with cast body, chassis, black plastic interior, tinted windows, fast wheels.
    1. Metallic gold body.
    2. Metallic blue body.
    3. Silver gray body.

430 ALFA ROMEO 6 71 mm 1/66 1982-1984
4-door sedan with cast body, chassis, black plastic interior, tinted windows, fast wheels.
    1. Red body.
    2. Orange body.

431 PEUGEOT 505 71 mm 2/66 1982-1984
4-door sedan with cast body, chassis, black plastic interior, tinted

windows, fast wheels.
- 1. Red body.

432 FIAT RITMO 70 mm 1/66 1982-1984

4-door sedan with cast body, chassis, black plastic interior, tinted windows, fast wheels.
- 1. Metallic green body.
- 2. Metallic blue body.

433 VOLVO F89 CRANE TRUCK 71 mm 1982-

Truck with cast cab, cabin, light gray plastic rear body, telescoping booms, hook, black chassis and grille, tinted windows, dome light, fast wheels.
- 1. Orange cab and cabin.
- 2. Blue cab and cabin.

434 VOLVO F89 FIRE ENGINE 71 mm 1982-

Truck with cast body, light gray plastic chassis-grille and parts, tinted windows, dome light, fast wheels.
- 1. Red body.

435 VOLVO F89 TANK TRUCK 71 mm 1982-

Tanker with cast cab, tank, black plastic chassis-grille, tinted windows, fast wheels, logo labels.
- 1. White cab and tank, BP logo.
- 2. White cab and tank, Shell logo.
- 3. White cab and tank, Texaco logo.

436 VOLVO F89 COVERED TRUCK 71 mm 1982-

Truck with cast cab, rear body, light gray plastic chassis-grille and cover, tinted windows, fast wheels.
- 1. Red cab and body.
- 2. Yellow cab and body.
- 3. Metallic blue cab and body.

437 RENAULT FUEGO 74 mm 1/66 1982-1984

2-door hatchback with cast body, chassis, black plastic interior, tinted windows, fast wheels.
- 1. Red body.
- 2. Yellow body.
- 3. Metallic blue body.

438 FORD ESCORT 75 mm 1/66 1982-1984

2-door hatchback with cast body, chassis-tow hook, black plastic interior, tinted windows, fast wheels.
- 1. Silver body and chassis.
- 2. Red body.
- 3. Yellow body.
- 4. Metallic green body.
- 5. Metallic blue body.

439 TALBOT SOLARA ? mm 1/66 1982-1984

No data.
- 1. Silver gray body.

440 VOLVO F89 MILK TANK TRUCK 71 mm 1982-1986?

Tanker with cast cab, white rear body and tanks, light gray plastic chassis-grille, tinted windows, fast wheels.
- 1. Red cab.
- 2. Orange cab.
- 3. Yellow cab.
- 4. Blue cab.

441 VOLVO F89 PROPANE TANKER 71 mm 1982-1986?

Tanker with cast cab, rear body and tank, light gray plastic chassis-grille, tinted windows, fast wheels.
- 1. Red cab, white rear body.

442 VOLVO F89 LADDER TRUCK 71 mm 1982-1988?

Fire truck with cast cab, unpainted ladder base, silver plastic rear body and ladder, light gray chassis-grille, tinted windows, dome light, fast wheels.
1. Maroon cab.

443 VOLVO F89 CONTAINER TRUCK 71 mm 1985-

No data.
1. "La pie qui chante" logo.
2. "L'Alsacienne" logo.

445 RENAULT CHERRY PICKER ? mm 1982-1986?

No data.
1. Yellow and green.

446 RENAULT CEMENT TRUCK 75 mm 1982-1988?

Truck with cast cab, plastic rear body, mixer, black chassis-grille-tow hook, tinted windows, fast wheels.
1. Red cab, blue rear, yellow mixer.
2. Yellow cab, green rear, orange mixer.

447 RENAULT BUCKET TRUCK 75 mm 1982-1988?

Truck with cast cab, rear body, and arms, green plastic bucket, black chassis-grille-tow hook, tinted windows, fast wheels.
1. Red cab, rear body and arms, white ?
2. Yellow cab, rear body and arms.
3. Blue cab, rear body and arms, white ?

448 RENAULT DUMP TRUCK 75 mm 1982-1988?

Dumper with cast cab and tipper, black plastic chassis-grille-tow hook, tinted windows, fast wheels.
1. Yellow cab and tipper.
2. Yellow cab, silver tipper.

3. Yellow cab, green tipper.

449 RENAULT CONTAINER TRUCK ? mm 1982-1986?

No data.
1. White cab, blue body.

450 RENAULT 9 ? mm 1/66 1982-1986

No data.
1. Green body.
2. "La pie qui chante" logo.

451 CITROEN BX ? mm 1/66 1984-

No data.
1. Green body.
2. Metallic green body.

452 RENAULT GARBAGE TRUCK 75 mm 1984-

Truck with cast cab, ivory plastic rear body, black chassis-grille-tow hook, tinted windows, fast wheels.
1. Yellow cab.

460 CHEVROLET CAMPER PICKUP 75 mm 1984-

Truck with cast body, white plastic camper, yellow chassis-grille, clear windows, fast wheels.
1. Metallic green body.
2. Blue body.
3. Blue body, "Circus" logo.

461 CHEVROLET FIRE VAN 75 mm 1984-

Truck with cast body, red plastic rear body, white ladder and chassis-grille, tinted windows, fast wheels.
1. Red body.
2. Red body, "Vroom" logo.

462 CHEVROLET COVERED TRUCK 75 mm 1984-
Truck with cast body, plastic cover and chassis-grille, tinted windows, fast wheels.
  1. Blue body, yellow cover.
  2. Bronze body, black cover.
  3. Tan body, black cover.
  4. Orange body, yellow cover, "Safari" logo.
  5. Blue body, yellow cover, "Service" logo.

463   CHEVROLET CAMPER WITH SURFBOARD   75 mm 1984-
Truck with cast body, white plastic camper shell, tinted windows, fast wheels.
  1. Red body.
  2. Green body.
  3. Tan body.

464 CHEVROLET WRECKER 75 mm 1984-
Wrecker with cast body, plastic rear and booms, white chassis-grille, tinted windows, fast wheels.
  1. Red body, yellow rear.
  2. Blue body and rear.
  3. Black body, yellow rear.
  4. Red body, yellow rear, "Vroom" logo.
  5. Black body, yellow rear, "Vroom" logo.

465 CHEVROLET PICKUP TRUCK 75 mm 1984-
Truck with cast body, plastic rear and chassis-grille, tinted windows, fast wheels.
  1. White body, blue rear, no logo.
  2. White body, blue rear, "Sheriff" logo.
  3. White body, blue rear, "Police" logo.
  4. Blue body, white rear, "Ranch" logo.

466 CHEVROLET AIRPORT TRUCK 75 mm 1984-
Truck with cast body, white plastic rear with steps, blue chassis-grille, tinted windows, fast wheels.
  1. White body.
  2. White body, "Air France" logo.

467 CHEVROLET CATTLE TRUCK 75 mm 1984-
Truck with cast body, green plastic stakes and chassis-grille, tinted windows, fast wheels.
  1. Light orange body.
  2. Orange body, "Ranch" logo.
  3. White body, "Tradition Charolaise" logo.

468   CHEVROLET PICKUP WITH MOTORCYCLE   75 mm 1984-
Truck with cast body, red plastic chassis-grille, red, green, or blue motorcycle, tinted windows, fast wheels.
  1. White body.
  2. Green body.
  3. Black body.

Original Mini-Jet (ex-Schuco) Numbers

809 BMW 2002 64 mm 1/66 1975-1982
2-door sedan with cast body, opening doors, unpainted chassis, black plastic interior, clear windows, fast wheels, #301809.
  1. Red body.
  2. Yellow body.

813 PORSCHE 911S 61 mm 1/66 1975-
Sports coupe with cast body, opening doors, unpainted chassis, black plastic interior, clear windows, fast wheels, #301813.

1. Metallic red body.
2. Metallic dark green body.
3. Blue body.

816 FORD CAPRI 1700 GT 65 mm 1/66 1975-
2-door sedan with cast body, opening doors, unpainted chassis, black plastic interior, clear windows, fast wheels, #301816.
1. Yellow body.
2. Green body.

839 OPEL MANTA 60 mm 1/66 1975-
No data.
1. Yellow body.
2. Silver gray body.

854 PORSCHE 917 65 mm 1/66 1975-
Sports-racing coupe with cast front and opening rear body, unpainted chassis, black plastic interior, clear windows, fast wheels, #306854.
1. Red body.
2. Yellow body.
3. Blue body.

861 RENAULT 17 COUPE 63 mm 1/66 1975-
Coupe with cast body, opening doors, unpainted chassis, black plastic interior, clear windows, fast wheels, #301861.
1. Red body.
2. Orange body.
3. Yellow body.
4. Green body.
5. Blue body.

871 RENAULT 5 52 mm 1/66 1975-1979
3-door car with cast body, opening doors, unpainted chassis, black plastic interior, clear windows, fast wheels, #301871.
1. Red body.
2. Yellow-green body.
3. Purple body.
4. Metallic brown body.

878 MATRA SIMCA BAGHEERA 60 mm 1/66 1975-1982>#402
See #402.

882 CITROEN GS 68 mm 1/66 1975-1982>#404
See #404.

883 CITROEN DS21 69 mm 1/66 1975-1982
4-door sedan with cast body, opening doors, unpainted chassis-interior, clear windows, fast wheels, #301883.
1. Red body.
2. Yellow-green body.
3. Blue body.
4. Metallic blue body.

884 PEUGEOT 504 68 mm 1/66 1975-1982>#405
See #405.

885 CITROEN DYANE 70 mm 1/66 1975-1982>#408
See #408.

886 RENAULT 12 69 mm 1/66 1975-1982>#407
See #407.

887 LIGIER JS2 68 mm 1/66 1975-1982>#401
See #401.

890 PEUGEOT 604 69 mm 1/66 1975-1982>#414
See #414.

891 CITROEN CX 69 mm 1/66 1975-1982>#406
See #406.

894 RENAULT 4L 61 mm 1/66 1975-1982>#409
See #409.

895 RENAULT 30TS 68 mm 1/66 1975-1982>#413
See #413.

896 PEUGEOT 604 69 mm 1/66 1975-1982>#414
See #414.

975 MASERATI BOOMERANG 67 mm 1/66 1975-1982>#411
See #411.

977 MERCEDES-BENZ AMBULANCE 69 mm 1/66 1975-1982 > #410
See #410.

#? PORSCHE 914 ? mm 1/66 1975-
No data.

#? RENAULT 4L FIRE CHIEF 61 mm 1/66 year?
5-door wagon with cast body, opening rear door, unpainted chassis, black plastic interior, tinted windows, fast wheels, black "Sapeurs pompiers."
　　1. Maroon body.

#? SIMCA 1308GT 64 mm 1/66 year?
4-door sedan with cast body, unpainted chassis, black plastic interior, tinted windows, fast wheels.
　　1. Silver body.

1/86 Scale Micro Miniatures

Note: The earliest issues had single-digit numbers before the 500 numbering system was introduced. Values: The 500 plastic cars and smallest vans are worth $8-12, the #515 Citroen van and diecast cars $10-15, the larger trucks and the bus $15-20, and the 526 Auto Transporter with five cars $25-30.

501 SIMCA VERSAILLES/ARIANE 52 mm 1/86 1959-1969
4-door sedan with plastic body, clear windows, silver chassis, grille, and headlights, red taillights. Ex 1-1 Versailles and 1-2 Ariane.
　　1. Dull olive body, red hubs, white tires (Versailles).
　　2. Light blue body, red hubs, white tires (Versailles).
　　3. Light tan body, silver hubs, black tires (Ariane).
　　4. Versailles also exists in yellow; Ariane in rose, orange, light green, light blue, blue, mauve, gray. No other data.

502 SIMCA ARONDE 48 mm 1/86 1959-1969
4-door sedan with plastic body, clear windows, silver chassis, grille, and headlights, red taillights, silver hubs, black tires.
　　1. Orange body.
　　2. Dull green body.
　　3. Gray body.

503 CITROEN 2CV AZ 45 mm 1/86 1957-1969
4-door sedan with plastic body, clear windows, silver chassis and grille, light green hubs, black tires. Ex #6.
　　1. Light red body.
　　2. Blue body.
　　3. Gray body.

504 CITROEN DS19 56 mm 1/86 1957-1969

4-door sedan with plastic body, clear windows, silver chassis, red hubs, white tires. Ex #2.
1. White body.
2. Orange body.
3. Yellow body.
4. Light blue body.
5. Lilac body.
6. Black body.

505 MERCEDES-BENZ 220SE 55 mm 1/86 1961-1969

4-door sedan with plastic body, clear windows, silver chassis, grille, and headlights, red taillights, silver hubs, black tires.
1. Light gray body.

506 PANHARD PL17 52 mm 1/86 1960-1969

4-door sedan with plastic body, clear windows, silver chassis and headlights, red taillights, silver hubs, black tires.
1. Light green body.
2. Light blue body.

507 RENAULT 4CV 42 mm 1/86 1958-1969

4-door sedan with plastic body, clear windows, silver chassis and headlights, red taillights, light green hubs, black tires. Ex #7.
1. Rose body.
2. Turquoise body.
3. Dark gray body.

508 RENAULT DAUPHINE 45 mm 1/86 1957-1969

4-door sedan with plastic body, clear windows, silver chassis and headlights, red taillights, light green hubs, black tires. Ex #4.
1. Light olive body.

509 RENAULT ESTAFETTE BUS 47 mm 1/86 1960-1969

Minibus with plastic body, clear windows, silver chassis, grille, and headlights, red taillights, silver hubs, black tires.
1. Yellow body.

510 RENAULT CARAVELLE 48 mm 1/86 1960-1969

Coupe with plastic body, clear windows, silver chassis and headlights, red taillights, silver hubs, black tires.
1. Light green body.
2. Light gray body.

511 RENAULT 4L 41 mm 1/86 1962-1969

Wagon with plastic or cast body, clear windows, silver chassis and headlights, ivory hubs, black tires.
1. Red plastic body.
2. Yellow plastic body.
3. Blue plastic body.
4. Gray plastic body.
5. Metallic gold cast body.

512 CITROEN AMI 6 45 mm 1/86 1962-1969

4-door sedan with plastic or metal body, clear windows, silver chassis and headlights, red taillights, silver hubs, black tires.
1. Yellow plastic body.
2. ? cast body.

513 RENAULT R4 VAN 42 mm 1/86 1963-1969

Light van with plastic body, clear windows, silver chassis, headlights and hubs, black tires, "Norev" logo.
1. Yellow body.
2. Aqua body.
3. Light blue body.
4. Light gray body.
5. Light gray body, "Pschitt" logo.

514 RENAULT R8 45 mm 1/86 1962-1969

4-door sedan with plastic or cast body, clear windows, silver chassis and headlights, red taillights, silver hubs, black tires.
1. Red plastic body.
2. Yellow plastic body.
3. Blue plastic body.
4. Gray plastic body.
5. ? cast body.

515 CITROEN 1200 KG VAN 50 mm 1/86 1959-1969

Van with plastic body, sliding door, clear windows, silver chassis, grille, and headlights, light green hubs, black tires, "Rapid-Lak" and numerous other logo types. Value $10-15.
1. Yellow body, "Teppaz" logo.
2. Green body, "Rapid-Lak" logo.
3. Light gray body, "Amora" logo.
4. See Argus for other promotional models.

516 PEUGEOT 403 VAN 51 mm 1/86 1960-1969

Covered pickup with plastic body, gray cover, clear windows, silver chassis, grille, and headlights, light green hubs, black tires.
1. Red body.
2. Yellow body.
3. Green body.
4. Blue body.
5. Dark blue body.

517 PEUGEOT 404 AND TRAILER ? mm 1/86 1961-1963

#518 car pulling plastic 2-wheel trailer with gray cover.
1. Pale blue trailer.

518 PEUGEOT 404 51 mm 1/86 1961-1969

4-door sedan with plastic body, clear windows, silver chassis, grille, and headlights, red taillights, silver hubs, black tires.

1. Pale blue body.
2. Blue body.

519 SIMCA 1000 44 mm 1/86 1963-1969

4-door sedan with plastic or metal body, clear windows, silver chassis, grille and headlights, silver hubs, black tires.
1. Red plastic body.
2. ? metal body.

520 UNIC DUMP TRUCK 82 mm 1/86 1958-1969

Quarry dumper with plastic cab, chassis, tipper, and hubs, clear windows, silver grille, black tires. Value $10-15.
1. Red cab and chassis, light gray tipper.
2. Yellow cab and chassis, light gray tipper.
3. Green cab and chassis, yellow tipper.
4. Blue cab and chassis, yellow tipper.
5. Olive cab and chassis, light gray tipper.

521 UNIC CEMENT TRUCK 171 mm 1/86 1960-1969

Cement carrier semi with plastic cab, chassis, semi, tanks, light gray tops and hubs, dark gray catwalks and pipes, clear windows, silver grille, black tires, spare wheel. Value $15-20.
1. Red cab and chassis, yellow semi and tanks.
2. Blue cab and chassis, yellow semi and tanks.

522 UNIC MILK TANK TRUCK 185 mm 1/86 1958-1969

Milk tank semi with plastic cab, chassis, semi, and hubs, cream sign and tanks, clear windows, silver grille, black tires, spare wheel, "France-Lait" logo on sign. Value $15-20.
1. Light blue cab and chassis, light gray semi and hubs.

523 UNIC PROPANE TRUCK 185 mm 1/86 1958-1969

Open semi with plastic cab, chassis, semi, silver gray bottles, light gray hubs, clear windows, silver grille, black tires, spare wheel, "Pri-

magaz" logo. Ex #8. Value $15-20.
1. Red cab, chassis and semi.
2. Maroon cab, red semi.

524   UNIC TITAN SEMI-TRAILER TRUCK   155 mm   1/86 1957-1969
Open semi with plastic cab, chassis, semi, opening tailgate, clear windows, silver grille, light gray hubs, black tires, spare wheel. Ex #3. Value $15-20.
1. Red cab and chassis, light blue semi and tailgate.
2. Red cab, chassis, semi and tailgate?

525   UNIC AUTO CARRIER   221 mm   1/86   1958-1969
Car carrier semi with plastic cab, chassis, semi parts, clear windows, silver grille, gray hubs, black tires, spare wheel. Ex #5. Value $15-20.
1. Red, rose, green or blue cab, with:
2. Blue, turquoise, gray or black semi.

526   UNIC AUTO CARRIER & 5 CARS   221 mm   1/86   1958-1968
#525 auto carrier with five 500 series cars. Ex #5A. Value $25-30.
1. Standard colors.

527   UNIC ESTEREL TANK TRUCK   142 mm   1/86   1964-1969
Tanker semi with plastic cab, chassis, semi, black chassis, clear windows, silver grille, light gray hubs, black tires, "Antar" or other logo. Value $15-20.
1. Red cab, chassis and semi, "Antar" logo.
2. Red cab, chassis and semi, "Esso" logo.
3. Yellow cab, chassis and semi, "Shell" logo.
4. Green cab and chassis, white semi, "BP" logo.
5. Dark blue cab, chassis and semi, "Azur" logo.

528   SAVIEM BUS   123 mm   1/86   1963-1969
Single deck bus with plastic body and interior, clear windows, silver grille, bumpers and hubs, black chassis and tires. Value $15-20.
1. White body, ? interior.
2. Red body, ? interior.
3. Maroon body, ? interior.
4. Light green body, red interior.
5. Blue body, gray interior.
6. Light gray body, red interior.

529   SIMCA 1500   49 mm   1963-1969
4-door sedan with plastic or cast body, clear windows, silver chassis, grille, and headlights, red taillights, silver or ivory hubs, black tires.
1. Red plastic body.
2. Yellow plastic body.
3. Light blue plastic body.
4. Red cast body.
5. Gray cast body.

530   PANHARD 24CT   49 mm   1/86   1963-1969
Coupe with plastic or cast body, clear windows, silver chassis, headlights, and hubs, red taillights, black tires.
1. Light green plastic body.
2. Pale blue-gray plastic body.
3. White cast body.
4. Red cast body.

531   RENAULT R16   48 mm   1/86   1965-1969
4-door hatchback with plastic or cast body, clear windows, silver chassis, grille, and headlights, ivory hubs, black tires.
1. White plastic body.
2. Blue plastic body.
3. Gold cast body.
4. Metallic blue cast body.

532 PEUGEOT 204 46 mm 1/86 1965-1969
4-door sedan with plastic or cast body, clear windows, silver chassis, grille, and headlights, silver or ivory hubs, black tires.
1. Cream plastic body.
2. Orange plastic body.
3. Light gray plastic body.
4. Dark green cast body.
5. Blue cast body.

Newer 500/1500 Series: value $10-15 each.

501 CAR AND BOAT TRAILER ? mm 1/43 1976-
#845 Citroen CX pulling trailer with cabin cruiser. Later #1501.
1. Gray trailer, ? cruiser.

502 CAR AND SPORTS CAR ON TRAILER ? mm 1/43 1976-
#839 Porsche Carrera (pulling or pulled?) Later #1502.
1. Gray trailer, ? cars.

503 CAR AND CARAVAN TRAILER ? mm 1/43 1976-
#842 Peugeot 504 pulling #93 caravan. Later #1503.
1. White caravan.

504 PRESIDENTIAL SET ? mm 1/43 1976-
#838 Citroen Presidentielle and two #230 motorcycles. Later #1504.
1. Standard colors.

506 MERCEDES AMBULANCE POLICE ESCORT 1/43 #1541>1987-
#874 ambulance with #230 police motorcycles. #1506.
1. Standard colors.

508 SAVIEM CRANE TRUCK 145 mm 1/43 1976-1981
Crane truck with cast cab, black chassis, plastic rear body and interior, clear windows, silver gray crane and drive train, black Saviem grille and tires, light gray hubs, "Maxi-Jet Depannage" logo.
1. Blue cab and rear body.

509 DAF CRANE TRUCK 145 mm 1/43 1976-1981
Same truck as #508 but with DAF grille.
1. Red cab and body.

510 VOLVO CRANE TRUCK 145 mm 1/43 1976-1981
Same truck as #508 but with Volvo grille.
1. Orange can and body.

511 TOUR DE FRANCE SET ? mm 1/43 1976-
#842 Peugeot 504 with two #230 motorcycles. Later #1511.
1. Colors?

512 CAR AND MOTORCYCLE TRAILER 209 mm 1/43 1976-
#856 Renault 30 TS, silver gray plastic trailer, and #230 motorcycle. Later #1512.
1. Standard colors.

513 POLICE CAR & MOTORCYCLES ? mm 1/43 1976-1988
#849 Peugeot 504 police car and #230 motorcycles. Later #1513.
1. Standard colors.

514 OFFICIAL CAR AND MOTORCYCLES ? mm 1/43 1976-1986
Adapted #857 Peugeot 604 and #230 motorcycles. Later #1514.
1. Colors?

515 SAVIEM BOTTLE TRUCK 132 mm 1/43 1976-1981
Flat truck with cast cab, plastic rear body, silver gray and orange bottle load, clear windows, silver gray drive train, light gray hubs, black chassis, grille, interior, bumpers and tires.
  1. Blue cab and rear body.

516 DAF BOTTLE TRUCK 132 mm 1/43 1976-1981
Same truck as #515 but with DAF grille.
  1. Red cab and rear body.

517 VOLVO BOTTLE TRUCK 132 mm 1/43 1976-1981
Same truck as #515 but with Volvo grille.
  1. Orange cab and body.

518 SAVIEM MOBILE SHOP 175 mm 1/43 1977-1981
Truck with cast cab, plastic rear body, orange rear doors, blue rear and black cab interiors, clear windows, light gray drive train, black chassis, grille, bumper and tires.
  1. Red cab, white rear body.

519 DAF MOBILE SHOP 175 mm 1/43 1977-1981
Same truck as #518 but with DAF grille.
  1. Light blue cab, white rear body.

520 VOLVO MOBILE SHOP 175 mm 1/43 1977-1981
Same truck as #518 but with Volvo grille. No other data.

521 SAVIEM MILK TANK TRUCK 129 mm 1/43 1976-1981
Tank truck with cast cab, plastic tank, white and silver gray rear body, white filler, silver gray cans, clear windows, black chassis, bumper, grille, silver drive train, gray hubs, black tires.
  1. Blue cab and tank.

522 DAF MILK TANK TRUCK 129 mm 1/43 1976-1981
Same truck as #521 but with DAF grille.
  1. Blue cab and tank.

523 VOLVO MILK TANK TRUCK 129 mm 1/43 1976-1981
Same truck as #521 but with Volvo grille.
  1. White cab and tank, orange rear body and filler.

524 SAVIEM FIRE TANK TRUCK ? mm 1/43 1976-1980
Tanker with Saviem grille. No other data.
  1. Red body.

525 DAF FIRE TANK TRUCK ? mm 1/43 1976-1981
Same truck as #524 but with DAF grille.
  1. Red body.

526 VOLVO FIRE TANK TRUCK ? mm 1/43 1976-1981
Same truck as #524 but with Volvo grille.
  1. Red body.

527 SAVIEM CATTLE TRUCK 132 mm 1/43 1976-1981
Truck with cast cab, plastic rear body, white inner body, clear windows, black chassis, grille, bumper, cab interior, and tires, silver gray drive train, gray hubs.
  1. Blue cab and rear body.

528 DAF CATTLE TRUCK 132 mm 1/43 1976-1981
Same truck as #527 but with DAF grille.
  1. Red cab and rear body.

529 VOLVO CATTLE TRUCK 132 mm 1/43 1976-1981
Same truck as #527 but with Volvo grille.
  1. Orange cab and rear body.

530 SAVIEM TOWER TRUCK 150 mm 1/43 1976-1981
Truck with cast cab, plastic rear body, white arms and bucket, black chassis, grille, bumper, jacks, and tires, gray hubs, stripe labels.
1. Blue cab and rear body.

531 DAF TOWER TRUCK 150 mm 1/43 1976-1981
Same truck as #530 but with DAF grille.
1. Red cab and rear body.

532 VOLVO TOWER TRUCK 150 mm 1/43 1976-1981
Same truck as #530 but with Volvo grille.
1. Orange cab and rear body.

533 CAR & CARAVAN TRAILER 234 mm 1/43 1977-1988
#857 Peugeot 604, caravan with white cast lower body, orange-brown upper body and hitch, tinted windows, fast wheels. Later #1533.
1. Standard car colors.

534 SAVIEM CIRCUS TRUCK ? mm 1/43 1978-1981
No data.

535 DAF CIRCUS TRUCK ? mm 1/43 1977-1981
Same truck as #534 but with DAF grille.
1. Colors?

536 VOLVO CIRCUS TRUCK ? mm 1/43 1977-1981
Same truck as #534 but with Volvo grille.
1. Colors?

537 SAVIEM BOX VAN ? mm 1/43 1978-1981
Box truck with "Norev International" logo. No other data.
1. Colors?

538 DAF BOX VAN ? mm 1/43 1978-1981
Same truck as #537 but with DAF grille.
1. Colors?

539 VOLVO BOX VAN ? mm 1/43 1978-1981
Same truck as #537 but with Volvo grille.
1. Colors?

540 SIMCA 1308 WITH CANOES ? mm 1/43 1978-
#860 Simca 1308 pulling boat trailer of #235.
1. Standard colors.

541 MERCEDES AMBULANCE & MOTORCYCLES 1/43 1978-1986>#1506
#874 Mercedes-Benz Ambulance and two #230 police motorcycles. #1541.
1. Standard colors.

542 CAR AND SAILBOAT ? mm 1/43 year?
#1542. No other data.

543 CAR & RALLY CAR ON TRAILER ? mm 1/43 year?
#1543. No other data.

1000 MERCEDES-BENZ AMBULANCE 124 mm 1/43 1988
Netherlands version of #874 ambulance. No other data.

1001 MERCEDES-BENZ AMBULANCE 124 mm 1/43 1988
ANWB version of #874 ambulance. No other data.

1509 CITROEN PRÉSIDENTIELLE & ESCORT 1/43 #838>1987-1988
Renumbered #838 with driver, two #230 police motorcycles.

1601 SAVIEM 044 BUS 254 mm 1/43 #98>1987-
Renumbered #98 bus. See #98 for details.
  1. Green lower, white upper body.

1602 SAVIEM 044 BUS 254 mm 1/43 #98>1987-
Same model as #1601 with different lower body color.
  1. Yellow lower, white upper body.

1604 SAVIEM 044 BUS 254 mm 1/43 #98>1987-
Same model as #1601 with different lower body color.
  1. Red lower, white upper body.

1606 SAVIEM 044 BUS 254 mm 1/43 #98>1987-
Same model as #1601 with different lower body color.
  1. Blue lower, white upper body.

2001 CITROEN CX & BOAT TRAILER ? mm 1/43 ca. 1977-1982
No data.

2002 PORSCHE RACING SET ? mm 1/43 ca. 1977
No data.

Diecast 1/43 Scale 600 Series: First Series

601 MATRA FORMULA III 93 mm 1/43 1971-
Racer with cast body and chassis, white plastic driver, clear windshield, silver suspension, gearbox, exhausts, and hubs, black tires. Value $15-20.
  1. Green body and chassis.
  2. Blue body and chassis.
  3. Metallic blue body and chassis.

602 FIAT 1100-D ? mm 1/43 (1971)
Not issued.

603 DKW JUNIOR 91 mm 1/43 1971-
Sedan with cast body, black plastic 3+ chassis, clear windows and headlights, red taillights, silver grille, bumpers, and hubs, black tires. Value $20-25.
  1. Ivory body.

604 VOLKSWAGEN 1500 98 mm 1/43 1971-
2-door sedan with cast body, black plastic chassis and interior, clear windows, silver headlights, bumpers, and hubs, black tires.
  1. Metallic maroon body. Value $20-25.

605 FORD ANGLIA ? mm 1/43 (1971)
Not issued.

606 SIMCA 1500 97 mm 1/43 1971-
4-door sedan with cast body, black plastic chassis and interior, clear windows, silver headlights, bumper, and hubs, black tires. Value $20-25.
  1. Gold body.
  2. Metallic rose body.

607 FIAT 1500 90 mm 1/43 1971-
4-door sedan with cast body, black plastic chassis, brown interior, clear windows, red taillights, silver grille, bumpers, and hubs, black tires. Value $15-20.
  1. Gold body.
  2. Red body.

609 CITROEN 2CV VAN ? mm 1/43 1972-
Van with plastic body, cast base, "Canard Duchene" logo. Value $15-20.
  1. Maroon body.
  2. Yellow body.

610 RENAULT 4L ? mm 1/43 1972-
Sedan with plastic body, cast chassis. Value $15-20.
    1. Colors?

611 CITROEN AMI 6 ? mm 1/43 (1972)
Not issued.

612 CITROEN 2CV AZ-LUXE ? mm 1/43 1972-
Sedan with plastic body, cast chassis. Value $15-20.
    1. Red body.
    2. Blue body.

613 VOLKSWAGEN 1300 93 mm 1/43 1972-
2-door sedan with cast chassis, plastic body, tan interior, clear windows and headlights, red taillights, silver hubs, black tires. Value $15-20.
    1. Pale yellow body.
    2. Green body.

614 PEUGEOT 404 ? mm 1/43 (1972)
Not issued.

615 PEUGEOT 404 BREAK ? mm 1/43 (1972)
Not issued.

616 CITROEN AMI 6 BREAK ? mm 1/43 (1972)
Not issued.

Second 600 Series: 1/66 scale Mini-Jet models.
Value $3-6 each.

601 CAR & CABIN CRUISER TRAILER ? mm 1/66 1984-
#438 Ford Escort pulling silver gray trailer with boat.
1. Metallic blue and white boat.

    2. Purple and orange boat.

602 CAR & SAILBOAT TRAILER ? mm 1/66 1984-
#438 Ford Escort pulling black trailer with boat.
    1. Green and white boat.

603 CAR & OPEN BOAT TRAILER ? mm 1/66 1984-
#437 Renault Fuego pulling orange trailer with boat.
    1. Red and white boat.

604 CAR & SPORTS CAR TRAILER ? mm 1/66 1984-
#438 Ford Escort pulling silver gray trailer with #412 Bertone Trapeze.
    1. Standard colors.

605 CAR & MOTORCYCLE TRAILER ? mm 1/66 1984-
#437 Renault Fuego pulling silver gray trailer with motorcycle.
    1. Green motorcycle.
    2. Blue motorcycle.

606 CAR & CARAVAN TRAILER ? mm 1/66 1984-
#438 Ford Escort pulling generic caravan.
1. White caravan.

607 CAR & HORSE TRAILER ? mm 1/66 1984-
#451 Citroen BX pulling horse trailer.
    1. Red trailer, green top.
    2. Tan trailer, green top.

608 COVERED TRUCK & TRAILER ? mm 1/66 1984-
#436 Volvo pulling covered trailer.
    1. Yellow truck and trailer, blue tops.

609   QUARRY DUMP TRUCK & TRAILER   ? mm   1/66 1984-
#448 Renault truck pulling trailer
    1. Yellow truck cab and trailer.

610   FIRE TRUCK & TRAILER   ? mm   1/66   1984-
#434 Volvo truck pulling trailer.
    1. Red truck and trailer.

611   DUMP TRUCK & TANK TRAILER   ? mm   1/66   1984-
#448 Renault truck pulling trailer.
    1. Orange and yellow-orange trailer.

612   CAMPER & CABIN CRUISER TRAILER   ? mm   1/66 1984-
#463 Chevrolet camper pulling trailer of #601.
    1. Colors?

613   CAMPER & SAILBOAT TRAILER   ? mm   1/66   1984-
#460 camper pulling trailer of #602.
    1. Colors?

614   CAMPER & OPEN BOAT TRAILER   ? mm   1/66   1984-
#460 camper pulling trailer of #603.
    1. Colors?

615   FOREST FIRE TRUCK & TRAILER   ? mm   1/66   1984-
#461 Chevrolet pulling trailer.
    1. Red truck and trailer.

616   CAMPER & CARAVAN TRAILER   ? mm   1/66   1984-
#463 camper with surfboard, pulling caravan.
    1. White caravan.

617   WRECKER & CAR ON TRAILER   ? mm   1/66   1984-
#464 wrecker pulling trailer of #604 with #412 Bertone Trapeze.
    1. Standard colors.

618   PICKUP & MOTORCYCLE TRAILER   ? mm   1/66 1984-
#468 pickup pulling trailer of #605.
    1. Standard colors.

619   FARM PICKUP & HORSE TRAILER   ? mm   1/66   1984-
#467 pickup pulling trailer of #607.
    1. Standard colors.

620   COVERED PICKUP & TRAILER   ? mm   1/66   1984-
#462 pickup pulling first aid trailer? (as #611?)
    1. Orange and yellow-orange trailer.

621   AIRPORT TRUCK & TRAILER   ? mm   1/66   1984-
#466 truck pulling trailer, "Air France" logo.
    1. White truck and trailer.

Diecast 1/43 Scale 700 Series

700   RENAULT 4 COCA-COLA VAN   86 mm   1/43   198_-
Light van with cast body, opening rear door, black plastic chassis and interior, clear windows, fast wheels, "Coca-Cola" labels. May also have another number. Value $10-15.
    1. Red body.

701   PEUGEOT 404 COUPE   104 mm   1/43   1971-1973
Coupe with cast body, opening doors, black plastic chassis, gray interior, clear windows, tinted headlights, red taillights, silver grille, bumpers and hubs, black tires. Value $25-30.
    1. Metallic maroon body.

2. Metallic light blue body.

702 FIAT 2300 COUPE 106 mm 1/43 1971-1973
Coupe with cast body, opening doors, black plastic chassis, gray interior, clear windows, tinted headlights, red taillights, silver grille, bumpers and hubs, black tires. Value $15-20.
1. Dark blue body.

702 PORSCHE 917 ? mm 1/43 1985?
Long-tailed version. No other data.

703 SIMCA 1100 COUPE 91 mm 1/43 1971-1973
Coupe with cast body, opening doors, black plastic chassis, gray interior, clear windows, tinted headlights, red taillights, silver grille, bumpers, and hubs, black tires. Value $15-20.
1. Metallic copper body.
2. Metallic blue body.

704 FORD TAUNUS 12M 98 mm 1/43 1971-1973
2-door sedan with cast body, opening doors, black plastic chassis, gray interior, clear windows, tinted headlights, silver grille, bumpers, and hubs, black tires. Value $15-20.
1. Metallic dark red body.

705 FORD CORTINA 99 mm 1/43 1971-1973
2-door sedan with cast body, opening doors, black plastic chassis, gray interior, clear windows, tinted headlights, red taillights, silver grille, bumpers, and hubs, black tires. Value $15-20.
1. Metallic blue body.

706 FIAT 124 89 mm 1/43 1971-1972
4-door sedan with cast body, opening trunk, black plastic chassis, gray interior, clear windows, red taillights, silver grille, headlights, bumpers, and hubs, black tires. Value $15-20.
1. Gold body.

707 SIMCA 1100S 90 mm 1/43 1971-1980
4-door sedan with cast body, opening hood and hatch, black plastic chassis, gray interior, clear windows, red taillights, silver grille, headlights, bumpers, and hubs, black tires or fast wheels. Revised as Talbot 1100S in 1977. Value $15-20.
1. Dark blue body.
2. Silver gray body.

708 VOLKSWAGEN 1600TL 95 mm 1/43 1971-1972
2-door fastback with cast body, opening doors, black plastic chassis, gray interior, clear windows, tinted headlights, red taillights, silver grille, bumpers, and hubs, black tires. Value $15-20.
1. Metallic green body.

708 RENAULT 5TL 79 mm 1/43 1983-1988
Same model as #808; regular version as #808, plus promotionals. Value $10-15.
1. White body, "Cidunati" logo.
2. White body, "Tollen" body.
3. White body, black roof panel, "Yoplait" logo.

709 MERCEDES-BENZ C-111 102 mm 1/43 1972-1980
Sports coupe with cast body, opening hoods, black plastic chassis and interior, red taillights, silver motor, grilles, and spoked hubs, black tires or fast wheels. Value $10-15.
1. Red body.
2. Metallic green body.

710 LIGIER JS3 81 mm 1/43 1972-1980
Sports-racing car with cast body and chassis, black plastic interior,

clear windows, silver motor, gearbox, roll bar, and spoked hubs, black tires, racing number decals. Value $5-10.

1. Yellow body, orange chassis.

711 RENAULT 5TL 79 mm 1/43 1972-1980

2-door hatchback with cast body, opening doors, silver gray plastic chassis, black roof. interior, and grille, clear windows, red taillights, silver hubs, black tires or fast wheels.. Value $10-15.

1. Light green body.

711 RENAULT R4 VAN 86 mm 1/43 1984-

Same model as #700, in numerous promotional versions. Value $5-20.

1. Lime green body, no logo.
2. See Argus for promotionals.

712 PORSCHE 917 107 mm 1/43 1972-1980

Sports-racing coupe with cast body, opening rear hood, silver gray plastic chassis and interior, clear windows and headlights, silver motor and spoked hubs, black tires or fast wheels, decals. Value $8-12.

1. Red body.

712 ALPINE A310 95 mm 1/43 1984-

Fastback coupe with cast body, red plastic chassis and interior, clear windows, fast wheels. Value $5-10.

1. White body.
2. Dark blue body.

713 LANCIA STRATOS RALLY 83 mm 1/43 1972-1980

Sports-racing coupe with cast body, opening doors, black plastic chassis and interior, clear windows, red taillights, silver spoked hubs, black tires or fast wheels, "Marlboro" decals. Value $5-10.

1. Red body, white trim.

2. White body.

714 CITROEN BERTONE CAMARGUE 93 mm 1/43 1972-1980, 1984-

Sports coupe with cast body, opening doors, black plastic chassis and interior, clear windows and headlights, red taillights, silver hubs, black tires or fast wheels. Value $5-10.

1. Metallic orange body.

718 LIGIER JS3 LE MANS 97 mm 1/43 1972-

Sports coupe with cast body, opening doors, black plastic chassis and interior, clear windows and headlights, fast wheels. Value $5-10.

1. Orange body.

718 LIGIER JS2 ? mm 1/43 1983-1988

Same model as #818; regular version as #818 plus promotional. Value $5-10.

1. Light orange body, "Kodak" logo.

722 CITROEN 2CV6 89 mm 1/43 1987-

4-door sedan with cast body, opening hood, blue plastic chassis, interior, motor, headlights and half-open roof, fast wheels, "chamallows" labels. Value $5-10.

1. Pink body.

726 CITROEN BX 2000 DOCTOR'S CAR ? mm 1/43 1987-1988

No data.

727 CITROEN CAMARGUE PROTOTYPE ? mm 1/43 year?

No data.

729 DE TOMASO PANTERA 96 mm 1/43 1984-
Same model as #829. No other data. Value $5-10.

730 TALBOT HORIZON ? mm 1/43 1988-
No data.

736 FIAT X1/9 89 mm 1/43 #836>1983-
Same model as #836. Regular version as #836 plus promotional. Value $5-10.
   1. Yellow and white body, "Poil de Carotte" logo.

742 PEUGEOT 504 103 mm 1/43 #842>1983-1985
Same model as #842. No other data. Value $5-10.

743 CITROEN 2CV6 88 mm 1/43 #843>year?
Same model as #843. Promotional versions only. Value $10-15.
   1. See Argus for promotionals.

750 CITROEN MEHARI ? mm 1/43 year?
No data.

757 PEUGEOT 604 106 mm 1/43 #857>1983-1988
4-door sedan with cast body, opening doors, black plastic chassis, grille and bumpers, light orange interior, clear windows and lights, fast wheels. Value $5-10.
   1. Silver body.

760 TALBOT 1510 ? mm 1/43 #860>1983-1988
Same model as #860. No other data. Value $5-10.

761 RENAULT 14TL 92 mm 1/43 #861>1983-
4-door sedan with cast body, opening hood, silver gray plastic chassis and motor, black interior and grille, tinted windows and headlights, red taillights, fast wheels, black and white decals. Value $5-10.
   1. Metallic green body.
   2. Light blue body, "Smarties" logo.

762 RENAULT 20 104 mm 1/43 #862>1983-1988
4-door hatchback with cast body, opening doors, black plastic chassis, interior, grille, and headlights, clear windows, fast wheels. Value $5-10.
   1. Silver body.

764 PORSCHE 924 97 mm 1/43 #864>1983-
Sports coupe with cast body, black plastic chassis and interior, tinted windows and opening hatch, fast wheels. Value $5-10.
   1. Red body.
   2. White body, "Kinder" logo.

773 FORD FIESTA 81 mm 1/43 #873>1983-
2-door hatchback with cast body, opening hatch, black plastic chassis, interior, and grille, clear windows and headlights, fast wheels. Value $5-10.
   1. Yellow body.
   2. Pink body, "Cambar" logo.

774 VW GOLF 87 mm 1/43 1983-1988
May be an error. See #778 below.

778 VW GOLF 87 mm 1/43 1983-1988
Same model as #878. Regular version as #878 plus promotionals. Value $5-15.
   1. Green body, "Ordonnans" logo.
   2. Blue body, "Lustucru" logo.

779 PEUGEOT 305 98 mm 1/43 #879>1983-1988
Same model as #879. Regular version as #879 plus police and promotionals. Value $5-15.
    1. White body, "Police" logo.
    2. White body, "Cidunati" logo.
    3. Red body, "Amora" logo.

780 TALBOT HORIZON 92 mm 1/43 #880>1983-
4-door hatchback with cast body, opening doors, black plastic chassis, interior, and grille, tinted windows and headlights, fast wheels. Value $5-15.
    1. Red body.
    2. Light green body, "Tic-Tac" logo.

781 RENAULT 18TL 102 mm 1/43 #881>1983-
4-door sedan with cast body, opening doors, black plastic chassis, interior, and grille, clear windows and headlights, fast wheels. Value $8-12.
    1. Yellow body.

782 CITROEN VISA II 86 mm 1/43 #882>1983-
Same model as #882. Regular version as #882 plus police and promotionals. Value $5-15.
    1. White body, "Police" logo.
    2. See Argus for promotionals.

792 FORD ESCORT 92 mm 1/43 1986-
Promotional version of #892. Value $10-15.
    1. Yellow body, "Banania" logo.

793 TALBOT SOLARA 100 mm 1/43 #893>1983-1988
Same model as #893. No other data. Value $5-10.

794 CITROEN BX 97 mm 1/43 #895>1986-
4-door sedan with cast body, black plastic chassis and interior, clear windows and headlights, fast wheels. Value $5-20.
    1. Orange body.
    2. See Argus for promotionals.

798 RENAULT 9 93 mm 1/43 1986-
Promotional version of #898. Value $10-15.
    1. Pink body, "Malabar" logo.

Diecast 1/43 Scale 800 Series

801 PEUGEOT 204 COUPE 84 mm 1971-1972
Coupe with cast body, opening hood, doors, and hatch, black plastic chassis, gray interior, clear windows, red taillights, silver motor, grille, headlights, bumpers, and hubs, black tires.
Value $25-30.
    1. White body.
    2. Metallic dark red body.

801 CITROEN VISA TROPHÉE ? mm 1/43 1983-1988
Rally version of #882? Value $5-10.
    1. White body, #7 and rally logo.

802 FIAT 1500 CONVERTIBLE ? mm 1/43 (1971)
Not issued.

802 RENAULT 20 PARIS-DAKAR ? mm 1/43 1983-1988
Rally version of #862? Value $5-10.
    1. Yellow body, #115 and Renault-Elf-Uniroyal logo.

803 OPEL REKORD 1700 103 mm 1/43 1971-1973
Coupe with cast body, opening doors and trunk, black plastic chassis,

gray interior, clear windows, tinted headlights, red taillights, silver hubs, black tires. Value $15-20.
  1. Metallic dark gold body.

803 PEUGEOT 505 DININ ? mm 1/43 1983-1988
Promotional version of #889? Value $5-10.
  1. Yellow body, #7 and "Dinin" logo.

804 PEUGEOT 304 95 mm 1/43 1971-1974?
4-door sedan with cast body, opening hood, 4 doors, and trunk, black plastic chassis and interior, clear windows, red taillights, silver motor, grille, headlights, bumpers and hubs, black tires. Value $12-18.
  1. Yellow body.
  2. Light gray body.

804 RENAULT FUEGO REXONA ? mm 1/43 1983-1988
Promotional version of #891? Value $5-10.
  1. Black body, #44 and "Rexona" logo.

805 RENAULT 12 101 mm 1/43 1971-1983
4-door sedan with cast body, opening hood, 4 doors, and trunk, black plastic chassis, gray interior, clear windows, red taillights, silver motor, grille, headlights, bumpers, and hubs, black tires. Value $10-15.
  1. Gold body.
  2. Maroon body.
  3. Dark blue body.

805 RENAULT 18 POLICE CAR 101 mm 1/43 1983-
4-door sedan with cast body, black plastic chassis and interior, clear windows and headlights, blue-orange-clear roof bar, red taillights, fast wheels, red-white-blue "Police" and black-white "Turbo" labels. Value $5-10.
  1. White body.

806 CITROEN DS21 112 mm 1/43 1972-1978
4-door sedan with cast body, opening hood, 4 doors, and trunk, black plastic chassis and interior, clear windows, red taillights, silver motor, headlights (two types), bumpers and hubs, black tires or fast wheels. Value $10-20.
  1. Metallic orange-red body.
  2. Yellow body, 30th Anniversary logo.

806 LIGIER JS3 81 mm 1/43 1983-1985
Sports-racing car with cast body and chassis, black plastic interior, clear windows, silver motor, roll bar, and hubs, black tires, racing number and other decals. Value $5-10.
  1. Green body, yellow chassis.

807 CITROEN SM 112 mm 1/43 1971-1980
2-door hatchback with cast body, opening hood, doors, and hatch, black plastic chassis, tan interior, clear windows and headlights, silver taillights, silver motor, bumper, and spoked hubs, black tires or fast wheels. Value $10-15.
  1. Metallic maroon body.
  2. Metallic blue body.

807 TALBOT 1100S 90 mm 1/43 1981-1983
4-door hatchback with cast body, opening hood and hatch, black plastic chassis, motor, and interior, clear windows, silver grille, headlights, and bumpers, fast wheels. Value $5-10.
  1. Silver body.
  2. Red body.
  3. Brown body.

808 CHRYSLER 180 104 mm 1/43 1971-1974
4-door sedan with cast body, opening hood, 4 doors, and trunk, black

plastic chassis, tan interior, clear windows, red taillights, silver motor, grille, headlights, bumpers, and hubs, black tires or fast wheels. Value $10-15.

1. Metallic blue body.
2. Metallic brown body.

808 RENAULT 5TL 79 mm 1/43 1981-1988

2-door hatchback with cast body, opening hood, doors, and hatch, silver gray plastic chassis, tinted windows and headlights, black roof panel, interior, and grille, red taillights, fast wheels. Value $5-10.

1. Metallic blue body.

809 ALPINE A220 108 mm 1/43 1972-1980

Sports-racing coupe with cast body, opening doors, and hoods, silver gray plastic chassis and interior, clear windshield and headlights, silver motor and spoked hubs, black tires or fast wheels, racing numbers and other decals. Value $6-12.

1. Metallic maroon body.

809 MERCEDES-BENZ C-111 101 mm 1/43 1981-

Sports coupe with cast body, black plastic opening hoods, interior, and chassis, clear windows, silver grilles, fast wheels. Value $5-10.

1. Red body.
2. Orange body.
3. Blue body.

810 CITROEN GS 93 mm 1/43 1971-1985

4-door sedan with cast body, opening hood and 4 doors, black plastic chassis, gray interior, clear windows, red taillights, silver motor, grille, headlights, bumpers, and hubs, black tires or fast wheels. Value $8-15.

1. Metallic gold body.

811 OPEL GT 1900 93 mm 1/43 1971-1980

Sports coupe with cast body, opening hood and doors, black plastic chassis, gray interior, clear windows, red taillights, silver motor, headlights, bumpers, and hubs, black tires or fast wheels. Value $8-15.

1. Yellow body.
2. Metallic blue body.
3. Metallic brown body.

812 ALPINE A310 95 mm 1/43 1972-1983

Sports coupe with cast body, opening hood and doors, silver gray plastic chassis and interior, clear windows and headlights, silver spoked hubs, black tires or fast wheels. Value $5-15.

1. Red body.
2. Maroon body.
3. Metallic green body.
4. Blue body.
5. Purple body.

813 LOLA T-294 90 mm 1/43 1972-1986

Sports-racing car with cast body, opening doors, black plastic chassis and interior, silver airfoil, roll bar, gearbox, headlights, and spoked hubs, black tires or fast wheels, racing number and other decals. Value $5-10.

1. Off-white body.

814 PORSCHE 917 ? mm 1/43 (1972)

Not issued.

814 BERTONE CAMARGUE 93 mm 1/43 1981-1986

Same model as #714. No other data. Value $5-10.

815 ALFA ROMEO 33 100 mm 1/43 1972-1979
Sports-racing coupe with cast body, opening doors and hoods, silver gray plastic chassis and interior, clear windows and headlights, silver motor, gearbox, and hubs, black tires or fast wheels. Value $5-10.
1. Light red body.
2. Green body.

815 LANCIA STRATOS MARLBORO ? mm 1/43 1981-1982?
Not issued?

815 RENAULT 18TL ? mm 1/43 (1983)
Not issued.

816 ALFA ROMEO MONTREAL 96 mm 1/43 1972-1981
Sports coupe with cast body, opening doors, silver gray plastic chassis and interior, clear windows, red taillights, silver grilles, headlights, and spoked hubs, black tires or fast wheels. Value $8-12.
1. Dark red body.
2. Metallic green body.

817 PORSCHE 914 ? mm 1/43 (1972)
Not issued.

817 LIGIER JS2 97 mm 1/43 1979-1980?
Not issued?

818 LIGIER JS2 97 mm 1/43 1972-1976
Sports coupe with cast body, opening doors, black plastic chassis and interior, clear windows and headlights, fast wheels. Value $5-10.
1. Red body.
2. Metallic dark green body.
3. Metallic dark blue body.

818 LIGIER JS2 LE MANS 102 mm 1/43 1977-81, 1986-88
Same car as #818 above plus green plastic airfoil, racing number and BP decals, fast wheels. Value $4-8.
1. Yellow body.

819 FERRARI 330P4 ? mm 1/43 (1972)
Not issued.

820 MASERATI GHIBLI 105 mm 1/43 1971-1980
Sports coupe with cast body, opening hood, doors, and trunk, silver gray plastic chassis and interior, clear windows, red taillights, silver motor, grille, bumpers, and spoked hubs, black tires or fast wheels. Value $8-12.
1. Metallic green body.
2. Blue body.
3. Metallic copper body.

820 VOLVO 265 FIRE CAR 113 mm 1/43 1987-1988
Based on #896. No other data. Was it issued?

821 MERCEDES-BENZ 350SL 98 mm 1/43 1971-
Sports coupe with cast body, opening hood and doors, silver gray plastic chassis and interior, clear windows, red taillights, silver motor, grille, bumpers, and hubs, black tires or fast wheels. Value $8-12.
1. Cream body.
2. Metallic red body.

822 RENAULT 15TS 98 mm 1/43 1972-1980
Hatchback coupe with cast body, opening hood and doors, black plastic chassis, gray interior, clear windows, red taillights, silver motor, grille, headlights, bumpers, and hubs, black tires or fast wheels. Value $8-12.
1. Yellow gold body.

2. Metallic green body.
3. Purple body.

823 RENAULT 17TS 98 mm 1/43 1972-1983
Hatchback coupe with cast body, opening hood and doors, black plastic chassis, gray interior, clear windows, red taillights, silver motor, grille, bumpers, and hubs, black tires or fast wheels. Value $8-12.
1. Metallic red body.
2. Orange body.
3. Yellow body.
4. Green body.
5. Blue body.

824 FERRARI DINO 246GTS 97 mm 1/43 1973-1981
Sports coupe with cast body, opening doors, black plastic roof and chassis, gray interior, clear windows and headlights, red taillights, silver bumpers, fast wheels. Value $8-12.
1. Orange-red body.
2. Metallic blue body.

824 FORD MUSTANG POLICE CAR 105 mm 1/43 1987-1988
Based on #887. No other data. Was it issued?

825 MATRA SIMCA BAGHEERA 91 mm 1/43 1973-1983
Sports coupe with cast body, opening doors, black plastic chassis, grille, and bumpers, gray interior, clear windows and opening hatch, red and yellow lights, fast wheels. Value $8-12.
1. White body.
2. Yellow body.
3. Blue body.
4. Gray body.
5. Metallic blue body: Talbot Bagheera, 1980.

826 PEUGEOT 104 82 mm 1/43 1973-1985
4-door sedan with cast body, opening doors, black plastic chassis and grille, gray interior, clear windows, silver headlights, and bumpers, fast wheels. Value $8-12.
1. Gold body.
2. White body.
3. Red body.
4. Green body.
5. Blue body.
6. Tan body.

827 PANHARD M3 VTT ? mm 1/43 (1975)
Not issued.

828 PEDALOREV ? mm 1974-1976?
Toy car, twin-boom design, with two figures. No other data.
1. Yellow body.

829 DE TOMASO PANTERA 96 mm 1/43 1973-1983
Sports-racing coupe with cast body, black plastic chassis, opening front hood, rear hood, and interior, clear windows, red taillights, silver spoked hubs, black tires, later fast wheels, "Pantera" and racing number decals. Value $6-10.
1. Yellow body.
2. Other colors.

830 NOREVBUG ? mm 1974-1976?
Toy car with driver and dog trailer. No other data.
1. Yellow body.

831 HELICOREV ? mm 1974-1976?
Toy car, 3-wheeler with two figures and rotor. No other data.
1. Blue body.

832 MATRA-SIMCA 670B SHORT 92 mm 1/43 197301984
Sports-racing car with cast body, opening doors and rear hood, black plastic chassis, interior, and roll bar, white airfoil and cowling, silver motor and spoked hubs, black tires or fast wheels, #4 and other decals. Value $6-10.
　　1. Blue body.

833 MATRA-SIMCA 670B LONG 104 mm 1/43 1973-1985
Sports-racing car with details like #832 but longer body. Value $6-10.
　　1. Blue body.
　　2. Blue body, Gitanes logo.

833 CITROEN CX TAXI 107 mm 1/43 1988
Taxi based on #845. No other data. Value $5-8.

834 CHEVRON B23 83 mm 1/43 1973-1983
Sports-racing car with cast body, opening rear hood, black plastic chassis, interior, and roll bar, clear windshield, silver motor and spoked hubs, black tires or fast wheels, #21 and "Côtes du Rhône" decals, later #39 decals. Value $4-8.
　　1. Blue body, #21 and "Côtes du Rhône" decals.
　　2. Blue body, #39 decals (no sponsor).

835 FERRARI 312P 90 mm 1/43 1975-1985
Sports-racing car with cast body, opening doors, black plastic chassis, interior, roll bar and airfoil, clear windshield, silver gearbox, exhausts and spoked hubs, black tires, or fast wheels, #3 and other decals. Value $6-10.
　　1. Red body.

836 FIAT X1/9 89 mm 1/43 1974-1983
Sports coupe with cast body, opening doors, black plastic chassis, interior, and rear panels, red taillights, fast wheels. Value $6-8.
　　1. Yellow body.

837 BMW 630 COUPE ? mm 1/43 1990-
No data.

838 CITROEN SM PRÉSIDENTIELLE 128 mm 1/43 1976-1985
Convertible with cast body, black plastic chassis and interior, clear windows and headlights, red taillights, silver bumpers, fast wheels, with or without (1979) three figures. Value $8-15.
　　1. Metallic silver gray body, 3 figures.
　　2. Metallic silver gray body, no figures.

839 PORSCHE CARRERA RSR 93 mm 1/43 1974-
Sports-racing coupe with cast body, opening doors, black plastic chassis and interior, clear windows and headlights, spoked hubs, black tires or fast wheels, various logo types. Value $8-12.
　　1. Metallic silver body, #26 and Martini logo.
　　2. Yellow body, "Jeans New Man" logo.
　　3. Metallic silver body, "Denver No. 2" logo.
　　4. White body, "Pepsi" logo.

840 ALPINE A440 92 mm 1/43 1974-81, 1986-88
Sports-racing car with cast body, opening doors, black plastic chassis and interior, white airfoil, red taillights, spoked hubs, black tires or fast wheels, #19 and "Elf" logo. Value $6-8.
　　1. Blue body.

841 RENAULT 16TX 97 mm 1/43 1974-1982
4-door hatchback with cast body, opening hood and hatch, black plastic chassis and interior, clear windows, red taillights, silver motor, grille, and bumpers, fast wheels. Value $6-10.
　　1. Metallic green body.
　　2. Metallic blue body.

842 PEUGEOT 504 103 mm 1/43 1976-1985
4-door sedan with cast body, opening hood, black plastic chassis, gray interior, clear windows, silver motor, grille, headlights, and bumpers, fast wheels. Value $6-8.
    1. Red body.
2, Metallic green body.
    3. Metallic blue body.

842 RENAULT 18 POLICE CAR ? mm 1/43 1988-
Police version of #843. No other data. Value $6-8.

843 CITROEN 2CV6 88 mm 1/43 1976-
4-door sedan with cast body, opening hood, silver gray chassis, open roof, interior, motor, and headlights, fast wheels. Value $6-8.
    1. Red body.

843 RENAULT 18TL ? mm 1/43 1989-
No data. Value $5-8.

844 FERRARI 512 ? mm 1/43
Not issued.

845 CITROEN CX 107 mm 1/43 1974-
4-door sedan with cast body, opening doors, black plastic chassis and interior, clear windows, red taillights, silver headlights and bumpers, fast wheels. Value $6-12.
    1. Silver body.
    2. Red body.
    3. Yellow body.
    4. Yellow gold body, "Orangina" logo.
    5. Dark blue body, "Orangina" logo.
    6. White body, "Cidunati" logo.
    7. White body, "Miniatures Lyon" logo (code 2).

846 RENAULT 17 RALLY 98 mm 1/43 1975-82, 1986-88
2-door hatchback with cast body, opening hood and doors, black plastic chassis, interior and grille, silver gray motor, clear windows, red taillights, fast wheels, "Elf" decals, +/- #8. Value $5-8.
    1. Orange body.

847 FIAT X1/9 ABARTH 88 mm 1/43 1975-1988
Sports coupe (based on #836) with cast body, opening doors, black plastic chassis, interior, bumpers and opening rear hood, clear windows, red taillights, fast wheels, #4 and Abarth decals. Value $5-8.
    1. Red body, green roof panel.

848 RENAULT 5LS 1300 ? mm 1/43
Not issued.

849 PEUGEOT 504 POLICE CAR 103 mm 1/43 1976-1988
4-door sedan (based on #842) with cast body, opening hood, black plastic chassis, gray interior, clear windows, red dome light, white antenna, silver grille, headlights and bumpers, fast wheels, "Police" labels. Value $8-12.
    1. Dark blue body.

850 RENAULT 5 DRIVING SCHOOL CAR 79 mm 1/43 1975-197_
2-door sedan (based on #711) with cast body, opening doors, silver gray plastic chassis, black interior and roof, clear windows and headlights, red taillights, white and red "Auto-Ecole" sign and labels, fast wheels. Value $8-12.
    1. Metallic blue-black body.

850 MERCEDES-BENZ FIRE KOMBI ? mm 1/43 1990
Portuguese fire department version. No data.

851 CAR WITH SKI RACK 90 mm 1/43 1975-1982
Usually #825 Matra Bagheera with red plastic ski rack. Value $8-12.
   1. Yellow body.
   2. Metallic blue body, #881 Renault 18.

851 MERCEDES-BENZ POLICE KOMBI ? mm 1/43 1990
Portuguese police version. No data.

852 RENAULT 16TX TAXI 97 mm 1/43 1975-1979
#841 Renault 16TX with white and red plastic "Taxi Radio" sign and labels. Value $8-12.
   1. Yellow body.

852 CITROEN CX TAXI 107 MM 1980-
#845 Citroen CX with white and red "Taxi Radio" sign and labels. Value $8-12.
   1. Red body.

852 VOLVO 264 TAXI 113 mm 1/43 1983>#853
#886 Volvo 264 with white and red "Taxi Radio" sign, light gray antenna, yellow and black labels. Value $6-8.
   1. Metallic red-brown body.

853 RENAULT 5TL RALLY 79 mm 1/43 1975-1978
2-door hatchback (based on #711) with cast body, white plastic opening doors, black interior, roof panel, and grille, clear windows and headlights, red taillights, fast wheels, #5 and "Elf" decals. Value $5-8.
   1. Light orange body.

853 MERCEDES-BENZ 280 TAXI 115 mm 1/43 1983>#854
Based on #890. No other data. Value $6-8.

853 VOLVO 264 TAXI 113 mm 1/43 #852>1984-1988
Same model as last #852 above. Value $6-8.

1. Metallic brown body.

854 BMW TURBO 94 mm 1/43 1975-1978
Sports prototype (ex-Schuco) with cast body, opening hoods and doors, unpainted chassis, black plastic interior and motor, clear windows, fast wheels. Value $10-15. May have "Club Norev" or "Michelin" logo.
   1. Red body.
   2. Yellow body.

854 MERCEDES-BENZ 280 TAXI 115 mm 1/43 #853>1984-1988
Renumbered #853. Varying decal types. Value $6-8.
   1. Metallic light blue body.

855 ALPINE A310 RALLY 94 mm 1/43 1975-1986
Sports coupe (based on #812) with cast body, opening hoods and doors, black plastic interior and chassis, clear windows and headlights, red taillights and roof panel, #4 and "Elf" decals. Value $5-8.
   1. Metallic dark blue body.

856 RENAULT 30TS 104 mm 1/43 1975-
4-door hatchback with cast body, opening doors, black plastic chassis, interior, grille, and rear panel, clear windows, silver headlights, red taillights, fast wheels. Value $6-10.
   1. Yellow body.
   2. Golden yellow body, "Treets" logo.

857 PEUGEOT 604 108 mm 1/43 1976-
4-door sedan with cast body, opening doors, black plastic chassis, interior, grille, and bumpers, clear windows, tinted headlights, red taillights, fast wheels.
   1. Silver body.
   2. Red body.

3. Light green body.
4. Blue body.
5. Silver gray body, government car.
6. White body, "Autophilie 1983" logo (code 2).
7. Red body, "Tour de France" logo.
8. Red body, Portuguese fire department logo.
9. Orange body, "Pepito" logo.

858 ALPINE A442 TURBO 92 mm 1/43 1976-1985

Sports-racing car with cast body, opening doors, black plastic chassis and interior, white airfoil, fast wheels, "Elf" and other decals. Value $5-8.
1. Orange body.
2. Blue body.

859 PEUGEOT 504 SAFARI 103 mm 1/43 1976-1988

4-door sedan (based on #842) with cast body, opening hood, black plastic chassis and roof equipment, clear windows, silver motor, grille, headlights, and bumper, fast wheels, #21 and other decals and labels. Value $6-8.
1. White body.

860 SIMCA 1308GT 97 mm 1/43 1976-1980

4-door hatchback with cast body, opening doors, silver gray plastic chassis and interior, clear windows, tinted headlights, red taillights, black grille, fast wheels. Value $8-10.
1. Metallic salmon body.
2. Metallic green body.

860 TALBOT 1510 ? mm 1/43 1981-1988

Fast wheels. No other data. Value $6-8.
1. Metallic yellow-green.

861 RENAULT 14TL 92 mm 1/43 1978-1983

4-door hatchback with cast body, opening hood, silver gray plastic chassis and interior, silver motor, black grille, clear windows, tinted headlights, fast wheels. Value $6-12.
1. Red body.
2. Metallic silver green body: 1980 updated type.
3. White body, "Ola" logo.
4. Red body, "Pompiers de Strasbourg" logo (code 2).

862 RENAULT 20TL 104 mm 1/43 1977-1988

4-door hatchback with cast body, opening doors, black chassis, interior, grille, and rear panel, silver bumpers and headlights, red taillights, fast wheels. Value $6-10.
1. Light green body.
2. Blue body.
3. White body, "VSD" logo.
4. Yellow body, "McDonald's" logo.

863 LANCIA STRATOS ALITALIA 83 mm 1/43 1977-1988

Sports coupe with cast body, opening doors, black chassis, interior and parts, clear windows and headlights, red taillights, fast wheels, #5 and "Alitalia" logo. Value $5-8.
1. Light gray body.

864 PORSCHE 924 97 mm 1/43 1978-1983

Sports coupe with cast body, black plastic chassis and interior, tinted windows and opening hatch, silver headlights, red taillights, fast wheels. Value $6-10.
1. Metallic gold body.
2. Red body.
3. White body, "Motor Expo Lisboa 88" logo.
4. Silver body, "Portugal 88 Salao Internacional" logo.

865 RENAULT R4 FIRE VAN 90 mm 1/43 1978-1988
Light van with cast body, opening rear door, silver gray plastic chassis and interior, tinted windows and dome light, black grille, light gray antenna, fast wheels, "Sapeurs Pompiers" labels. Value $8-12.
  1. Dark red body.

866 RENAULT R4 POLICE VAN 90 mm 1/43 1978-1988
Light van with details as #865 except red taillights, "Gendarmerie" labels. Value $8-12.
  1. Dark blue body.

867 RENAULT R4 MAIL VAN 90 mm 1/43 1978-1988
Light van with details as #865 except red taillights, "PTT" labels. Value $10-15.
  1. Dark yellow body.
  2. Red body, "PTT Post" logo: Netherlands issue.

868 BMW 633CF COUPE 108 mm 1/43 1978-1988
Coupe with cast body, opening doors, black plastic chassis, grille, and interior, tinted windows, red taillights, fast wheels. Value $6-8.
  1. Silver body.
  2. White body.
  3. Orange body.

869 BMW 633 PROTOTYPE 108 mm 1/43 1978-1988
Coupe with details as #868 plus white front and rear spoilers, #12, "Esso-Castrol" and red-white-blue stripe decals. Value $5-8.
  1. White body.
  2. White body, #14, "Motul" logo.
  3. Silver gray body.
  4. Blue body, "Norev" logo.

870 DE TOMASO PANTERA PROTOTYPE 110 mm 1/43 1977-1985
Sports coupe with cast body (as #829), black plastic hoods, spoilers, chassis, and interior, clear windows, fast wheels. Value $5-8.
  1. Dark red body.

871 ALPINE A310 POLICE CAR 94 mm 1/43 1977-1985
Sports coupe (as #855) with cast body, opening hood and doors, black plastic chassis and interior, clear windows and headlights, red dome and taillights, light gray antenna, fast wheels, "Gendarmerie" labels. Value $6-8.
  1. Blue body.

872 PORSCHE 917 ? mm 1/43 (1981)
Not issued.

872 RENAULT 18TL POLICE CAR 89 mm 1/43 1983-
4-door wagon with cast body, opening doors, black plastic chassis, grille, and interior, clear windows, red-blue-clear roof bar, red taillights, fast wheels, "Police" labels. Value $8-10.
  1. White body.

873 FORD FIESTA ? mm 1/43 1978-1983
Value $6-8. No data except:
  1. Red body.

874 MERCEDES-BENZ 250 AMBULANCE 124 mm 1/43 1978-1982
Ambulance with cast body, black plastic chassis and interior, clear windows, white opening rear door and stretcher, light gray antenna, blue dome lights, silver grille and headlights, fast wheels. Value $10-20.

1. White body, "SAMU" logo.
2. White body, "Ambulance" logo.
3. Red and white body, "Ambulance" logo.
4. White body, "BV Penacovia Ambulancia" logo.
5. White and red body, "Broeder de Vries" logo (code 2).
6. White and blue body, "Het Witte Kruis den Haag" logo.
7. White and blue body, "ANWB Alarm Centrale" logo.
8. Red body, "BV Porto Ambulancia" logo.
9. Blue and white body, "Policia Emergencia 115 Ambulancia" logo.

875 RENAULT 5 DOCTOR'S CAR 79 mm 1/43 1977-1988

2-door sedan (as #711) with cast body, opening doors, silver gray plastic chassis, black interior, grille, and roof panel, blue dome light, clear windows and headlights, red taillights, light gray antenna, fast wheels, "SOS Medecin" labels. Value $8-10.
1. White body.

876 SIMCA 1308 "EUROPE 1" 97 mm 1/43 1978-1982

4-door hatchback with cast body, opening doors, silver gray plastic chassis, black interior and grille, clear windows, tinted headlights, red taillights, light gray antenna, fast wheels, black and orange "Europe 1" logo. Value $10-15.
1. Orange body.
2. Talbot 1510, otherwise as type 1: 1982.

876 FERRARI 204/246GTS 97 mm 1/43 1983-1989

Same basic model as #824. Value $8-10. No other data except:
1. Unchanged from #824.
2. Black and white body, "Apple" logo.

877 LIGIER JS2 LE MANS 102 mm 1/43 1978-1984

Sports coupe (as #818) with cast body, opening doors, black plastic chassis and interior, green airfoil, tinted windows, clear headlights, red taillights, fast wheels, #115, "BP" and other decals. Value $5-8.
1. Orange body.

878 VOLKSWAGEN GOLF 87 mm 1/43 1978-

2-door hatchback with cast body, opening hatch, black plastic chassis, grille and interior, tinted windows, fast wheels. Value $5-8.
1. Gold body.
2. Red body.
3. White body, red and green trim, "TAP AIR PORTUGAL" logo.

879 PEUGEOT 305SR 98 mm 1/43 1978-

4-door sedan with cast body, opening doors, black plastic chassis, grille, and interior, tinted windows and headlights, red taillights, fast wheels. Value $5-8.
1. White body.
2. Red body.
3. Metallic copper red body.
4. Metallic green body.

880 SIMCA HORIZON GLS 92 mm 1/43 1977-1984

4-door hatchback with cast body, opening doors, black plastic chassis, grille, and interior, tinted windows and headlights, red taillights, fast wheels. Value $8-10.
1. Gold body.
2. Red body.
3. Metallic maroon body.
4. Yellow body, Talbot Horizon: 1982.
5. Red body, "Ponpiers de Strasbourg" logo (code 2): 1984.

881 RENAULT 18TL 102 mm 1/43 1980-1983
4-door sedan with cast body, opening doors, black plastic chassis, grille, and interior, tinted windows and headlights, red taillights, fast wheels. Value $6-10.
1. Silver body.
2. Metallic copper body.
3. Light orange body.
4. Metallic light blue body.
5. White body, "Police" logo.
6. White body, "Tollen" logo (code 2).
7. Orange body, "Paris Match" logo.
8. Light green body, "Pierrot Gourmand" logo.
9. Blue and white body, Portuguese "Policia" logo.

882 CITROEN VISA 86 mm 1/43 1980-1983
4-door hatchback with cast body, opening doors, silver gray plastic chassis, grille, and interior, tinted windows and headlights, red taillights, fast wheels. Value $6-10.
1. Silver body.
2. Metallic green body.

883 VW GOLF POLICE CAR 87 mm 1/43 1980-1988
2-door hatchback (as #878) with cast body, opening hatch, black plastic chassis, grille, and interior, tinted windows and dome light, light gray antenna, red taillights, fast wheels. Value $8-10.
1. Cream body "Polizei" labels.
2. White and red body, "Rijkspolitie" labels.

884 VW GOLF AUTO CLUB CAR 87 mm 1/43 1980-1983
Same model as #883 but with black "ADAC" labels. Value $8-10.
1. Light orange body.

885 PORSCHE 924 POLICE CAR 97 mm 1/43 1980-1988
Sports coupe (as #864) with cast body, black plastic chassis and inte-rior, tinted windows, dome light and opening hatch, light gray antenna, red taillights, fast wheels. Value $8-12.
1. White body, green panels with white "Polizei" lettering.
2. White body, red "Rijkspolitie" logo.

886 VOLVO 264 112 mm 1/43 1981-1989
4-door sedan with cast body, opening doors, black plastic chassis and interior, tinted windows, silver grille and headlights, red taillights, fast wheels. Value $8-12.
1. White body.
2. Metallic copper red body.
3. Metallic silver blue body.
4. Blue body.
5. White body, "R.M.C." logo.
6. White body, "Politi PO3" logo.
7. White body, Belgian "SOS 901" logo.
8. White body, red stripe, "SOS 901" logo.
9. Red body, Marlboro Briquets" logo.

886 CITROEN CX 2400 RALLY ? mm 1/43 (1980)
Not issued.

887 FORD MUSTANG 105 mm 1/43 1981-
Sports coupe with cast body, opening doors, black plastic chassis, grille, and interior, tinted windows and headlights, red taillights, fast wheels. Value $6-10.
1. Metallic green body.
2. Metallic blue body.
3. Orange body, "Benco Demarrez Plein Pot" logo.
4. Dark blue body, red-white-blue "N.A.R.T." logo.

887 CITROEN 2CV ? mm 1/43 (1980)
Not issued.

888 ALFA ROMEO 6 108 mm 1/43 1981-
4-door sedan with cast body, opening doors, black plastic chassis, grille, and interior, tinted windows, red taillights, fast wheels. Value $6-10.
1. Red body.
2. Orange body.
3. Metallic green body.
4. Metallic blue body.
5. Pink body, "Les Chnapis Pata Poum" logo.

889 PEUGEOT 505STI 105 mm 1/43 1981-
4-door sedan with cast body, opening doors, black plastic chassis, grille, and interior, tinted windows and headlights, red taillights, fast wheels. Value $6-10.
1. Maroon body.
2. Metallic blue body.
3. Yellow body, New York "Taxi" sign and labels (code 2).
4. Green and black body, "Taxi Lisboa" logo.
5. Green and black body, "Taxi Porto" logo.

890 MERCEDES-BENZ 280SE 115 mm 1/43 1981-
4-door sedan with cast body, opening doors, silver gray plastic chassis and interior, clear windows, silver grille and headlights, red taillights, fast wheels. Value $6-10.
1. White body.
2. Metallic maroon body.
3. Yellow body
4. Red body, "Chips Vico" logo.
5. Yellow body, "Jeans New Man" logo.

891 RENAULT FUEGO 100 mm 1/43 1982-
2-door hatchback with cast body, opening doors, silver gray plastic chassis, grille, and interior, clear windows and headlights, red tail-lights, fast wheels. Value $6-10.
1. Silver body.
2. Yellow body.
3. Orange body, "Oasis" logo.

892 FORD ESCORT 92 mm 1/43 1982-
2-door hatchback with cast body, black plastic chassis, grille, spoiler, and interior, clear windows and headlights, red taillights, fast wheels. Value $6-10.
1. Yellow body.
2. Metallic silver blue body.
3. Silver body, black trim with "XR 3" lettering: 1984.
4. Orange body, "XR 3" lettering as above.
5. Metallic copper body, "XR 3" lettering as above.
6. Metallic lilac body, "XR 3" lettering as above.
7. White body, "GNR Brigada de Transito" logo.
8. White and red body, #8, "Briquets Marlboro" logo.
9. Red body, #8 and "Marlboro Briquets" logo.

893 TALBOT SOLARA 100 mm 1/43 1982-1983
4-door sedan with cast body, opening doors, silver gray plastic chassis, grille, and interior, tinted windows and headlights, red taillights, fast wheels. Value $8-10.
1. Metallic light blue body.
2. Yellow body, "La pie qui chante" logo.

894 RENAULT 18 WITH SURFBOARD 102 mm 1/43 (1983)
Not issued.

895 CITROEN BX 97 mm 1/43 1983-
4-door hatchback with cast body, black plastic chassis and interior, clear windows and headlights, fast wheels. Value $8-15.
1. White body.

2. Metallic green body.
3. Metallic light blue body.
4. White body, red, blue and black stripes: rally version.
5. Orange body, "Service" logo.
6. Metallic green body, "Autobedrijfeyzinga 65 Jaar" logo.

896 VOLVO 264 WAGON 113 mm 1/43 1982-
4-door wagon with cast body, opening doors, black plastic chassis and interior, clear windows, silver grille and headlights, red taillights, fast wheels. Value $6-12.
1. Red body.
2. Metallic green body.
3. Metallic blue body.
4. Silver body.
5. White body, "Volvo" lettering.
6. White body, "Volvo Auto-Sueco LDA" logo.
7. White body, "Auto Show 89" logo.
8. White body, "Radiotelevisao Portugesa" logo.
9. Tan body, logo as type 8.
10. Red body, "Pin Pon" logo.
11. Green body, "Garde Forestier" logo.

897 RENAULT 18TL BREAK 102 mm 1/43 1982-
4-door wagon with cast body, opening doors, black plastic chassis, grille, and interior, clear windows and headlights, red taillights, fast wheels. Value $6-12.
1. Yellow body.

2. Green body.
3. Metallic light blue body.
4. Blue body.
5. White body, "2e Expo Mini Rochetailee" logo.
6. White body, "Mamie Nova" logo.
7. White body, "Proto" logo (code 2).
8. White body, "Tollen" logo (code 2).
9. Cream body, "Paul Bocuse" logo.
10. Red body, "Correios" logo.
11. Red body, "Sapeurs Pompiers Strasbourg" logo (code 2).
12. Red body, "Pompiers de Strasbourg" logo (code 2).

898 RENAULT 9 93 mm 1/43 1983-
4-door sedan with cast body, opening doors, black plastic chassis, grille, and interior, clear windows and headlights, red taillights, fast wheels. Value $6-10.
1. White body.
2. Orange body.

899 VW GOLF RALLY 87 mm 1/43 1984-1988
2-door hatchback (as #878) with cast body, opening hatch, black plastic chassis, grille, and interior, clear windows, red taillights, fast wheels. Value $6-8.
1. White body, #5, blue and yellow trim and other labels.
2. Red body, labels as type 1.
3. Blue body, "Norev No. 9" labels.

QUIRALU

The firm of Quiralu was founded in Luxeuil in 1933 by a man named Quirin, and those two names, plus "aluminum," give us a good idea of how it got its name. The firm produced a variety of merchandise over the years, including at least an occasional toy, as I have a fascinating hand-drawn fire hose reel and three figures in what seem to be Napoleonic-era uniforms. Everything is held on a sheet of cardboard by metal clips, and the general atmosphere is quaint, to say the least. The firm is known to have made aluminum soldier figures, and I suspect the "firemen" were fugitives from their ranks. Other than that, Quiralu seems to have been best known for its cooking pots. But in 1955 the firm began to make 1/43 scale diecast models, some of which are quite interesting and all of which are rather rare today. They generally feature black sheet-metal bases, turned metal hubs, white or black rubber tires and sometimes clear plastic windows. The last new models appeared in 1959, and production must have ended within a few years of that date. I am not absolutely sure whether the numbers by which the models are listed here are Quiralu's own or were added by an early chronicler, but I believe they are authentic.

As for values, I think it is safe to say that any Quiralu model in mint condition is worth at least $75, and some of them should be worth $100 or more–much more in a few cases–whether boxed or not. Many thanks to Mike Sarvas for the information he kindly contributed on colors and values.

1 SIMCA TRIANON 107 mm 1955
Four-door sedan with cast body, sheet metal base, turned hubs, white tires, silver bumpers, grille, and headlights, red taillights, single body color. Value $75-85.
    1. Cream body.
    2. Green body.
    3. Blue body.
    4. Gray body.

2 SIMCA VERSAILLES 107 mm 1955
Same casting and parts as #1, with roof painted a second color. Value $75-85.

1. Cream body, green roof.
2. Dark green body, cream roof.
3. Blue body, cream roof.
4. Gray body, green roof.

3 SIMCA RÉGENCE   107 mm   1955

Same casting and parts as #1, with body sides and rear painted a second color. Value $75-85.
1. Cream and green body.
2. Gray and green body.
3. Gray and blue body.
4. Gray and black body.

4 PEUGEOT 403   102 mm   1956

Four-door sedan with cast body, sheet metal base, turned hubs, white tires, silver bumpers, grille, and headlights, red taillights, single body color. Value $75-85.
1. Blue body.
2. Black body.
3. Other body colors not known.

5 PEUGEOT 403   102 mm   1956

Same casting and parts as #4, with roof painted a second color. Value $85-95.
1. Blue body, light blue roof.
2. Other body and roof colors not known.

6 PEUGEOT 403   102 mm   1956

Same casting and parts as #4 plus clear plastic windows, single body color. Value $85-95.
1. Probably exists in black.
2. Other body colors not known.

7 PEUGEOT 403   102 mm   1956

Same casting and parts as #4 plus clear plastic windows, roof painted a second color. Value $85-95.
1. Black body, white roof.
2. Black body, cream roof.
3. Other body and roof colors not known.

8 MERCEDES-BENZ 300SL   106 mm   1956

Sports coupe with cast body, sheet metal base, turned hubs, white tires, silver emblem, bumpers, grille, and headlights, single body color. Too wide to be an accurate model of the 300SL. Value $100-125.
1. Red body.
2. Blue body.
3. Gray body.

9 MERCEDES-BENZ 300SL   106 mm   1956

Same casting and parts as #8, with roof in second color. Value $100-125.
1. Red body, cream roof.
2. Red body, gray roof.
3. Blue body, cream roof.
4. Gray body, green roof.

10 SIMCA MARLY BREAK   106 mm   1957

Station wagon with cast body, sheet metal base, turned hubs, black, or white tires, silver bumpers, grille, and headlights, red taillights, front roof panel in second color. Value $75-85.
1. Red body, yellow roof panel.
2. Yellow body, red roof panel.
3. Blue body, light blue roof panel.
4. Blue body, gray roof panel.
5. Gray body, light blue roof panel.

11 SIMCA MARLY BREAK 106 mm 1957
Same casting and parts as #10 plus clear plastic windows, front roof panel in second color. Value $75-85.
1. White body, blue roof panel.
2. Yellow body, black roof panel.
3. Blue body, gray roof panel.
4. Gray body, green roof panel.

12 SIMCA MARLY AMBULANCE 106 mm 1957
Same casting and parts as #10 plus clear plastic windows, blue cross on roof. Value $100-120.
1. White body.

13 PORSCHE CARRERA 91 mm 1957
Sports coupe with cast body, sheet metal base, turned hubs, white tires, silver bumpers and headlights, single body color. Value $300-350.
1. Red body.
2. Yellow body.
3. Blue body.

14 PORSCHE CARRERA 91 mm 1957
Same casting and parts as #13, roof in second color. Value $300-350.
1. Red body, cream roof.
2. Red body, black roof.
3. Yellow body, black roof.
4. Cream body, green roof.
5. Blue body, cream roof.
6. Blue body, light blue roof.

15 JAGUAR XK 140 104 mm 1957
Sports roadster with cast body, sheet metal base, turned hubs, black or white tires, silver bumpers, grille, and headlights, cream folded top, red or blue interior, single body color. Value $100-120.

1. White body, no other data.
2. Red body, blue interior.
3. Blue body, red interior.
4. Black body, red interior.

16 MESSERSCHMITT 81 mm 1958
Bubblecar with cast body, sheet metal base, three turned hubs, white tires, plastic driver and clear canopy, silver bumper, headlight, and emblem, red taillights, fenders in second color. Value $75-85.
1. Red body, cream fenders.
2. Red body, black fenders.
3. Green body, cream fenders.
4. Light green body, dark green fenders.
5. Light blue body, dark blue fenders.
6. Blue body, light blue fenders.
7. Gray body, red fenders.
8. Gray body, blue fenders.
9. Gray body, different shade gray fenders.

17 ROLLS-ROYCE 107 mm 1958
Four-door sedan with cast body, sheet metal base, turned hubs, white tires, silver bumpers, grille, and headlights, red taillights. First color = hood, roof and rear body sides, second color = sides and trunk. The model is of a special body type by Hooper, rather jazzy for a Rolls. Value $100-120.
1. Cream and red body.
2. Cream and green body.
3. Cream and gray body.
4. Gray and red body.
5. Gray and blue body.
6. Gray and navy blue body.
7. Gray and dark gray body.

18 VESPA 400 2CV 81 mm 1958

Two-door minicar with cast body, sheet metal base, turned hubs, white tires, silver bumpers, grille, and headlights, roof panel in second color. Big model of small car. Value $75-85.

1. Cream body, gray roof.
2. Red body, cream roof.
3. Green body, cream roof.
4. Blue body, cream roof.

19 VELAM ISETTA 67 mm 1958

Bubblecar with cast body, sheet metal base, turned hubs, white tires, clear plastic windows, silver bumpers, red lights, roof in second color. Value $75-85.

1. White body, gray roof.
2. Cream body, gray roof.

20 RENAULT ÉTOILE FILANTE 107 mm 1958

Speed record car with cast body, sheet metal base, white plastic driver, clear windshield, turned hubs, white tires, silver grilles, red and white trim decals. Value $90-100.

1. Blue body.
2. Dark blue body.

21 RENAULT ÉTOILE FILANTE 107 mm 1958

Same casting and parts as #20 without decals, with trim painted on, trim lines cast into body. Value $85-95.

1. Blue body, red and white trim.

22 PEUGEOT D4A VAN 87 mm 1958

Light van with cast body, sheet metal base, turned hubs, white tires, silver bumper, grille, and headlights, cream stripe/blue "Primagaz" logo decals. Value $300-350.

1. Red body.

23 PEUGEOT D4A VAN 87 mm 1958

Same casting and parts as #22, with green-white-black "Thomson" and "Ducretet-Thomson" decals, one on each side. Value $300-350.

1. Mustard yellow body.
2. Apple green body.
3. Green body, "Thomson" decals on both sides.

24 PEUGEOT D4A ARMY AMBULANCE 87 mm 1958

Same casting and parts as #22, with red crosses in white circles.

1. Khaki brown body. Value $350-375.

25 BERLIET GBO COVERED TRUCK 225 mm 1959

Same castings and most parts as #26 below, plus cloth cover on wire hoops. No other data. Value $250-300.

1. Two-tone blue?

26 BERLIET GBO DUMP TRUCK 225 mm 1959

Dump truck with cast aluminum cab-chassis, tipper, frame, opening side panels and tailgate, and hubs, black tires, spare wheel, sheet metal front chassis, silver grille and headlights, black bumper and fuel tank, wire controls. Value $250-300.

1. Red cab, chassis and trim, tan tipper and hubs.
2. Two-tone blue?

27 GBO COVERED TRAILER 170 mm 1959

Four-wheel truck trailer based on rear body of #25, with cast aluminum body parts and hubs, black tires, cloth cover, wire hoops. Value $100-125.

1. Tan body, red trim.

R.A.M.I.

Whether you write it R.A.M.I. as in its catalogs, RAMI or Rami, the four letters stand for "les Retrospectives Automobiles Miniature," and most of the models represent actual antique cars on display at the Musée Français de l'Automobile (French Automobile Museum) in the castle of Rochetaillée, near Lyons. Other models, the catalog says, represent old-time cars found in other museums.

This series of 1/43 scale diecast miniatures began in 1958 with the production of the first five models. The series was expanded by the addition of several models every year through 1968, a single model (number 38, the highest catalog number used) in 1969, and a last lone addition (number 2, replacing the original model to bear that number) in 1971. Production seems to have wound down through the seventies, when the firm, or at least the dies, had passed to the German firm of Ziss. The Danhausen catalog of 1974 still lists all the models, and some, but by no means all, of the models appear in that dealer's 1978 and 1979 editions By 1980, only three models are offered, and none at all after that date.

R.A.M.I. models are certainly interesting. Though some of them portray well-known old-timers like the Model T Ford, others represent relatively unknown and, in some cases, slightly fantastic real cars. Their quality, while not outstanding, is certainly good, and they have enjoyed considerable popularity throughout their existence and are still quite desirable collectors' items, worth $40 to $55 apiece today. Speaking of quality, models #32 through #38 were also listed as "Luxe" models #1 through #7, presumably indicating a higher standard of quality; in practice, this seems to have meant the use of more chrome-plated parts. Each model was issued in only one combination of colors, which makes it easy for us to present a complete list of them.

1 RENAULT 1907 TAXI DE LA MARNE 88 mm 1958
Open-cab car with cast body, chassis, gold lights and radiator, yellow spoked hubs, black tires. Value $40-50.

1. Black upper body and chassis, red lower body.

2 DE DION-BOUTON 1900 VIS-À-VIS 55 mm 1958-1970
Open vis-à-vis with cast body, black seats and chassis, gold tiller, green spoked hubs, black tires. Value $40-50.
1. Gray body.

2 MOTOBLOC 1902 TONNEAU 68 mm 1971
Open four-seater with cast body, chassis, white seats, gold grille and lights, chrome spoked hubs, black tires. Value $40-50.
1. Red body, black chassis.

3 LION-PEUGEOT 1907 DOUBLE PHAETON 72 mm 1958
Open four-seater with cast body, chassis, red front seats. gold grille, lights, and levers, yellow spoked hubs, black tires. Value $40-50.
1. Blue body, black chassis.

4 CITROEN 1924 5CV ROADSTER 73 mm 1958
Open two-seater with cast body, chassis, black folded top, red seats, silver grille, lights, and windshield frame, gray disc hubs, black tires. Value $40-50.
1. Yellow body, black chassis.

5 DE DION 1900 CAB 56 mm 1958
High closed car with cast upper and lower body, black chassis, gold light, yellow spoked hubs, black tires. $40-50.
1. Green upper, yellow lower body.

6 BUGATTI 1928 TYPE 35 85 mm 1959
Two-seat racing car with cast body, chassis, red seats, unpainted grille, front springs, and exhaust pipe, chrome spoked hubs, black tires. Value $40-50.
1. Blue body, black chassis.

7 CITROEN 1925 B2 LIMOUSINE 88 mm 1959
Four-door sedan with cast body, roof, black hood, and chassis, yellow seats, silver grille and lights, gray disc hubs, black tires. Value $40-50.
1. Yellow body, gray roof.

8 SIZAIRE & NAUDIN 1906 RACING CAR 74 mm 1959
Two-seat sports-racing car with cast body, chassis, red seats, gold grille, front springs, lights, and levers, white spoked hubs, black tires. Value $40-50.
1. White body and chassis.

9 ROCHET-SCHNEIDER 1895 VIS-À-VIS 68 mm 1960
Open four-seater with cast body, chassis, red seats, white parasol, gold grille, lights, tiller, and panel, white spoked hubs, black tires. Value $40-50.
1. Yellow-orange body, black chassis.

10 HISPANO-SUIZA 1934 TOWN CAR 97 mm 1960
Open-cab town sedan with cast body, chassis, red seats, black roof, unpainted grille, windshield, lights, and bumpers, chrome disc hubs, black tires, spare wheel. Value $40-50.
1. Light yellow body, black chassis.

11 GOBRON-BRILLIÉ 1899 DOUBLE PHAETON 64 mm 1961
Four-seater, rear top up, with cast body, black top, seats and fenders, gold grille, lights, and steering wheel, yellow spoked hubs, black tires. Value $40-50.
1. Orange body.

12 GAUTHIER-WEHRLÉ 1897 CAB 61 mm 1961
Open-front two-seat coupe with cast body, top, red seat, gold windshield, lights, and tiller, white spoked hubs, black tires.
    1. Gray body, orange top. Value $40-50.

13 PACKARD 1912 LANDAULET 89 mm 1962
Open-cab car with cast body, black chassis and top, red front seat, gold grille, lights, and levers, white spoked hubs, black tires. $45-55.
    1. Orange body.

14 PEUGEOT 1898 COUPE 75 mm 1962
Coach with cast body, roof, black chassis, red open front seat, gold dash, lights, and controls, white spoked hubs, black tires. $40-50.
    1. Light blue body, gray roof.

15 FORD 1908 MODEL T 84 mm 1963
Top-up three-seater with cast body, chassis, gray top, red seats, gold grille, windshield, lights, and horn, tan spoked hubs, black tires. Value $40-50.
    1. Yellow body and chassis.

16 FORD 1907 MODEL R TOURER 84 mm 1963
Top-up four-seater with cast body, chassis, top, seats, gold grille, windshield, lights, and horn, white spoked hubs, black tires. $40-50.
    1. Black body, chassis. top and seats.

17 PANHARD & LEVASSOR 1908 LA MARQUISE 99 mm 1964
Roofed-cab closed car with cast body, hood, black chassis, gray roof, red front seat, gold grille, windshield, levers, and lights, white spoked hubs, black tires. Value $40-50.
    1. Lilac body, orange hood.

18 PANHARD & LEVASSOR 1899 TONNEAU BALLON 80 mm 1964
Roofed-cab closed car with cast body, roof, black chassis and hood, red front seat, gold grille, lights, and levers, white spoked hubs, black tires. Value $40-50.
    1. Ivory body, gray roof.

19 HAUTIER 1898 ELECTRIC TAXI 90 mm 1964
Closed cab with cast body, opening doors, red rear driver's seat, gold lights, white spoked hubs, black tires. Value $45-55.
    1. Black body, orange doors.

20 DELAUNAY-BELLEVILLE 1904 85 mm 1964
Four-seat tourer with cast body, hood, gray raised top, black chassis, red seats, gold grille, lights, and levers, white spoked hubs, black tires. Value $40-50.
    1. Pale blue body, orange hood.

21 GEORGES RICHARD 1902 TONNEAU 68 mm 1964
Roofed four-seater with cast body, roof, black chassis, white seats, gold grille, lights, and levers, white spoked hubs, black tires. Value $40-50.
    1. Red body, gray roof.

22 SCOTTE 1892 STEAM CAR 70 mm 1965
Roofed/closed car with cast body, chassis, roof, red front seat, gold boiler, lights, and controls, bronze cast spoked wheels. Value $45-55.
    1. Blue body, orange chassis, gray roof.

23 RENAULT 1900 TONNEAU 72 mm 1965
Open four-seater with cast body, chassis, maroon seats, gold grille, lights, and levers, bronze spoked hubs, black tires. Value $40-50.
    1. White body, black chassis.

24 LORRAINE-DIETRICH 1911 93 mm 1965

Four-door sedan with cast body, hood, black chassis and roof, gold grille, lights, and horn, gray tank and toolbox, white spoked hubs, black tires, spare wheel. Value $40-50.

   1. Yellow body, orange hood.

25 PANHARD & LEVASSOR 1895 TONNEAU 65 mm 1965

Open four-seater with cast body, chassis, yellow front and orange facing rear seats, gold lights and controls, white spoked hubs, black tires. Value $40-50.

   1. Blue body, gray chassis.

26 DELAHAYE 1904 PHAETON 73 mm 1965

Top-up four-seater with cast body, chassis, top, white seats, gold grille, lights, and levers, white spoked hubs, black tires. $40-50.

   1. Red body, black chassis and top.

27 AUDIBERT & LAVIROTTE 1898 69 mm 1966

Open four-seater with cast body, chassis, orange seats, gold grille, lights, and levers, bronze spoked hubs, black tires. Value $40-50.

   1. Green body, black chassis.

28 LÉON BOLLÉE 1911 DOUBLE BERLINE 94 mm 1966

Two-section sedan with cast body, hood, chassis, blue roof, gold grille and lights, tan spoked hubs, black tires. Value $40-50.

   1. Red body and hood, dark blue chassis.

29 S. P. A. 1912 SPORTS CAR 103 mm 1966

Open roadster with cast body, chassis, white seats, gold grille, windshield, tank, lights, and lever, chrome spoked hubs, black tires, two spares. Value $40-50.

   1. Red body and chassis.

30 AMÉDÉE BOLLÉE 1878 LA MANCELLE 92 mm 1966

Steam carriage with cast body, top, gray roof over rear seats, black chassis, red seats, gold boiler and lights, bronze spoked wheels. Value $40-50.

   1. Green body, tan top.

31 LUC COURT 1901 RACING CAR 70 mm 1967

Open two-seater with cast body, chassis, white and maroon seats, gold grille, lights, and lever, tan spoked hubs, black tires. Value $40-50.

   1. Yellow body, black chassis.

32 BRASIER 1908 LANDAULET 82 mm 1967

Open-front car with cast body, hood, black chassis, top, and front seats, gold grille, dash, lights, and levers, chrome irons and spoked hubs, black tires. Also Luxe #1. Value $40-50.

   1. Yellow body, green hood.

33 BERLIET 1910 LIMOUSINE 95 mm 1968

Two-section sedan with cast front and rear body, orange hood, black chassis, gray roof and toolbox, gold grille, dash, lights, and trim, chrome spoked hubs, black tires. Also Luxe #2. Value $40-50.

   1. Green front, cream rear body.

34 MIEUSSET 1903 RUNABOUT 68 mm 1968

Top-up two-seater with cast body, black chassis and top, white seats, gold grille, lights, levers, and irons, chrome spoked hubs, black tires. Also Luxe #3. Value $40-50.

   1. Rose red body.

35 DE DION-BOUTON 1902 RACING CAR 84 mm 1968

Two-seater with cast body, chassis, blue seats, gray tank, gold grille and lever, louver decals, chrome spoked hubs, black tires. Also Luxe #4. Value $40-50.

   1. Ivory body, red chassis.

36 LACROIX DE LAVILLE 1898 84 mm 1968
Three-wheeler with cast body, chassis, blue seats, silver tiller, gold dash, light, and horn, chrome spoked hubs, black tires. Also Luxe #5. Value $40-50.
    1. Cream body, black chassis.

37 DELAGE 1932 TORPEDO 117 mm 1968
Open sports car with cast body, chassis, orange seats, chrome grille, windshield, lights, and spoked hubs, black rumble seat cover and tires. Also Luxe 6. Value $45-55.
    1. Maroon body, white chassis.

38 MERCEDES 1927 SSK 100 mm 1969
Open sports car with cast body, chassis, white seats, chrome grille, windshield, exhaust pipe, lights, and spoked hubs, black tires, two spares. Also Luxe #7. Value $45-55.
    1. Red body, black chassis.

———

SAFIR

Safir became the successor to Jadali in 1961 and expanded Jadali's two old-time car models to a series that grew to include some two dozen models by the end of the sixties. Making effective use of various interchangeable parts that ranged from chassis to parasols, the firm produced a number of picturesque models that never got as much exposure as they deserved–though other firms, especially in Hong Kong, paid them the ultimate compliment.

In 1969 the Safir firm moved into other areas, producing the first of its series of "Champion" racing and sports cars in 1/43 and smaller scales, and in 1975 Safir began to reissue numerous trucks and military vehicles made from France Jouets dies. The last new models, a small series of four Formula I racing cars, appeared in 1977, and a year later the firm went out of business, after having produced a wide variety of colorful, reasonably priced, interesting models that I always enjoyed collecting.

Veteran Cars
1 PEUGEOT 1892 VIS-À-VIS 64 mm 1/43 1961-
Open-roofed car with cast body and chassis, ivory plastic top, black seats, gold lights and controls, white spoked hubs, black tires. Same body and chassis as #2 through #6. Value $10-15.
    1. Red body, cream chassis.
    2. Light blue body, cream chassis.

2 PEUGEOT 1898 VICTORIA 75 mm 1/43 1961-
Open car with cast body and chassis, ivory front body, parasol and folded top, black seats, gold lights and controls, white spoked hubs, black tires. Value $10-15.
    1. Yellow body, red chassis.
    2. White body, red chassis.
    3. Red body, black chassis.

3 PEUGEOT 1899 VICTORIA 75 mm 1/43 1961-
Top-up car with cast body and chassis, black plastic top and front floor, red seats, gold lights and controls, clear hubs, black tires. Value $10-15.
1. Black body, yellow chassis.
2. Black body, cream chassis.

4 PEUGEOT 1896, TOP DOWN 64 mm 1/43 1961-
Top-down car with cast body and chassis, black plastic folded top, ivory seat, gold trunk, lights, and controls, white spoked hubs, black tires. Value $10-15.
1. Red body, yellow chassis.
2. Green body, yellow chassis.

5 DECAUVILLE 1901 VIS-À-VIS 64 mm 1/43 1961-
Top-up version with cast body and chassis, black plastic top, gray seats, gold lights and controls, clear hubs, black tires. Value $10-15.
1. Yellow body, red chassis.

6 DELAHAYE 1901 VIS-À-VIS 64 mm 1/43 1961-
Parasol version with cast body and chassis, red plastic parasol, ivory seats, gold lights and controls, brown spoked hubs, white tires. Value $10-15.
1. Black body, yellow chassis.

7 RENAULT 1902 PARIS-VIENNA 84 mm 1/43 1962-
Racing car with cast body and chassis, black plastic seats, front frame and spare tire, gold radiators, lights, and controls, red spoked hubs, black tires. First made by Jadali. Value $10-15.
1. Red body and chassis.

8 FORD 1911 MODEL T ROADSTER 79 mm 1/43 1962-
Roadster with cast body and chassis, black plastic folded top and rear axle, gold front axle, headlights, windshield frame, grille, and spoked hubs, black tires. First made by Jadali. Value $10-15.
1. Red body, black chassis.

9 CITROEN 1924 10 HP TAXI 84 mm 1/43 1963
Open-cab taxi with cast chassis-hood and unpainted grille-headlights and windshield frame, plastic body, black roof and seats, gold lights and horn, yellow disc hubs, black tires and spare. Same chassis as #11-13, 21-23. Value $10-15.
1. Red body, black chassis.
2. Yellow body, black chassis.

10 RENAULT 1900 35 HP COUPE 63 mm 1/43 1963-
Coupe with cast chassis, plastic body, black roof and grille, gold radiator shell and lights, white spoked hubs, black tires. Same chassis as #14 through 18. Value $10-15.
1. White body, red chassis.
2. Green body, red chassis.

11 CITROEN 1923 FIRE TRUCK 84 mm 1/43 1963-
Van with cast chassis-hood, plastic body with ladders on roof, red seats and hubs, gold radiator shell, windshield frame, lights, and horn, black grille and tires. Value $15-20.
1. Red body and chassis, with spare wheel.
2. Red body and chassis, with hose reel.

12 CITROEN 1923 AMBULANCE 84 mm 1/43 1963-
Van with cast chassis-hood, unpainted grille-headlights and windshield frame, plastic body, gold horn, white hubs, black tires, red cross flags, blue logo. Value $15-20.
1. White body and chassis.
2. White body, black chassis.

13 CITROEN 1923 MAIL TRUCK 84 mm 1/43 1963
Van with cast-chassis-hood, unpainted grille-headlights and windshield frame, plastic body, tan mailbags, gold horn, yellow hubs, black seats and tires, cream logo. Issued briefly. Value $15-25.
    1. Green body, black chassis.

14 FIAT 1901 8 HP 72 mm 1/43 1963-
Four-seater, top up, with cast chassis, plastic body and hood, gray top, brown seats, gold lights, white spoked hubs, black grille and tires. Also exists with top down. Value $10-15.
    1. White body and hood, black chassis, top up.
    2. White body and hood, top down.

15 MERCEDES 1901, TOP UP 61 mm 1/43 1963-
Two-seater with cast chassis, plastic body and hood, brown top and seat, gold grille, lights, and controls, tan trunk, brown spoked hubs, white tires. Value $10-15.
    1. Green body and hood, yellow chassis.

16 RENAULT 1899 WITH ROOF 64 mm 1/43 1964-
Two-seater with cast chassis, plastic body and hood, red top and spoked hubs, gold grilles, lights, horn, and controls, black seat, trunk, and tires. Value $10-15.
    1. Red body and hood, yellow chassis.

17 PANHARD 1898, TOP DOWN 76 mm 1/43 1964-
Four-seater with cast fenders, plastic body, hood, ivory seats, gold lights and controls, black folded top, chassis, and tires. Also exists with top up. Value $10-15.
    1. Green body and hood, red fenders, top down.
    2. Maroon body, yellow chassis, top up.

18 PEUGEOT 1900 COUPE 67 mm 1/43 1964-
Coupe with cast chassis, plastic body, gold lights and controls, black roof, top, seats, and grille, white spoked hubs, black tires. Value $10-15.
    1. Maroon body, yellow chassis.

19 PEUGEOT 1892 TOIT BOIS 67 mm 1/43 1965-
Vis-à-vis with cast body and chassis, brown roof, gold lights and grille, white spoked hubs, black seats and tires. Value $10-15.
    1. Yellow body, red chassis.

20 MERCEDES 1901 9 HP ? mm 1/43 1963?
Same as #15, but with top down. Value $10-15.
    1. Green body and hood, red chassis.

21 CITROEN 1924 TAXI ? mm 1/43 1967?
Apparently a variant of #22 and 23, with open cab and rear top. Value $10-15.
    1. Black body, roof, chassis, and hood.

22 CITROEN 1924 TAXI 90 mm 1/43 1967-
Covered-cab taxi with cast chassis and hood, plastic body and roof, black seats, grille, hubs, and tires, gold radiator shell, windshield frame, lights, and horn, wicker labels. Value $10-15.
    1. Black body, roof, chassis, and hood.

23 CITROEN 1924 TAXI 90 mm 1/43 1967-
Same as #22 but with open cab. Value $10-15.
    1. Black body, roof, chassis, and hood.

24 RENAULT 1906 TOWN CAR 96 mm 1/43 1967-
Town car with cast chassis, plastic body and hood, black roof, seats, and closed rear top, clear windows, gold grille, lights, and controls, brown spoked hubs, black tires and spare. Value $10-15.
    1. Red body and hood, black chassis.

25 RENAULT 106 TOWN CAR 96 mm 1/43 1967-
Same as #24 but with open rear top. Value $10-15.
  1. Black body and hood, yellow chassis.

26 UNIC 1908 TAXI 98 mm 1/43 1968-
Town car with cast chassis, plastic body, black roof, rear top, driver's seat, grille, and frame, gold radiator shell, lights, and controls, clear windows, tan spoked hubs, black tires. Open cab. Value $10-15.
  1. Maroon body, green chassis.
  2. Dark green body, black chassis?

27 UNIC 1908 TAXI 98 mm 1/43 1968-
Same as #26 but with closed cab. Value $10-15.
  1. Maroon body, black chassis.

101 GREGOIRE 1910 TRIPLE BERLINE 130 mm 1/43 1965
3-section sedan with cast chassis-hood, plastic upper and lower body, brown trunks, gold radiator shell, lights, and parts, clear windows, white spoked hubs, black grille and tires, spare wheel. Value $15-20.
  1. Red lower body, black upper body and chassis.

Super Champion 1/43 Scale Sports and Racing Cars

30 LOLA T70 TEMPORADA 96 mm 1/43 1970-
Sports-racing coupe with unpainted cast chassis and motor, plastic body, black interior, clear or tinted windows, silver gray hubs, black tires, blue and white stripes. Value $10-15.
  1. Red body, #50, VDS team logo.

31 LOLA T70 AUSTRIAN G.P. 96 mm 1/43 1970-
As above except "Wrangler" and "Peter Quelle" logo. Value $10-15.
  1. Green body, #32, David Piper team logo.

32 LOLA T70 PARIS 1000 KM 96 mm 1/43 1970-
As above except "Koni," "Ferodo," etc. Value $10-15.
  1. Light blue body, #102, Ulf Norinder team logo.

33 LOLA T70 DAYTONA 96 mm 1/43 1970-
As above except red-white-black trim. Value $10-15.
  1. Dark blue body, #8.

34 LOLA T70 NÜRBURGRING 96 mm 1/43 1970-
As above except for team logo. Value $10-15.
  1. Yellow and red body, #55, Bonnier-Müller logo.

35 LOLA T70 MONZA 96 mm 1/43 1970-
As above except green stripes. Value $10-15.
  1. White body, #33, Sidney Taylor team logo.

40 PORSCHE 917 TEMPORADA 98 mm 1/43 1971-
Sports-racing coupe with unpainted cast chassis and motor, plastic short-tailed body, clear windows, black interior, silver gray hubs, black tires, green trim. Value $15-20.
  1. White body, #28.

41 PORSCHE 917 DAYTONA 98 mm 1/43 1971-
As above except red stripes. Value $15-20.
  1. White body, #3, Porsche Austria team logo.

42 PORSCHE 917 MONZA 98 mm 1/43 1971-
As above except orange and black stripes. Value $15-20.
  1. Light blue body, #7, Gulf Porsche team logo.

43 PORSCHE 917 LE MANS 98 mm 1/43 1971-
As above except white stripes. Value $15-20.
  1. Orange-red body, #23, Shell logo.

44 PORSCHE 917 BRANDS HATCH 98 mm 1/43 1971-
As above except green trim. Value $15-20.
  1. Blue body, #12, Textar logo.

45 PORSCHE 917 HOLLAND 98 mm 1/43 1971-
As above except red trim. Value $15-20.
  1. Dark yellow body, #18, David Piper team logo.

50 PORSCHE 917 LE MANS 111 mm 1/43 1971-
Sports-racing coupe with unpainted cast chassis and motor, plastic
long-tailed body, clear windows, black interior, silver gray wing and
hubs, black tires, green trim, Martini logo. Value $15-20.
  1. Dark blue body, #3, Larrousse-Kauhsen logo.

51 PORSCHE 917 LE MANS 111 mm 1/43 1971-
As above except white trim. Value $15-20.
  1. Blue trim, #3, Cibie logo.

52 PORSCHE 917 LE MANS 111 mm 1/43 1971-
As above except black wing and wheels, red trim, Shell logo. Value
$15-20.
  1. White body, #25, Elford-Ahrens logo.

53 PORSCHE 917 HOCKENHEIM 98 mm 1/43 1971-
As above except short body, white trim. Value $15-20.
  1. Blue body, #12.

54 PORSCHE 917 DAVID PIPER 98 mm 1/43 1971-
As above except short tail, silver trim. Value $15-20.
  1. Orange-red body, David Piper team logo.

55 PORSCHE 911 KYALAMI 98 mm 1/43 1971-
As above except short tail, red trim, Martini logo. Value $15-20.
  1. Yellow body, #2, Siffert-Ahrens logo.

60 FERRARI 512M FRANCORCHAMPS 95 mm 1/43 1972-
Sports-racing coupe with unpainted cast chassis and motor, plastic
body, red interior and flaps, clear windows, gold hubs, black tires.
Value $15-20.
  1. Yellow body, #9, Camel Racing Team logo.

61 FERRARI 512M SUNOCO 95 mm 1/43 1972-
As above except yellow interior, wing, trim, and hubs. Value $15-20.
  1. Blue body, #6, Kirk F. White team logo.

62 FERRARI 512M MONTJUICH 95 mm 1/43 1972-
As above except green interior, wing, and trim. Value $15-20.
  1. Yellow body, #15, Tergal logo.

63 FERRARI 512M GELO 95 mm 1/43 1972-
As above except yellow flaps and trim. Value $15-20.
  1. Red body, #10.

64 FERRARI 512M N.A.R.T. 95 mm 1/43 1972-
As above except dark blue and white stripes, red intake and flaps.
Value $15-20.
  1. Red body, #12.

65 FERRARI 512M FILIPINETTI 95 mm 1/43 1972-
As above except blue hubs, light blue and white stripes, white intake
and flaps. Value $15-20.
  1. Red body, #6.

70 PORSCHE 917 LE MANS 98 mm 1/43 1971-
Sports-racing coupe similar to #40 but with high tail fins, with silver
gray hubs, blue and red trim, Martini logo. Value $15-20.
  1. White body, #22, Marko-Lennep logo.

71 PORSCHE 917 JOHN WYER 98 mm 1/43 1971-
As above except orange and black stripes, Gulf Porsche logo. Value $15-20.
    1. Light blue body, #19.

72 PORSCHE 917 DAYTONA 98 mm 1/43 1971-
As #40 (squared tail, no fins), with red and blue trim, Porsche Audi and Martini & Rossi Racing logo. Value $15-20.
    1. Silver body, #3, Larrousse-Elford logo.

73 PORSCHE 917 NÜRBURGRING 98 mm 1/43 1971-
As #70 (high fins) with green stripes, Team Auto Usdau logo. Value $15-20.
    1. Yellow body, #55, Joest-Kauhsen logo.

74 PORSCHE 917 GULF PORSCHE-WYER 111 mm 1/43 1971-
As #50 (long tail) with orange and black stripes, Gulf-Porsche-Wyer logo. Value $15-20.
    1. Light blue body, Rodriguez-Oliver logo, #18.

75 PORSCHE 917 MARTINI 111 mm 1/43 1971-
As above (long tail) with two-tone blue and red trim, Martini logo. Value $15-20.
    1. Silver body, #21, Elford-Larrousse logo.

80 FERRARI 312 T2 96 mm 1/43 1976-
Racing car with cast body, white plastic chassis and intake, silver airfoils, black seat and mirrors. Value $15-20.
    1. Red body, white cockpit area, #12.

81 LIGIER-MATRA JS5 96 mm 1/43 1977-
Racing car with cast body, white plastic chassis and intake, silver airfoil, black seat and mirrors. Value $15-20.
    1. Blue and white body.

82 TYRRELL P34 #4 98 mm 1/43 1977-
Racing car with cast body (rounded nose), blue plastic intake, airfoil, and cockpit, black chassis, motor, suspension, and seat. Value $15-20.
    1. Dark blue body, #4, driver Depailler.

83 TYRRELL P34 33 96 mm 1/43 1977-
Racing car almost identical to #82, but with straight nose. Value $15-20.
    1. Dark blue body, #3, driver Stewart.

Reissues of F.J. models: Commercial Vehicles

BERLIET COVERED TRUCK 92 mm 1/45 ca. 1975
Truck with cast cab and black chassis, plastic rear body and cover, black interior, clear windows, silver gray hubs, black tires, logo decals. Value $8-12.
    1. Yellow cab and rear body, black cover, "Calberson" logo.
    2. Yellow cab and rear body, white cover, "Professionels Reunis" logo.

BERLIET DUMP TRUCK 97 mm 1/45 ca. 1975
Truck with cast cab and black chassis, plastic tipper, black interior, clear windows, silver gray hubs, black tires. Value $8-12.
    1. Orange cab and tipper.

BERLIET FIRE TRUCK 94 mm 1/45 ca. 1975
Ladder truck with cast cab and black chassis, silver gray plastic rear bed and aerial ladder, red mount, black interior, clear windows, silver gray hubs, black tires. Value $10-15.
    1. Red cab.

BERLIET GARBAGE TRUCK 105 mm 1/45 ca. 1975
Garbage truck with cast cab, rear body, and opening rear, black chassis, black plastic interior, clear windows, silver gray hubs, black tires. Value $8-12.
    1. Blue cab, gray rear body parts.

BERLIET STAKESIDE TRUCK 92 mm 1/45 ca. 1975
Stake truck with cast cab, black chassis, plastic rear bed, stakes, black interior, clear windows, silver gray hubs, black tires, "Franciade" logo decals. Value $8-12.
    1. Green cab and stakes, yellow rear bed.

BERLIET STRADAIR CIRCUS TRUCK 104 mm 1/45 ca. 1975
Cage truck with cast cab, black chassis, plastic rear bed and body, red bars, black interior, clear windows, red hubs, black tires, "Cirque Jean Richard" logo decals. Value $10-15.
    1. Red cab and rear bed, blue rear body.

BERLIET STRADAIR BOTTLE TRUCK 104 mm 1/45 ca. 1975
Bottle truck with cast cab, red chassis, plastic rear body, black interior, clear windows, red hubs, black tires, "Kanterbräu" logo decals. Value $8-12.
    1. Yellow cab and rear body.

BERLIET STRADAIR WRECKER 104 mm 1/45 ca. 1975
Wrecker with cast cab, black chassis, plastic rear bed, red boom, black interior, clear windows, silver gray hook and hubs, black tires, "Allo SOS" logo decals. Value $8-12.
    1. White cab, gray rear bed.

MERCEDES-BENZ CEMENT MIXER 101 mm 1/45 ca. 1975
Cement truck with cast cab, black chassis, plastic rear body, barrel, chute, black interior, clear windows, silver gray hubs, black tires, black and red "Unibeton" logo decals. Value $8-12.
    1. Blue cab, yellow rear body, barrel, and chute.

MERCEDES-BENZ COVERED TRUCK 91 mm 1/45 ca. 1975
Covered truck with cast cab, black chassis, plastic rear body, white cover, black interior, clear windows, silver gray hubs, black tires, red "aux Professionels Reunis" logo decals. Value $8-12.
    1. Yellow cab and rear body.

MERCEDES CRANE TRUCK 103 mm 1/45 ca. 1975
Crane truck with cast cab, black chassis, plastic rear bed, blue boom and hook, white mount, black interior, clear windows, silver gray hubs, black tires. Value $8-12.
    1. Blue cab, silver gray rear bed.

MERCEDES-BENZ TANK TRUCK 91 mm 1/45 ca. 1975
Tanker with cast cab and chassis, plastic tank, black interior, clear windows, silver gray hubs, black tires, logo decals. Value $10-15.
    1. White cab and tank, red chassis, "Esso" logo.
    2. Blue cab, black chassis, white tank, "Elf-Caltex" logo.
    3. Yellow-orange cab and tank, red chassis, "Shell" logo.
    4. White cab and tank, "BP" logo, no other data.

Trucks and Trailers
BERLIET COVERED TRUCK & TRAILER 175 mm 1/45 ca. 1975
Covered "Calberson" truck as above with similar 4-wheel trailer. Value $12-18.
    1. Yellow cab and bodies, black covers.

BERLIET FIRE TRUCK & TRAILER 175 mm 1/45 ca. 1975
Ladder truck as above with water tank trailer, "Service departmentale

d'Incendie du Var" logo decals. Value $15-25.
    1. Red cab and tank, silver gray rear body and ladder.

BERLIET STRADAIR CIRCUS TRUCK & TRAILER 188 mm 1/45 ca. 1975

Stradair circus truck as above with similar cage trailer. Value $15-25.
    1. White cab and beds, blue bodies, red chassis and bars.

MERCEDES-BENZ COVERED TRUCK & TRAILER 175 mm 1/45 ca. 1975

Covered truck as above with similar trailer, "aux Professionels Reunis" logo decals. Value $12-18.
    1. Yellow cab and bodies, white covers.

MERCEDES-BENZ TANK TRUCK & TRAILER   175 mm 1/45 ca. 1975

Shell tank truck as above with similar trailer. Value $15-25.
    1. Yellow-orange cab and tanks, red chassis, "Shell" logo.
    2. White cab and tanks, "BP" logo.
    3. May also exist in Elf and Esso versions.

Dodge Civilian and Military Trucks
DODGE COVERED TRUCK 96 mm 1/45 ca. 1975

Truck with cast or plastic body, plastic windshield frame, cover, silver gray hubs, black tires, two figures. Value $8-15.
    1. Yellow truck, light brown cover, "Cirque Pinder" logo.
    2. Olive body and cover, red crosses, British Army ambulance.
    3. Light brown body and cover, French Army emblems.
    4. White body, light brown cover, red crosses, U.S. Army ambulance.

DODGE OPEN TRUCK 96 mm 1/45 ca. 1975

As above but without rear cover. Value $8-15.

    1. Red body, mount, and ladder, "Baskerville Fire" logo.
    2. Light brown body, mount, and searchlight, Israeli Army logo.
    3. Light brown body, mount, and searchlight, U.S. Army logo.
    4. Light brown body, mount, and radar dish, U.S. Army logo.
    5. Olive body, mount, and radar dish, USSR Army logo.
    6. White body, mount, and AA guns, USSR Army logo.
    7. Olive body, mount, and guns, USSR Army logo.

DODGE WRECKER 96 mm 1/45 ca. 1975

Wrecker with cast body, plastic windshield frame, silver gray boom, unpainted cast hook, silver gray hubs, black tires, "SOS Autoroute" logo. Value $8-12.
    1. Orange body and windshield frame.

Dodge Trucks and Trailers
DODGE COVERED TRUCK & CANNON 177 mm 1/45 ca. 1975

Covered truck with USSR Army logo, pulling plastic two-wheel cannon. Value $10-15.
    1. White body, cover, and cannon.

DODGE ROCKET TRUCK & TRAILER 160 mm 1/45 ca. 1975

Open truck and plastic two-wheel trailer with launchers, USSR Army logo. Value $10-15.
    1. Dark green body and launchers.

Jeeps
1 TAXI JEEP 84 mm 1/45 ca. 1975

Jeep with cast body, matching plastic windshield frame, light brown top, driver figure, silver gray hubs, black tires, "Grand Canyon Taxi" decals. Value $8-12.
    1. Olive body.

2 U.S AIR FORCE JEEP 84 mm 1/45 ca. 1975
Military police Jeep. No other data. Value $8-12.

3 LOVE JEEP 84 mm 1/45 ca. 1975
Jeep with cast body, matching plastic windshield frame, olive top, driver figure, silver gray hubs, black tires, "Love" and flower decals. Value $8-12.
    1. Purple body.

4 RED CROSS JEEP 84 mm 1/45 ca. 1975
Jeep with cast body, matching plastic windshield frame, olive top, driver figure, silver gray hubs, black tires, "Croix Rouge" decals. Value $10-15.
    1. White body.

5 U.S. ARMY JEEP 84 mm 1/45 ca. 1975
Jeep with cast body, matching plastic windshield frame, driver figure, silver gray hubs, black tires, white lettering and emblems. Value $8-12.
    1. Olive body.

6 FFL JEEP 84 mm 1/45 ca. 1975
No data. Value $8-12.

7 ISRAELI ARMY JEEP 84 mm 1/45 ca. 1975
Jeep with plastic (or cast?) body and windshield frame, driver figure, "Tel Aviv" and Star of David logo. Value $8-12.
    1. Tan body.

8 PROTECTION CIVILE JEEP 84 mm 1/45 ca. 1975
No data. Value $8-12.

9 USSR MILITARY JEEP 84 mm 1/45 ca. 1975
Jeep with cast or plastic body, plastic windshield frame, driver figure, silver gray hubs, black tires, red star and CCCP logo. Value $8-12.
    1. White body.

#? CIRCUS JEEP 84 mm 1/45 ca. 1975
Jeep with plastic body and windshield frame, driver figure, silver gray hubs, black tires, "Cirque Pinder" logo. Value $10-15.
    1. Yellow body.

#? FIRE JEEP 84 mm 1/45 ca. 1975
Jeep with cast body, plastic windshield frame, driver figure, silver gray aerial ladder and hubs, black tires, "Sapeurs Pompiers" logo. Value $10-15.
    1. Red body.

#? POLICE JEEP 84 mm 1/45 ca. 1975
Jeep with cast body, plastic windshield frame, light brown top, driver figure, silver gray hubs, black tires, "Frontier Police Patrol" logo. Value $8-12.
    1. Blue body.

#? RANGER JEEP 84 mm 1/45 ca. 1975
Jeep with cast body, plastic windshield frame, olive top, driver figure, silver gray hubs, black tires, "U.S. Ranger Police Commissioner" decals. Value $8-12.
    1. Orange body.

#? JEEP 84 mm 1/45 ca. 1975
Jeep with cast body, plastic windshield frame, light brown top, driver figure, silver gray hubs, black tires, no decals. May not be in original condition. Value?
    1. Olive body.

Jeeps and Trailers

ISRAELI JEEP & TRAILER   133 mm   1/45   ca. 1975
Jeep with cast body, plastic windshield frame, tan top and two-wheel box trailer, driver figure, silver gray hubs, black tires, "Tel Aviv" and Star of David decals. Value $12-18.

> 1. Tan body.

USSR JEEP & GUN   159 mm   1/45   ca. 1975
Jeep with cast body, plastic windshield frame, white top and cannon on wheels, driver figure, silver gray hubs, black tires, red star and other lettering decals. Value $12-18.

> 1. White body.

Champion 1/66 Scale Racing Cars: First Series

FERRARI FORMULA I   70 mm   1/66   1969-
Racing car with cast body and chassis, silver plastic parts, white driver, clear windshield, racing number and other decals. Value $8-12.

> 1. "Monza": Red body and chassis, red airfoil, #10, driver Amon.
> 2. "Rouen": Red body and chassis, yellow stripes, #26, driver Ickx.

HONDA FORMULA I   68 mm   1/66   1969-
Racing car with cast body and chassis, plastic parts as above, decals. Value $8-12.

> 1. "Monza": White body and chassis, red trim and airfoil, #14, driver Surtees.
> 2. "Rouen": White body and chassis, red stripes, #16.

LOTUS-FORD FORMULA I   71 mm   1/66   1969-
Racing car with cast body and chassis, plastic parts as above, decals. Value $8-12.
1. "Monaco": Red body and chassis, gold trim, #9, driver Hill.

2. "Mexico": Red body, chassis, and airfoil, gold trim, #10, driver Hill.

LOTUS STP INDIANAPOLIS   72 mm   1/66   1969-
Racing car with cast body and chassis, plastic parts as above, decals. Value $8-12.

> 1. "Indianapolis": Red body, yellow chassis, #60.
> 2. "Indy": Metallic dark red body and chassis, #70.

MATRA FORMULA I   70 mm   1/66   1969-
Racing car with cast body and chassis, plastic parts as above, decals. Value $8-12.

> 1. "Zandvoort": Blue body, chassis, and airfoil, #7, driver Beltoise.
> 2. "Madrid": Blue body and chassis, yellow stripes, #15, driver Pescarolo.

McLAREN FORMULA I   70 mm   1/66   1969-
Racing car with cast body and chassis, plastic parts as above, decals. Value $8-12.

> 1. "Monza": Yellow body, chassis, and airfoil, #1, driver McLaren.
> 2. "Spa": Light orange body and chassis, green stripe, #2, driver Hulme.

Second Series

B.R.M. FORMULA I   65 mm   1/66   ca. 1972
Racing car with unpainted cast chassis, plastic body, airfoil, intake, white driver, black wheels, decals. Value $5-10.

> 1. Green body, yellow cowling, white intake and airfoil, #6, driver Rodriguez.
> 2. White body, silver gray intake and airfoil, #14, driver Siffert.
> 3. White body and airfoil, red cowling, black intake, #17, driver Beltoise.

MARCH 711 FORMULA I 64 mm 1/66 ca. 1972
Racing car with unpainted cast chassis, plastic body, airfoils, white driver, black wheels, decals. Value $5-10.
 1. Red body and airfoils, #14, "STP" decals.
 2. Yellow body, silver gray airfoils, #17, "STP" decals.
 3. Red body, white airfoils, #27, "Motul" decals, driver Pescarolo.

MATRA MS120 FORMULA I 64 mm 1/66 ca. 1972
Racing car with unpainted cast chassis, plastic body, airfoil, intake, white driver, black wheels, decals. Value $5-10.
 1. Blue body, white cowling, intake, and airfoil, #16, driver Amon.
 2. Purple body, silver gray intake, otherwise as type 1.
 3. Red body, white cowling and airfoil, black intake, #19, driver Amon.
 4. Blue body, white cowling and intake, silver gray airfoil, #21, driver Beltoise.
 5. Purple body, silver gray intake, white airfoil, otherwise as type 4.

TYRRELL-FORD FORMULA I 61 mm 1/66 ca. 1972
Racing car with unpainted cast chassis, plastic body, airfoil, intake, white driver, decals. Value $5-10.
 1. Dark blue body, red intake, white airfoil, #9, driver Cevert.
 2. Light blue body, white intake, red airfoil, #11, driver Stewart.
 3. Green body, white intake, red airfoil, #21, driver Stewart.
 4. Blue body, otherwise as type 3.

Champion 1/66 Scale Sports Cars: First Series
1-2-3 CHAPPARAL 2D 67 mm 1/66 1969-
Sports-racing car with unpainted cast chassis, plastic body, interior, clear windows, silver gray hubs, black tires, decals. Value $5-12.
 1. "Le Mans": Dark blue body, red interior, #1, Shell emblem.
 2. "Can-Am": Dark orange body, black interior, #2, BP emblem.
 3. "Nürburgring": White body, black interior, #3, Shell emblem.
 4. Red body, black interior, #1, red and white stripes.
 5. Yellow body, black interior, #77, black and white checkers.
 6. Blue body, red interior, no #, red and white stripes, STP emblem.

4-5-6 FERRARI P4 66 mm 1/66 1969-
Sports-racing car with unpainted cast chassis, plastic body, interior, clear windows, silver gray hubs, black tires, decals. Value $5-12.
 1. "Monza": Red body, black interior, #4, Ferrari emblem, Italian flag.
 2. "Spa": Yellow body, black interior, #5, BP emblem, Belgian flag.
 3. "Silverstone": Green body, red interior, #6, Union Jack.
 4. White body, black interior, #5, red and white stripes.
 5. Red body, black interior, #11, black and white checkers.
 6. Blue body, red interior, #4, red and white stripes.

7-8-9 LOLA T70 65 mm 1/66 1969-
Sports-racing car with unpainted cast chassis, plastic body, interior, clear windows, silver gray hubs, black tires, decals. Value $5-12.
 1. "Can-Am": Green body, red interior, #7, Shell emblem.
 2. "Daytona": Red body and interior, #8, Esso emblem.
 3. "Sebring": Yellow body, red interior, #9, Mobil emblem.
 4. White body, red interior, #81, red and white stripes.
 5. Red body, black interior, #7, yellow stripes.
 6. Red body, black interior, #9, Firestone emblem.
 7. Yellow body, black interior, #81, red-white-blue trim.
 8. Purple body, red interior, #51, red-white-blue trim.

10-11-12 FORD GT II 68 mm 1/66 1969-

Sports-racing car with unpainted cast chassis, plastic body, interior, clear windows, decals. Value $5-12.

1. "Sebring": Dark blue body, red interior, #10, Esso emblem.
2. "Le Mans": Red body, black interior, #11, Italian flag.
3. "Daytona": White body, red interior, #12, French flag. Mobil emblem.
4. White body, black interior, #31, Ford and Champion emblems.
5. Red body, cream interior, #92, Spa-Sofia-Liege logo.
6. Red body, black interior, no #, red and white stripes.
7. Yellow body, red interior, no #, Dunlop emblem.
8. Green body, red interior, #43, Spa-Sofia-Liege logo.
9. Blue body, red interior, #43, Spa-Sofia-Liege logo.

Second Series:
FERRARI 512 S 68 mm 1/66 ca. 1971

Sports-racing car with unpainted cast chassis, plastic body, clear windows, black wheels, decals. Value $8-12.

1. Green body, yellow stripes, #4.
2. Yellow body, green trim, #9, Escuderia Montjuich team logo.
3. Red body, white and blue stripes, #58, Filipinetti team logo.

MATRA 650 68 mm 1/66 ca. 1971

Sports-racing car with unpainted cast chassis, plastic body, clear windows, black wheels, decals. Value $8-12.

1. Green body, white cowling, red-white-blue stripes, #10.
2. Blue body, otherwise as type 1.
3. Red body, white cowling, #32, driver Beltoise.
4. Blue body, otherwise as type 3.
5. Blue body, white cowling, #33, driver Pescarolo.

PORSCHE 917 SHORT 66 mm 1/66 ca. 1971

Sports-racing car with unpainted cast chassis, plastic body, clear windows, black wheels, decals. Value $8-12.

1. Light blue body, #7, Gulf-Porsche logo, orange and black trim.
2. White body, #22, Martini logo. red-blue-dark blue trim.
3. Red body, #23, Bosch logo, white stripes.

PORSCHE 917 LONG 74 mm 1/66 ca. 1971

Sports-racing car with unpainted cast chassis, plastic body, clear windows, black wheels, decals. Value $8-12.

1. Purple body, #2, white stripes, driver Siffert.
2. Yellow body, #3, Martini logo, red trim.
3. White body, #25, Bosch logo, red trim.

Champion 1/66 Truck Series
SAVIEM BOX VAN 71 mm 1/66 year?

Truck with unpainted cast chassis, plastic cab and rear body, clear windows, black fast wheels, logo decals. Value $5-10.

1. White cab and body, red floor, "Bonbel/La Vache qui rit" logo.
2. Yellow cab, red box and floor, "S.E.V. Marchal" logo.

SAVIEM DUMP TRUCK 71 mm 1/66 year?

Dump truck with unpainted cast chassis, plastic cab, tipper, clear windows, black fast wheels, logo decals. Value $5-10.

1. Green cab, yellow tipper, "C.S.S." logo.
2. Red cab, green tipper, "Les Sabliers de France" logo.

SAVIEM GARBAGE TRUCK 73 mm 1/66 year?

Garbage truck with unpainted cast chassis, plastic cab, tipping rear body, clear windows, black fast wheels, logo decals. Value $5-10.

1. Red cab, silver gray rear body, "Attention Ouvriers" logo.
2. Blue cab, white rear body, same logo as type 1.

SAVIEM FLAT TRUCK WITH LOAD 70 mm 1/66 year?

Flat truck with unpainted cast chassis, plastic cab, rear bed, load, clear windows, black fast wheels. Value $5-10.

1. Yellow cab, blue bed, boat wit white hull, red deck.
2. Blue cab, yellow bed, boat with red hull, white deck.
3. Yellow cab, green bed, red site hut.
4. Red cab, green bed, airplane with white fuselage, yellow wings.

SAVIEM ARMY TRUCK WITH ROCKET 71 mm 1/66 year?

Flat truck with unpainted cast chassis, plastic cab, rear bed, red and white rocket. Value $5-10.

1. Tan cab and bed, red rocket with white nose.
2. Olive cab and bed, white rocket with red nose.

Vans and Rally Vehicles
CITROEN 2CV 65 mm 1/66 year?

Car with unpainted cast chassis, plastic body, opening hood, roof panel, black interior, clear windows, black fast wheels, logo decals. Value $5-10.

1. Red body and hood, closed roof, #112, Credit Agricole logo.
2. Cream body and hood, open roof, #87, Paris-Persepolis logo.
3. Light blue body and hood, closed roof, no #, Cibie logo.
4. Green body and hood, open roof, no #, duck figure.

LAND ROVER SAFARI 72 mm 1/66 year?

Land Rover with unpainted cast chassis, plastic body, rigid or simulated canvas rear cover, clear windows, black fast wheels, logo decals. Value $5-10.

1. Red body and rigid cover, Raid Paris-Le Cap logo.
2. Red body, cream canvas cover, Sapeurs-Pompiers du Var logo.

3. Yellow body, white rigid cover, East African Safari logo.
4. Olive body and canvas cover, French Army ambulance.

RENAULT ESTAFETTE VAN 67 mm 1/66 year?

Van with unpainted cast chassis, plastic body, sliding side door, windows, black fast wheels, logo decals. Value $5-10.

1. White body, blue windows and dome light, red crosses, ambulance.
2. White body, clear windows, Allo SOS logo.
3. Yellow body, clear windows, Renault Service Competition logo.
4. Blue body, clear windows, Transports 2000 logo.

RACING

These all-plastic 1/43 scale models were made by Safir and marketed under the name of Racing; they represent the same Lola and Porsche models as those of the 1/43 Champion series.

LOLA T-70 96 mm 1/43 1972-

Sports-racing car with plastic body, black interior, tinted windows, clear headlights, silver gray chassis, motor, and hubs, black tires, decals. Value $10-15.

1. White body, amber windows, #89, Wynn's logo, red stripes.
2. Orange-red body, green windows, #67, Champion logo, white trim.
3. Yellow body, green windows, #60, Ferodo logo, red trim.
4. Blue body, amber windows, #68, Ferodo logo, red stripes.

PORSCHE 917 SHORT 100 mm 1/43 1972-

Sports-racing car with plastic body, interior, clear windows and headlights, silver gray chassis, motor, and hubs, black tires, decals. Value $10-15.

1. Red body, cream interior, #32, Martini logo.

2. Green body, red interior, #17, Wynn's logo.
3. Light blue body, red interior, #77, Ferodo logo.
4. Purple body, red interior, #2, Ferodo logo.

PORSCHE 917 LONG 113 mm 1/43 1972-
Sportracing car with plastic body, interior, clear windows and head-

lights, silver gray chassis, motor, and hubs, black tires, decals. Value $10-15.
1. White body, black interior, #5, Motul logo.
2. Orange-red body, black interior, #24, Ferodo logo.
3. Yellow body, black interior, #39, Martini logo.
4. Blue body, red interior, #31, Martini logo.

OTHER BRANDS

Many other brand names have appeared on the scene in France. In some cases we have full information on their products, in other cases our data are very fragmentary. Here they are in alphabetical order.

ADOR
Paolo Rampini's book shows a caravan trailer model made by Ador.

CARAVAN TRAILER ? mm 1/43? ca. 1953
Caravan with plastic body, clear windows?, red hubs, black tires, tin tow hook. Value?
1. Cream body.

BONUX
Bonux models were made by the Cle firm for promotional and other uses. There are probably many more of them than we know of; the following ready-made and kit models are known to exist.

ISOTTA-FRASCHINI 1902 61 mm 1/43? year?
Open two-seater with plastic body, black seat and tires, white spoked hubs, lights, and controls. Resembles Politoys #112. Value $4-8.
1. Red body.

PEUGEOT 203 91 mm 1/48 year?
Sedan with plastic body, matching chassis, black hubs, white tires, "Bonux" cast on roof. Value $10-15.
1. Gray body and chassis.

ROAD ROLLER 58 mm 1/? year?
Roller with plastic body, silver gray canopy, front mount, and rollers. Value $4-8.
1. Yellow body.

Plastic 1/50 Scale Kits
FIAT TORPEDO 1901 ? mm 1/50 ca. 1960
No data.

FORD 1903   ? mm   1/50   ca. 1960
No data.

LEYLAND DOUBLE-DECK BUS 1920   87 mm   1/50   ca. 1960
Open-top double-decker with plastic body parts, black spoked hubs, light brown seats, brown driver, "Global" and "London Transport" decals. Value $10-15.
    1. Red body parts.

PACKARD 1912 TOWN SEDAN   ? mm   1/50   ca. 1960
No data.

PEUGEOT 1898 BROUGHAM   84 mm   1/50   ca. 1960
Coach with plastic body parts, other parts missing, black spoked wheels. Value $4-8.
    1. Red body parts.

REGAL 1914 SEDAN   ? mm   1/50   ca. 1960
No data.

RENAULT 1910 TRUCK   ? mm   1/50   ca. 1960
No data.

ROLLS-ROYCE 1907 SILVER GHOST TORPEDO   ? mm   1/50   ca. 1960
No data.

ROLLS-ROYCE 1911 SILVER GHOST LANDAU   ? mm   1/50   ca. 1960
No data.

SIZAIRE-NAUDIN 1906 RACING CAR   ? mm   1/50   ca. 1960
No data.

BOURBON

As far as we know, this firm produced only two 1/43 scale models: a Peugeot D4A van of the fifties with various logo types, and a newer Berliet tanker semi, which would lend itself to several logo varieties but seems to exist only with an Elf logo.

The firm also has made somewhat larger plastic models of Poclain heavy equipment. I have no data on them but can show you a few.

PEUGEOT D4A VAN   ? mm   1/43?   year?
Similar but not identical to Quiralu version. No other data. Value?
    1. Argentil-Lion Noir logo.
    2. Hilti logo.
    3. Shell logo.

BERLIET TANKER SEMI   217 mm   1/43?   year?
Tanker semi with plastic cab and semi, white tank, clear windows, red hubs, white tires, red and black Elf logo. Value $30-40?
    1. Blue cab and semi.

B.S.

During the fifties the firm of Beuzen et Sordet made at least eighteen simple plastic models of cars (1/43 scale) and trucks (1/70), presumably for sale at low prices in variety stores. They are not high-quality scale models, and they are probably not worth very much, but they deserve to be better known–or so the one B.S. model I have would lead me to believe.

ACMA VESPA SCOOTER   ? mm   1/43?   1952
No data.

FIRE TRUCK   ? mm   1/70   1954
Large ladder. No other data.

FIRE TRUCK   ? mm   1/70   1954
Small ladder. No other data.

FIRE PUMPER   ? mm   1/70   year?
No data.

FIRE RESCUE TRUCK   ? mm   1/70   year?
No data.

FORD 1903   ? mm   1/43   1954
No data.

FORD 1903 BERGER   ? mm   1/43?   1954
No data.

CITROEN 2CV   / mm   1/43   1955
No data.

CITROEN DS19   ? mm   1/43   1956
No data.

PEUGEOT 203   ? mm   1/43   1956
No data.

PEUGEOT 403   ? mm   1/43   1956
No data.

SIMCA VERSAILLES   ? mm   1/43   1956
No data.

SIMCA ARONDE   ? mm   1/43   1957
No data.

VELAM ISETTA   ? mm   1/35   1957
No data.

ACMA VESPA 400   ? mm   1/43   1958
No data.

SIMCA ARIANE   99 mm   1/43   1959
4-door sedan with plastic body, gray chassis-grille-lights-bumpers, white plastic wheels. Value $4-8.
    1. Yellow body.

RENAULT FLORIDE   ? mm   1/43   1959
No data.

CALABUT
    Only one model made by this firm is known. It was made in the early fifties and resembles the plastic toy trucks made in the USA at that time.

CAROUSEL TRUCK   ? mm   1/?   195_
Flat truck with plastic body, merry-go-round parts and wheels. No other data. Value?

COFALU
    This firm, once thought to have made numerous diecast Tour de France models (see Salza), made at least three plastic 1/40 scale models, two of them Tour-de-France-related, in the early sixties.

PEUGEOT 203 WITH BICYCLES   ? mm   1/40   1960
No data. Value $10-20?

PEUGEOT 404 WITH BICYCLES   133 mm   1/40   1962
Sedan with plastic body, red chassis-interior and rack, three colored

bicycles. Ford France and Belgian flag labels. Value $10-20?

    1. White body.

GO-KART 59 mm 1/40 1962

Kart with plastic chassis, silver gray motor, black wheels, blue steering wheel, varying driver colors, #4 on driver. Value $10-20?

    1. Orange chassis.

D.E.L.

    This firm made a series of 1/45 scale plastic old-time car models, largely inspired by Rami and Dugu models, during the sixties. Just when I thought I had a complete list of them, one more turned up, and even more may exist. They are of fairly good quality and probably worth upwards of $10 each, but beyond that...?

CITROEN 1925 B2 85 mm 1/45 196_

4-door sedan with plastic body, seats, black chassis, roof, hood, disc wheels, and spare, gold grille and lights. Resembles Rami.

    1. Maroon body and seats.

FIAT 1899 NO. 1 ? mm 1/45 196_

Resembles Dugu. No other data.

FIAT 1902 12 HP ? mm 1/45 196_

Resembles Dugu. No other data.

FIAT 1906 F2 ? mm 1/45 196_

Resembles Dugu. No other data.

FIAT 1910 TIPO 2 ? mm 1/45 196_

Resembles Dugu. No other data.

FIAT 1926 509 TORPEDO 83 mm 1/45 196_

Tourer with plastic body, black chassis, lowered top and spoked wheels, cream seats, gold grille and windshield frame. Resembles Dugu.

    1. Maroon body.

GOBRON-BRILLIÉ 1898 DOUBLE PHAETON ? mm 1/45 196_

Resembles Rami. No other data.

LANCIA 1925 LAMBDA 89 mm 1/45 196_

4-door sedan with plastic body, black chassis, roof, interior, spoked wheels, and spare, gold grille. Resembles Dugu.

    1. Maroon body.

LEGNANO 1908 ? mm 1/45 196_

Resembles Dugu. No other data.

LION-PEUGEOT 1908 DOUBLE PHAETON 70 mm 1/45 196_

Tourer with plastic body, dark green seats, black chassis, louvers, and spoked wheels. Resembles Rami.

    1. Light gray body.

RENAULT 1902 PARIS-VIENNA 82 mm 1/45 196_

2-seat racing car with plastic body, light gray seats and grilles, black controls, lights, and spoked wheels. Resembles Safir.

    1. Red body.

VOISIN 1934 CARÉNÉ 88 mm 1/45 196_

2-door sedan with plastic body, black chassis, roof, disc wheels, and spare, maroon interior, gold grille and lights.

    1. Cream body.

DESORMEAUX

This firm produced only two 1/43 scale lead models of French antique cars in 1957 and 1958. Both models have been valuable rarities for many years.

CITROEN 5 CV 1923 70 mm 1/43 1957

Roadster with cast body, black chassis, seat, and folded top, unpainted windshield frame, grille, and lights, black disc wheels. Value $100 and up.

    1. Yellow body.

LE ZEBRE 1910 66 mm 1/43 1958

Roadster with cast body, black chassis and folded top, tan windshield frame and seat, gold grille and lights, red spoked wheels. Value $100 and up.

    1. Green body.

ERIA

This firm produced ten 1/46 scale diecast models between 1957 and 1961. I have never seen one and have no idea what they are worth.

31 PEUGEOT 403 ? mm 1/46 1957

32 RENAULT DAUPHINE ? mm 1/46 1958

33 SIMCA P60 ARONDE ? mm 1/46 1959

34 PANHARD PL17 ? mm 1/46 1960

35? RENAULT ESTAFETTE VAN ? mm 1/46 1960?
Cannot verify catalog number.

36 JAGUAR D-TYPE ? mm 1/46 1960

37 PEUGEOT 404 ? mm 1/46 1961

38 CITROEN ID19 AMBULANCE ? mm 1/46 1961

39 CITROEN ID19 BREAK ? mm 1/46 1961

FARACARS

In 1969 this firm produced a very popular model of the Indianapolis STP turbine car. It was, alas, the only Faracars model produced, and is much in demand today.

101 STP TURBINE CAR 88 mm 1/43 1969

Indianapolis racing car with cast body and chassis, black plastic seats, suspension, and parts, gray hubs, black tires. Value $75-95.

    1. Red body and chassis.

GEGE

Gege produced both 1/20 and 1/43 scale models of the same nine cars in the late fifties. I have never seen the 1/20 scale models, so I can only assume that they are similar in construction to the 1/43 items, which have plastic bodies, diecast chassis, and flywheel motors.

CITROEN DS19 116 mm 1/43 1956

4-door sedan with cast chassis, plastic body, brown interior, clear windows, silver bumpers, unpainted metal hubs, white tires. Value $60-75.

    1. Brown body, cream roof.

FORD VENDOME ? mm 1/43 1956
No data.

FORD VEDETTE ? mm 1/43 1956?
No data.

PEUGEOT 203 ? mm 1/43 1956
No data.

PEUGEOT 403 108 mm 1/43 1956
4-door sedan with cast chassis, plastic body, gray interior, clear windows, silver grille, bumpers, and headlights, red taillights, unpainted metal hubs, white tires. Value $60-75.
    1. Blue-gray body.

RENAULT FRÉGATE AMIRAL ? mm 1/43 1956
No data.

SIMCA ARONDE 99 mm 1/43 1956
4-door sedan with cast chassis, plastic body, gray interior, clear windows, silver grille, bumpers, and trim, red taillights, unpainted metal hubs, white tires. Value $60-75.
    1. Light gray body.

SIMCA TRIANON ? mm 1/43 1956?
No data.

SIMCA VERSAILLES ? mm 1/43 1956
No data.

GULLIVER
    Gulliver produced three diecast models in the late thirties and one more in 1950–and the most recent one might just be the rarest!

BERLIET BUS 151 mm 1/42? 193_
Single-deck bus with cast body and 6 hubs, rubber tires, windup motor, grille detail. Value $100 and up.
    1. Unpainted body and hubs.

BERLIET COVERED TRUCK 134 mm 1/42? 193_
Covered truck with cast cab-chassis, tipper, and 6 unpainted hubs, brown fabric cover, rubber tires, "Berliet Diesel" and grille decals. Value $75-95.
    1. Blue body, silver painted windows.

RENAULT CELTAQUATRE 103 mm 1/42? 193_
Sedan with cast body and four silver wheels. Value $100 and up.
    1. Blue body.

RENAULT 4CV ? mm 1/43? 1950
No data. Value presumably over $100.

J. E. P.
    In 1958 and 1959, J. E. P. produced a small series of five 1/43 scale cars with plastic bodies and diecast chassis. Their quality is good, and they have ranked as desirable models for many years.

1611 PANHARD DYNA 55 106 mm 1/43 1958-1959
4-door sedan with unpainted cast chassis, plastic body, red interior, clear windows and headlights, gray hubs, white tires. Value $65-75.
    1. Olive green body.
    2. Light gray body.

1612 PEUGEOT 403 104 mm 1/43 1958-1959
4-door sedan with unpainted cast chassis, plastic body, red interior, clear windows and headlights, silver grille, red taillights, gray hubs, white tires. Value $65-75.
    1. Dark gray body.

1613 SIMCA VERSAILLES 101 mm 1/43 1958-1959

4-door sedan with unpainted cast chassis, plastic body, red interior, clear windows, silver grille, red taillights, gray hubs, white tires. Value $65-75.

　　1. Yellow body, black roof.
　　2. Light gray body, ivory roof.

1614 CITROEN DS19 111 mm 1/43 1958-1959

4-door sedan with unpainted cast chassis, plastic body, red interior, clear windows and headlights, red taillights, gray hubs, white tires. Also numbered 7374. Value $65-75.

　　1. Yellow body, black roof.

1615 RENAULT DAUPHINE 90 mm 1/43 1958-1959

4-door sedan with unpainted cast chassis, plastic body, red interior, clear windows and headlights, red taillights, gray hubs, white tires. Value $65-75.

　　1. Yellow body.

J. F.

This firm produced two plastic models of Citroen racing and record cars in 1938.

CITROEN RACING CAR ? mm 1/? 1938

Open-cockpit racing car with plastic body, black wheels, tin base, windup motor. No other data.

CITROEN RECORD CAR 98 mm 1/? 1938

Closed-cockpit record car with plastic body, black wheels, gears, and hook for rubber band drive. Value $50-75.

　　1. Blue-green body.

JOUEF

Jouef has produced an assortment of plastic toy vehicles in various scales. I suspect that the list below is far from complete! More research needs to be done on Jouef, as very little is known of its products. The two versions of the Simca Aronde and the HO scale models date from the fifties; the little tractor is probably a bit newer. In the seventies Jouef made O gauge slot cars, two of which will be shown in the illustrations, as they make rather nice static models once they've been taught not to steer.

PANAMERICAINE 92 mm 1/43? 1952

4-door Simca Aronde with plastic body, black wheels, tin chassis-grille-bumpers, clockwork motor, control lever projects through slot in hood. #3 cast in body. Value?

　　1. Red body.

SIMCA ARONDE 92 mm 1/43? 1955

Same body as Americaine; no other data.

FARMALL TRACTOR 32 mm 1/? year?

Tractor with plastic body, black wheels, "Farmall" cast in body, "Jouef" in rear wheels. Value?

　　1. Red body.

CHAUSSON BUS 108 mm 1/87 195_

Single-deck bus with plastic body, red interior, silver roof rack and trim, gray chassis and wheels. Luggage on roof rack probably not original. Value $20-30?

　　1. Dark blue body.

CITROEN DS19 54 mm 1/87 195_

4-door sedan with plastic body, gray chassis-grille-bumpers, white wheels, silver headlights, red taillights. Value $15-25.

1. Gray body.

PANHARD DYNA 49 mm 1/87 195_
4-door sedan with details as above. Value $15-25.
1. Black body.

PEUGEOT 203 49 mm 1/87 195_
4-door sedan with details as above. Value $15-25.
1. Pale aqua body.
2. Pale blue body.

PEUGEOT 403 51 mm 1/87 195_
4-door sedan with details as above. Value $15-25.
1. Yellow body.

SIMCA ARIANE 50 mm 1/87 195_
4-door sedan with details as above. Value $15-25.
1. Gray-blue body.

SIMCA ARONDE 46 mm 1/87 195_
4-door sedan with details as above. Value $15-25.
1. Light gray body.

LE JOUET MÉCANIQUE

Only one model made by this firm is known; it dates from about 1955 and is a 1/45 scale diecast model with a clockwork motor.

PANHARD DYNA ? mm 1/45 ca. 1955
Sedan with cast body and clockwork motor. No other data.

JOUSTRA

It would not surprise me to learn that these Joustra models were Gama trucks made under license, as they bear a close resemblance to early Gama models. There may well be more of them.

#? MEILLER EXCAVATOR TRUCK 160 mm 1/? year?
Truck with cast chassis-cab, cabin, black shovel, cream sheet metal arm, crank, chains, yellow plastic hubs, black tires. Value $35-45?
1. Orange chassis-cab and cabin.

4002 MEILLER DUMP TRUCK 110 mm 1/? year?
Dumper with cast chassis-cab, tipper, tin tipping mechanism, cream plastic hubs, black tires. Value $35-45?
1. Orange chassis-cab, red tipper.

LAVIROLETTE

Only one Lavirolette model is known; it is a streamlined coupe, about 110 mm long, made of plastic. It is shown in "Ma Collection" No. 25 and described as being in the styling of 1939.

AERODYNAMIC COUPE ca. 110 mm 1/43? year?
No data.

LES ROULIERS

This brand, not to be confused with Les Routiers, also offers only one model, a plastic 1/43 scale Renault Étoile Filante record car.

1b RENAULT ÉTOILE FILANTE 106 mm 1/43 1961
Record car with plastic body, black chassis, red and white trim, silver hubs, white tires. Value $40-50?
1. Light blue body.

POCLAIN

The firm of Poclain makes real earth-moving equipment and, in or before 1973, also sold a series of plastic models of their own products, some, if not all, made by Bourbon, and presumably for showroom use, though Multi-Sports of Paris sold them to collectors as well. I have no idea what they are worth and can only describe the two I have and list the rest.

CG TRACK BACKHOE ? mm 1/43 ca. 1973

GY WHEEL BACKHOE ? mm 1/43 ca. 1973

GY WHEEL LOADER ? mm 1/43 ca. 1973

HC 300 TRACK BACKHOE ? mm 1/43 ca. 1973

HC 300 TRACK LOADER ? mm 1/43 ca. 1973

LC 80 TRACK EXCAVATOR ? mm 1/43 ca. 1973

LY 2P WHEEL EXCAVATOR ? mm 1/43 ca. 1973

TCB TRACK EXCAVATOR ? mm 1/43 ca. 1973

TCS TRACK EXCAVATOR ? mm 1/43 ca. 1973

TC 45 TRACK EXCAVATOR 158 mm 1/43 ca. 1973
Backhoe-type shovel with plastic cab, arms, shovel, black chassis, hubs, and treads, gray and black panels, black and red lettering. Value?
    1. Red cab, arms, and shovel.

TX WHEEL EXCAVATOR ? mm 1/43 ca. 1973

TY 45 WHEEL EXCAVATOR 122 mm 1/43 ca. 1973
Scoop-type shovel with plastic chassis, cab, rams, shovel, black wheels, gray, and black panels, black and red lettering. Value?
    1. Red chassis, cab, rams, and shovel.

TY 5 TRACK EXCAVATOR ? mm 1/43 ca. 1973

P.R.
The firm of P.R. made two diecast advertising vans that were already highly desirable collectors' items when I added them to my collection almost thirty years ago. They were made in 1957 and 1958, and represent publicity vehicles associated with the Tour de France bicycle race. They must certainly have three-figure values today.

SAVON LE CHAT VAN 99 mm 1/43 1957-1958
Unusually styled van with cast body, black tin chassis, yellow plastic block with white cat figure, clear windows, unpainted metal hubs, black tires, red trim. Value over $100.
    1. Green and yellow body, white front and rear.

WATERMAN INK VAN 108 mm 1/43 1957-1958
Streamlined van with cast body, black tin chassis, unpainted metal hubs, black tires, silver grille, multicolored cast-in logo. Value over $100.
    1. Cream body, blue bumpers.

PRIMO
This firm made a plastic model of a Renault Frégate sedan that was depicted in an issue of "Ma Collection." This appears to be all that is known of this manufacturer.

RENAULT FRÉGATE 1951 83 mm 1/45? 195_
Sedan with plastic body and wheels. No other data.

RHODANIENNE
The only Rhodanienne model I know of is a one-piece (and I do mean one-piece!) aluminum casting, including non-turning wheels, of a civilian or military ambulance. It is more of a paperweight than a

model vehicle, and I have no idea what it is worth.

AMBULANCE 84 mm 1/? year?
Ambulance with cast aluminum body including wheels, red painted crosses, painted windows and hubs. Value?
    1. Silver body, white windows?
    2. Olive body, silver windows and hubs.

ROLUX
Rolux made lead models of an American-type fastback of World War II vintage and the same vehicle as an army staff car. All my information on them comes from "Ma Collection."

LIMOUSINE ? mm 1/42? 194_
Fastback with lead body, aluminum chassis, rubber wheels, silver grille and bumpers. Value?
    1. Color unknown.

ARMY STAFF CAR ? mm 1/42? 194_
Same model as above in military livery. No other data.

SALZA
Salza is the brand that many of us assumed was Cofalu until we were enlightened. Both brands make Tour de France models, but while Cofalu models are made of plastic, Salza models are rather crudely cast in aluminum. Apparently the same models are made year after year and sold only in conjunction with the Tour de France. Some of them include wire racks holding cast bicycles. "Ma Collection" includes thorough information on this series.

ASPRO AMBULANCE 114 mm 1/42? year?
Van-type ambulance with cast body, black chassis and wheels, silver painted hubs, "Aspro Service Sanitaire" logo. Value?
    1. White body.

JEEP WITH BICYCLES 90 mm 1/40 year?
Open Jeep with cast body and cycles, wire rack, plastic driver, black wheels, silver painted hubs. Value?
    1. White body.

GENDARMERIE JEEP 90 mm 1/40? year?
Same casting as above. No other data. Value?

PRESS JEEP 90 mm 1/40? year?
Same casting as above. No other data. Value?

PEUGEOT 203 CONVERTIBLE 134 mm 1/36? year?
Convertible with cast body, rack, cycles, black plastic wheels, silver painted hubs, two flags, "L'Equipe" and Union Jack logo. Value?
    1. White body and rack.

PEUGEOT 404 SEDAN 135 mm 1/40? year?
Sedan with cast body, cycles, black chassis and wheels, silver painted hubs, "Wiel's Groene Leeuw" and "L'Equipe" logo. Value?
    1. White body.

PEUGEOT D4A VAN 101 mm 1/42? year?
Van with cast body, black chassis and wheels, silver painted hubs, various logo types. Value?
    1. Gray body, "L'Equipe," "Spar," "Rokado," and other advertising.
    2. Other logo types include Bianchi, BIC, Brooklin, Flandria, GAN, Gitanes, KAS, Keshol, Molteni, Peugeot, SCIC, Super Ser, Watney.

PEUGEOT D4A LOUDSPEAKER VAN 101 mm 1/42? year?
Same van as above with blue plastic speakers, white signboards.
Value?
  1. Yellow body, "Voiture Balai," "L'Equipe," "Gilac," and other advertising.

SHELL
Since this model uses a familiar trade mark, I assume it was made for promotional purposes. It would not surprise me to learn that there were more of them.

FERRARI V8 FORMULA I 95 mm 1/43? year?
Racing car with plastic body, black chassis, white driver, silver intakes and exhausts, clear windshield, racing number labels. Value $5-10?
  1. Red body.

MAKERS UNKNOWN
This list covers a multitude of models and eras, from pre-war celluloid to post-war plastic. I have some of the listed models, have borrowed others, and can only refer to "Ma Collection" for information on the rest. As for their values, I'd rather not guess!

SPORTS COUPE 84 mm 1/43? prewar?
Coupe with celluloid body, 4 wooden wheels, silver grille, windows, and spare.
  1. Pink body.

BUGATTI LE MANS 84 mm 1/43? prewar?
Sports car with celluloid body, 4 black wheels, silver grille and louvers.
  1. Light blue body.

BUGATTI FORMULA I 95 mm 1/40? 1956?
Racing car with plastic body including base, black and silver plastic wheels. Model of front-engined car vaguely like 1956 8-cylinder Gordini, but labeled Bugatti–as the 1956 Bugatti appeared so rarely, maybe someone didn't notice it was rear-engined!
  1. Blue body.

CISITALIA-PORSCHE 105 mm 1/40? Fifties?
Racing car with plastic body (may have included base), black and silver plastic wheels.
  1. Red paint over blue plastic body.

CITROEN 2CV VAN ? mm 1/50? year?
Light van with plastic body and wheels too big for it. No other data.

JEEP 75 mm 1/43? year?
Open Jeep with plastic body, windshield frame, steering wheel, wheels, and spare.
  1. All parts dark green.

PEUGEOT 203 ca. 100 mm 1/40? year?
Fastback sedan with plastic body, presumably plastic hubs. Not a good model of a Peugeot 203, but looks more like it than like anything else. No other data.

RENAULT 1908 101 mm 1/43 year?
Old-time town car with plastic body, hood, black chassis, roof, and seats, golden brown radiator, yellow spoked hubs, black tires and spare. Glued together; appears to be a kit model.
  1. Yellow body and hood.

RENAULT DAUPHINOISE VAN ? mm 1/50? year?
Light van, presumably by same maker as the Citroen van above,

likewise with plastic body and too-big wheels. No other data.

RENAULT FRÉGATE   104 mm   1/40?   year?
Sedan with plastic body, black chassis, white wheels, cream painted grille, lights, and bumpers.
> 1. Light blue body.

RENAULT FRÉGATE AMIRAL   ? mm   1/43?   year?
Sedan with sheet metal body and chassis, metal hubs and white tires. No other data.

SIMCA 9 ARONDE   84 mm   1/50?   year?
Sedan with plastic body and mottled wheel-axle units.
> 1. Orange body.

SIMCA P60 ARONDE   ? mm   1/43   1958 or later
Sedan with plastic body, white wheels, two-tone paint, closed windows. No other data.

TALBOT COUPE   ? mm   1/?   year?
Streamlined sports coupe with rubber body. Something of the kind was available in the USA some years ago, but was not made in France.

FASTBACK SEDAN   89 mm   1/?   year?
Four-door fastback with celluloid body, black wheels, "Au Chrrdon Bleu, 32 Rue Alex. Roche, Roanne" lettering on roof.
> 1. Yellow body, black trim, silver grille.

FOUR-SEAT ROADSTER   121 mm   1/?   year?
Open four-seater with celluloid body, wooden wheels, silver trim, "GG 11" license.
> 1. Blue-gray body.

SPORTS COUPE   97 mm   1/?   year?
Coupe with celluloid body, wooden wheels, silver trim, "R 66" license.
> 1. Green body.

SEDAN   107 mm   1/?   year?
Sedan with celluloid body, wooden chassis, metal hubs, rubber tires, cream trim.
> 1. Red body.

SMALL SCALE MODELS

There were a few French firms that specialized in small-scale models, some of them approximately 1/87 (HO) scale, some even smaller. The smallest models, those by Gitanes, are the least known.

GITANES
These little models appear to date from the late fifties, and may have been produced for promotional uses. Nobody seems to know how many there were, so I can only list the four I have. I have no idea what they are worth.

ASTON MARTIN   46 mm   1/?   year?
Sports-racing car with cast body, red seat, unpainted chassis and wheels, racing number.
> 1. Metallic green body.

CITROEN 2CV   37 mm   1/?   year?
Sedan with cast body, unpainted chassis and wheels, silver grille, lights, and bumper.
> 1. Gray body.

GORDINI FORMULA I 43 mm 1/? year?
Racing car with cast body, red seat, unpainted chassis and wheels, racing number.
    1. Metallic blue body.

RENAULT MAIL VAN 45 mm 1/? year?
Van with cast body, unpainted base, green wheels, silver grille, lights, and bumper.
    1. Green body.

JADALI

In addition to a series of HO scale diecast models rather reminiscent of early Matchbox vehicles, Jadali made two Seat cars–the Spanish branch of Fiat, perhaps for sale in Spain–and two 1/43 scale old-time cars which were later produced by Jadali's successor, Safir.

50 TRACTOR WITH TIPPER ? mm 1/86 1957
No data.

51 ESSO TANK TRUCK 51 mm 1/86 1957
Tanker with cast body and unpainted wheels, gold grille and headlights, Esso decals. Value $30-40.
    1. Red body.

52 DUMP TRUCK ? mm 1/86 1957
No data.

53 EXCAVATOR ? mm 1/86 1957
No data.

54 DUMP TRUCK ? mm 1/86 1958
No data.

55 AIR COMPRESSOR TRUCK 46 mm 1/86 1958
Truck with cast body and unpainted wheels, silver painted parts. Value $30-40.
    1. Yellow body.

56 ROAD ROLLER 53 mm 1/86 1958
Roller with cast body, light gray plastic rollers, gold driver and panels. Value $30-40.
    1. Orange body.

57 BULLDOZER ? mm 1/86 1958
No data.

58 CATERPILLAR TRACTOR ? mm 1/86 1958
No data.

#? SEAT 1957 ? mm 1/86 1958
No data.

#? SEAT 1400 1957 ? mm 1/86 1958
No data.

#? FORD MODEL T 77 mm 1/43 1957
Roadster with cast body, black chassis, black plastic folded top, gold grille, windshield frame, and front axle, black rear axle, gold spoked hubs, black tires. Value $75-100.
    1. Red body.

#? RENAULT 1902 PARIS-VIENNA ? mm 1/43 1958
No data. See Safir #7 for its successor.

LES ROUTIERS
All fourteen 1/90 scale Les Routiers models were produced in 1959.

They may well be worth as much as $50 apiece today, but that is just a guess on my part. The Byrrh tank truck, built like a wine barrel on wheels, certainly should be worth more. The names of some models are just a bit mystifying.

1 PANHARD TANK TRUCK   ? mm   1/90   1959
No data.

2 UNIC SEMI-TRAILER   ? mm   1/90   1959
No data.

3 BERLIET DUMP TRUCK   57 mm   1/90   1959
Dumper with cast cab-chassis and tipper, gray wheels, silver grille.
    1. Yellow cab-chassis, light blue tipper.

4 CITROEN WRECKER   57/69 mm   1/90   1959
Wrecker with cast body, rear bed, unpainted boom, gray wheels, silver grille.
    1. Red body, light blue rear bed.

5 CITROEN DUMP TRUCK   58 mm   1/90   1959
Dumper with cast cab-chassis, tipper, gray wheels, silver grille.
    1. Green cab-chassis, yellow tipper.

6 CATERPILLAR DUMPING TRACTOR   ? mm   1/90   1959
No data.

7 RICHIER ROAD ROLLER   52 mm   1/90   1959
Roller with cast body, front wheel mount, roof, unpainted rollers.
    1. Green body and mount, brown roof.

8 CATERPILLAR ROAD GRADER   ? mm   1/90   1959
No data.

9 CATERPILLAR QUARRY BUCKET   ? mm   1/90   1959
No data.

10 TRACTOMOTIVE EXCAVATOR   ? mm   1/90   1959
No data.

11 RENAULT BYRRH TANK TRUCK   52 mm   1/90   1959
Tanker with cast body, gray wheels, silver grille and lights, blue and white "Byrrh" decals. Value over $50.
    1. Red body.

12 RENAULT ÉTOILE FILANTE   ? mm   1/90   1959
No data.

13 BUS   ? mm   1/90   1959
No data.

14 MOBILE CRANE   ? mm   1/90   1959
No data.

MIDGET TOYS

With one exception, Midget Toys were made to 1/86 scale; the Vespa 400 was also made to 1/43 scale, but as it is a model of a very small car, it is not so very big. All the Midget Toys were made in 1959, and presumably they all had numbers, but I have only been able to determine about half of them. Once again, I can only guess at their values and say that the 1/86 models should be worth $30 to $45 and the 1/43 Vespa something over $50.

1 FLAT TRUCK   55 mm   1/86   1959
Flatbed with cast cab, bed, and silver wheels.
    1. Red cab, olive bed.

2 LUMBER SEMI-TRAILER TRUCK 90 mm 1/86 1959
Log semi with cast cab, semi, and silver wheels. Did it carry a load originally?
    1. Green cab, olive semi.

3 QUARRY DUMP TRUCK 57 mm 1/86 1959
Dumper with cast cab-chassis, tipper, and silver wheels.
    1. Red cab-chassis, gray tipper.

4 FARM TRACTOR 57 mm 1/86 1959
Tractor with cast body, silver and black wheels.
    1. Green body.

5 OPEN SEMI-TRAILER TRUCK 72 mm 1/86 1959
Open semi with cast cab, semi, and silver wheels.
    1. Tan cab, gray semi.

6 DYNA-PANHARD 57 mm 1/86 1959
Sedan with cast body, silver chassis, wheels, and bumpers.
    1. Dull aqua body.

14 CRANE TRUCK 56 mm 1/86 1959
Truck with cast cab, chassis, swiveling boom, and wheels, wire hook.
    1. Gray cab, chassis, and boom.

#? DYNA-PANHARD CONVERTIBLE ? mm 1/86 1959
No data.

#? CITROEN DS19 56 mm 1/86 1959
Sedan with cast body, silver chassis, wheels, and bumpers.
    1. Green body, cream roof.

#? JAGUAR D-TYPE 46 mm 1/86 1959

Sports-racing car with cast body, chassis, silver wheels, silver and white driver's number decal.
    1. Dark green body and chassis.

#? TRANSFORMER SEMI-TRAILER 90 mm 1/86 1959
Flat semi with cast cab, semi, gray and cream transformer, silver wheels.
    1. Red cab, silver semi.

#? 3-AXLE SEMI-TRAILER ? mm 1/86 1959
No data.

#? VANWALL FORMULA I 46 mm 1/86 1959
Racing car with cast body, chassis, silver wheels and exhaust pipes, silver and white driver, number decal.
    1. Dark green body and chassis.

#? VESPA 400 45 mm 1/86 1959
Mini-car with cast body, silver chassis, wheels, bumpers, and lights, cream and/or silver interior.
    1. Light olive body.
    2. Blue body.

#? VESPA 400 65 mm 1/43 1959
Same car as above with cast body, silver chassis, wheels, bumpers, and lights, cream and silver interior.
    1. Light olive body.
    2. Blue body.

EPILOGUE: J. P. CARS

    In the seventies a French enthusiast, Jean Pastre of Niort, resurrected the time-honored practice of making miniature cars of plaster and flour. Some of the models had metal chassis, and the first one on the list is made entirely of metal, while at least one is made of resin. Many of them seem to have been based on pre-war models by firms such as C.I.J. and J.R.D., but others appear to have been M. Pastre's own creations, though I do not have enough information on old-time plaster models to say for sure. These models were available directly from M. Pastre, and I think they make an ideal conclusion to this book, for they bring us back to more or less where we began.

1 DELAHAYE 235 COACH
Metal body. No other data.

10 DELAHAYE 235 COACH
Resin body. No other data.

11 DELAHAYE RACING CAR 97 mm
Racing car with plaster body, wooden wheels, silver grille and lights, blue driver.
    1. Red body.
    2. Blue body.

12 BUGATTI LE MANS "TANK" 99 mm
Sports-racing car with plaster body, silver hubs, black tires and grille, white driver.
    1. Blue body.

13 MASERATI RACING CAR 90 mm
Racing car with plaster body, silver hubs, black tires, black grille, silver exhaust pipes, brown driver.
    1. Red body.

14 RACING CAR 93 mm
Racing car with plaster body, black wheels, silver grille, brown driver.
    1. Blue body.

15 PEUGEOT 402 CABRIOLET 116 mm
Convertible with plaster body, metal hubs, black tires, spare wheel, cast-in driver and passenger, gray folded top, silver grille.
    1. Tan body.

16 BARCLAY CAR
I assume this was based on an American model by Barclay.

17 CITROEN TRACTION AVANT COUPE
No data.

18 CITROEN PETITE ROSALIE 85 mm
Record car with plaster body, black wheels, silver grille, brown seat cover and driver.
    1. Dark green body.

19 CITROEN ROSALIE VI 82 mm
Sports-racing car with plaster body, black wheels and grille, blue and brown driver, brown seat cover and hood strap.
    1. Dark blue body.

20 CITROEN P45
6-wheel truck tractor? No data.

21 CITROEN C4 ROADSTER 85 mm
Convertible with plaster body, metal chassis, black wheels, light gray folded top, silver radiator shell with black grille, brown driver and passenger.
    1. Green body, black chassis.

22 CITROEN C4 ROADSTER MOTEUR FLOTTANT 85 mm
Same basic model as #21 but with silver Citroen grille.
    1. Dark green body, black chassis.

23 CITROEN C4 FALSE CABRIOLET

24 CITROEN C4 SEDAN 90 mm
4-door sedan with plaster body, metal chassis, black wheels and spare, black roof, clear windows, silver grille.
    1. Dark blue body, black chassis.

25 CITROEN C4 FIRE TRUCK
No data.

26 CITROEN C4 BARREL TRUCK 87 mm
Flat truck with plaster body, metal chassis, black wheels, 3 tan barrels, clear windows, silver grille.
    1. Dark green body, black chassis.

27 CITROEN C4 LIVESTOCK TRUCK 91 mm
Stake truck with plaster body, metal chassis, black wheels, clear windows, silver grille, 3 pink pigs.
    1. Dark blue cab, tan rear body, black chassis.

28 CITROEN C4 FARM TRUCK
No data.

29 CITROEN P45 FLAT TRUCK WITH SACKS
No data.

30 CITROEN P45 CABLE TRUCK
No data.

31 CITROEN P45 MILK TRUCK
No data.

32 RENAULT 14/18 ARMY TANK
No data.

33 RENAULT NERVASPORT 96 mm
Record car with plaster body, spoked plastic hubs, black tires, silver windows, orange grille, blue-on-white name decal.
    1. Green body.

34 RENAULT FIRE TRUCK 98 mm
Fire truck with plaster body, ladder, metal chassis, tin racks, black wheels, 2 cast-in firemen, 2 white hose reels, silver grille.
    1. Red body, chassis, and ladder

35 RENAULT STREET SPRINKLER 92 mm
Truck with plaster body, metal chassis, black wheels, silver grille and windows, black filler cap.
    1. Green body, black chassis.

36 RENAULT BREWERY TRUCK 90 mm
Truck with plaster body, metal chassis (mine appears to be non-original, likewise the wheels), clear windows, silver grille.
    1. Red body, yellow, and black bottle cases.

37 RENAULT COAL TRUCK 90 mm
Truck with plaster body, metal chassis, black wheels, clear windows, silver grille, brown bags of black coal.
    1. Dark blue body, black chassis.

38 RENAULT OPEN TRUCK 90 mm
Truck with plaster body, metal chassis, black wheels, clear windows, silver grille, tan rear interior.
    1. Dark green body, black chassis.

39 RENAULT FLAT TRUCK WITH BARRELS
Truck with plaster body, metal chassis, load of barrels. No other data.

40 CITROEN C4 TANK TRUCK

Presumably similar to above in construction. No other data.

41 CITROEN P45 WRECKER

Presumably similar to above in construction. No other data.

42 CITROEN P45 FIRE AMBULANCE 104 mm

Closed van with plaster body and chassis, metal hubs, white tires, black and silver grille, silver windows.
>   1. Red body and chassis.

101 CITROEN U23 FIRE TRUCK 126 mm

Tanker with plaster body and chassis, silver plastic ladder, red metal racks, red and white cast metal hose reels, white hose, black wheels, black interior, silver lights.
>   1. Red body and chassis.

102 CITROEN U23 OPEN TRUCK

No data.

PRICE GUIDE

Please regard this guide as a guide and nothing more. The values given are for mint boxed models; for mint unboxed models, subtract about 10%; for non-mint models, subtract an appropriate portion of the value. Two prices will be given, when possible, to set a range within which a model might be valued. Please realize that different color or logo variations of the same model can have very different values. And please do not expect models listed in this guide to be priced within the figures stated here; every individual has his or her own opinion of what a model is worth–so please do not accuse anyone of overcharging you if that person's price is higher than what is given here. That person may well know more about the value of that model than I do.

EARLY BRANDS

A.R. cars: $100 and up.
A.R. Peugeot 301 trucks: $75-100.
A.R. other models: probably $100 and up.
C.D. cars and trucks: $100 and up.
Citroen: $100 and up.
S.R. small models:$15-30; others: ?

C.I.J.

Plaster and flour models: $50 and up.
Aircraft, smaller: $40-60.
Aircraft, larger: $75-100.
Renault Viva: $100 and up.
3/1 De Rovin: $75-95.
3/2 Étoile Filante: $80-95.
3/3 Facel Vega: $75-95.
3/4 Citroen Estate Car: $75-95.
3/5 Panhard Dyna Junior: $75-95.
3/6 Citroen Ami 6: $50-65.
3/7 Simca 1000: $50-65.
3/8 Simca 1000 Police: $50-65.
3/9 Simca 1000 Bertone: $50-65.
3/10 Volkswagen: $60-75.

3/12 Mercedes-Benz 220: $60-75.
3/13 Peugeot 404: $50-65.
3/15 Chrysler Windsor: $125-150.
3/16 Plymouth Belvedere: $125-150.
3/20 Panhard BP Tanker: $60-75.
3/21 Renault Shell Tanker: $60-75.
3/23 Berliet GLR Tanker: $70-80.
3/24 Berliet Shell Tanker: $75-85.
3/25 Renault Covered Truck: $50-65.
3/26 Renault Covered Trailer: $40-50.
3/27 Caravan Trailer: $50-65.
3/28 Cattle Trailer: $50-65.
3/30 Fire Engine: $100-125.
3/31 Sugar Beet Trailer: $50-65.
3/32 Seed Trailer: $50-65.
3/33 Renault Tractor: $100-125.
3/34 Renault Tractor & Trailer: $150-175.
3/35 Water Tank Trailer: $50-65.
3/36 Sling Cart Trailer: $50-65.
3/37 Tipping Trailer: $50-65.
3/38 Tractor and Tipping Trailer: $150-175.
3/39 Tractor and Sling Cart: $150-175.
3/40 Renault Bus: $75-95.
3/41 Citroen Ambulance: $85-95.

3/42 Renault Prairie: $50-60.
3/43 Renault Savane: $50-60.
3/44 Renault Colorale: $50-60.
3/45 Renault Prairie Taxi: $50-60.
3/46 Peugeot 403 Break: $50-65.
3/46E Peugeot 403 Ambulance: $75-85.
3/46H Peugeot 403 Break: $50-65.
3/46P Peugeot 403 Police: $50-65.
3/47 Panhard Dyna: $60-75.
3/48 Renault 4CV: $60-75.
3/49 Renault 4CV Police: $65-75.
3/50 Renault Alpine: $50-65.
3/51 Renault Frégate: $50-65.
3/52 Renault Grand Pavois: $50-65.
3/53 Renault Domane: $50-65.
3/53A Renault Domane Ambulance: $70-85.
3/54 Panhard Dyna: $50-65.
3/54T Panhard Taxi: $60-75.
3/55 Renault Colorale Ambulance: $70-85.
3/56 Renault Dauphine: $50-65.
3/56T Renault Dauphine Taxi: $50-65.
3/57 Renault Dauphine Police: $50-65.
3/58 Renault Floride: $50-65.
3/60 Renault Van, plain: $50-60.
3/60 Primistere Van: $85-95.
3/60A Astra Van: $85-95.
3/60B Boucherie Van: $85-95.
3/60P French Mail Van: $85-95.
3/60P German & Belgian Mail Vans: $120-130.
3/60S Shell Van: $85-95.
3/60T Renault Van & Trailer: $110-120.
3/61 Renault Ambulance: $110-115.
3/61M Renault Army Ambulance: $100-115.
3/62 Renault SNCF Bus: $85-95.
3/62N Nettoyer Van: $85-95.
3/63 Renault Police Van: $75-85.
3/65 Renault Police & Trailer: $100-110.
3/66 Renault Dauphinoise: $50-60.
3/67 Renault 300 KG Van: $50-60.
3/68 Renault Mail Van: $65-75.
3/68PB Belgian Mail Van: $95-110.
3/69 Renault Police Car: $60-75.
3/70 Renault Semi: $75-85.
3/72 Renault Shell Tanker: $100-110.
3/73 Renault Logger Semi: $80-90.
3/75 Renault Atomic Transporter: $175-195.

3/76 Citroen 2CV Mail Van: $75-85.
3/76A Sailboat Trailer: $50-60.
3/77 Berliet Semi: $100-120.
3/78 Unic & Railroad Car: $125-150.
3/79 Saviem Bottle Truck: ?
3/80 Renault Dump Truck: $75-85.
3/81 Renault/Saviem Crane: $85-95.
3/82 Renault/Saviem Shovel: $85-95.
3/83 Renault Wrecker: $85-95.
3/84 Berliet Mobile Crane: $90-100.
3/88 Renault Excavator: ?
3/89 Citroen Police Van: $60-75.
3/89B Citroen Brandt Van: $85-95.
3/90 Renault Estafette: $65-75.
3/91 Renault Police Van: $70-80.
3/92 Renault Estafette Bus: $65-75.
3/93 Renault Police Bus: $70-80.
3/94 Renault Bottle Truck: $90-100.
3/95 Renault Fire Engine: $110-125.
3/96 Renault Searchlight & Trailer: $100-110.
3/97 Saviem Missile Launcher: $90-100.
3/98 Renault Radar Truck: $90-100.
3/99 Renault Gun Truck: $90-100.
3/? Farm Tractor: $110-125.
4/20 Panhard BP Tanker: $75-85.
4/21 Renault Shell Tanker: $75-85.
4/30 Fire Engine: $125-150.
4/42 Renault Prairie: $65-75.
4/43 Renault Savane: $65-75.
4/44 Renault Colorale: $65-75.
4/45 Renault Prairie Taxi: $65-75.
4/47 Panhard Dyna: $70-80.
4/48 Renault 4CV: $70-80.
4/50 Renault Cattle Truck: $75-85.
4/51 Renault Frégate: $60-70.
4/68 Saviem Army Tanker: $90-100.
4/69 Saviem Shell Tanker: $110-125.
4/70 Saviem Mobil Tanker: $110-125.
4/71 Saviem BP Tanker: $110-125.
4/72 Somua Transformer Carrier: $110-125.
4/73 Saviem Cement Truck: $85-95.
4/74 Saviem Army Truck: $80-90.
4/75 Saviem Cable Carrier: $100-115.
4/76 Saviem Covered Truck: $75-85.
4/77 Berliet Covered Trailer: $40-50.
4/78 Saviem Dump Truck: $75-85.

4/80 Saviem Dump Truck: $75-85.
4/81 Berliet Garbage Truck: $90-100.
4/84 Sand Bin: ?
Accessories and Sets: ?
Micro Series: $35-50 each.

CLE

Series of 25: $5-10 each.
Other Modem Cars: $5-10 each.
1/90 Scale Trucks: $4-8 each.
Sports & Racing Cars: $4-8 each.
La Belle Epoque: $4-8 each.

FRANCE JOUETS

100 Series Berliet: $60-75 each.
200 Series Pacific: $100 and up.
300 Series GMC Trucks: $60-75 each.
400 Series Dodge Trucks: $60-75 each.
500 Series Jeeps: $50-65 each.
600 Jeeps & Trailers: $60-75 each.
700 Series Stradair Trucks: $60-75 each.

JRD

Plaster and Flour Models: ?
106 Citroen Police Van: $60-75.
107 Citroen Red Cross Van: $75-85.
108 Citroen EDF Van: $60-75.
109 Citroen Fire Van: $80-90.
110 Citroen 2CV: $60-75.
111 Citroen 2CV Van: $50-70.
112 Citroen 11CV: $75-85.
113 Citroen Esso Van: $85-95.
114 Citroen Covered Truck: $60-70.
115 Citroen Army Truck & Trailer: $75-85.
116 Citroen DS19: $65-75.
117 Citroen Road Service: $75-85.
118 Citroen Air France Van: $75-85.
120 Berliet Kronenbourg Semi: $150-175.
121 Berliet Total Tanker Semi: $150-165.
122 Unic Antar Tanker: $125-135.
123 Unic & Railroad Car: $175-200.
124 Unic Circus Train: $175-200.
125 Berliet Weitz Crane: $120-135.
126 Unic Hafa Van: $150-165.
127 Unic Transports Internationaux: $150-165.

128 Unic Milk Tanker: $140-150.
129 Fruehauf Trailer: $100-110.
130 Unic Liquid Transporter: $125-135.
131 Berliet Garbage Truck: $125-135.
132 Berliet Antargaz Semi: $140-150.
133 Berliet Fire Truck: $150-165.
134 Berliet Bottle Truck: $140-150.
151 Peugeot 404: $50-65.
152 Citroen DS19 Cabriolet: $50-65.
153 Mercedes-Benz 220S: $50-65.
154 Citroen Ami-6: $50-60.
155 Simca 1000: $50-60.
Reissues: Market prices.

MINIALUXE

Tacots Old-timers: $5-10 each.
C-2 Berliet Bus: $15-20.
S Series Cars: $5-10 each, except:
S-1 Siata-Fiat: $10-15.
S-2 BMW 1500: $10-15.
S-3 Simca 1300: $8-12.
S-4 Ford Consul: $8-12.
S-5 Peugeot 204: $8-12.
Other Cars: $5-10 each, except:
Citroen DS19: $8-12.
Citroen 11CV: $10-15.
Ford Anglia: $8-12.
Ford Taunus: $8-12.
Gordini Formula 1: $10-15.
Hotchkiss-Gregoire: $40-50.
Jaguar D-Type: $10-15.
Mercedes-Benz Formula 1: $10-15.
Panhard PL17: $10-15.
Panhard PL17 Cabriolet: $10-15.
Peugeot 203 Break: $10-15.
Peugeot 403: $8-12.
Peugeot 404: $8-12.
Renault Floride Coupe: $10-15.
Renault Ondine: $8-12.
Renault Ondine Police: $8-12.
Simca 9 Aronde: $8-12.
Simca Oceane: $8-12.
Simca Plein Ciel: $8-12.
Vespa: $8-12.
Minibus: $10-15.

Somua Paris Bus: $15-20.
Specials and Sets: $5-15 each.

NOREV

1 Simca Aronde: $45-55.
1 Opel Rekord: $10-15.
2 Ford Vedette: $30-40.
2 Citroen Ami 6: $12-16.
3 Citroen 15CV: $50-60.
3 Renault 16: $6-12.
4 Panhard Dyna: $35-45.
4 Panhard PL17: $25-35.
5 Renault 4CV: $35-45.
5 Simca Elysée: $30-40.
5 Peugeot 204: $5-10.
6 Simca Versailles: $35-45.
6 Peugeot 201: $15-25.
7 Simca Trianon: $30-40.
7 Peugeot J7 Van: $20-30.
8 Peugeot 203: $35-45.
8 Peugeot 1927: $15-20.
9 Peugeot 403: $30-40.
9 Renault 10: $10-15.
10 Citroen DS19: $35-45.
10 Renault Juvaquatre: $15-25.
11 Renault Grands Pavois: $30-40.
11 Renault Amiral: $30-40.
11 Alfa Romeo Giulietta: $20-30.
12 Mercedes-Benz Formula 1: $35-45.
12 Maserati 200S: $20-25.
13 Renault Dauphine: $30-40.
13 Mercedes-Benz Formula 1: $30-40.
14 Ford Vedette Ambulance: $35-45.
14 Peugeot 203: $35-45.
14 Renault Gordini: $8-15.
14 Renault 8: $8-12.
15 Citroen 15 Police: $55-65.
15 Peugeot 403: $30-35.
16 Citroen 2CV Van: $30-40.
16 Porsche Carrera: $25-35.
17 Jaguar 2.4: $25-30.
17 Renault 4CV: $25-30.
18 Simca Plein Ciel: $25-30.
18 Vespa 400: $20-25.
18 Monteverdi: $8-12.

19 Simca Oceane: $25-30.
19 Jaguar X: $20-25.
20 Maserati 200S: $20-25.
20 Fiat Jardinière: $10-15.
21 Porsche Carrera: $30-35.
21 Peugeot with Skis: $40-45.
21 Simca Miramas: $35-40.
21 Mercedes-Benz 250SE: $10-15.
22 Panhard with Skis: $40-45.
22 Lancia Aurelia: $25-30.
22 Simca Aronde: $20-25.
22 Volkswagen 1600TL: $10-15.
22 Chrysler 180: $8-12.
23 Renault Grand Pavois: $35-40.
23 Simca 1937: $20-25.
24 Jaguar 2.4: $25-30.
24 Simca 5 1936: $20-25.
25 Lancia Aurelia: $25-30.
25 Peugeot J7 Bus: $20-25.
26 Citroen 2CV Van: $20-40.
27 Citroen 2CV: $20-25.
27 Citroen SM: $6-12.
28 Peugeot 404 Break: $5-10.
29 Panhard PL17: $10-15.
29 Citroen 11A: $20-25.
30 Simca 1300: $8-12.
31 DAF Variomatic: $8-12.
32 Simca Oceane: $20-25.
32 Peugeot 204 Break: $5-10.
33 Simca Plein Ciel: $25-30.
33 Rolls-Royce Silver Shadow: $15-20.
34 Ford Vedette Wrecker: $25-30.
35 Ford Vedette Wrecker: $25-30.
35 Simca Versailles: $30-35.
35 Citroen Rosalie: $20-25.
36 Fiat 1000-D: $10-15.
37 DKW Junior: $10-15.
38 Fiat 2300: $10-15.
39 Simca Beaulieu: $25-30.
39 Panhard 1927: $20-25.
40 Simca Chambord: $20-25.
40 Citroen ID19: $20-25.
41 Simca Marly Ambulance: $25-30.
42 Renault Estafette: $20-30.
43 Ford Taunus: $10-15.
44 Volvo P-1800: $10-15.
45 Fiat 1500: $8-12.

46 Citroen 1922: $20-25.
47 Chrysler New Yorker: $25-35.
47 Simca 1501: $8-12.
48 Citroen DS19 1960: $25-35.
48 Citroen DS19 1963: $20-25.
49 Mercedes-Benz 220SE: $10-15.
50 Renault Ondine: $20-25.
50 Renault Dauphine: $15-20.
51 Peugeot 404: $8-12.
52 Renault Floride: $15-25.
53 Renault 4L: $8-12.
54 Citroen Ami 6: $10-15.
55 Renault Estafette Bus: $10-15.
56 Citroen AZ-Luxe: $8-12.
56 Citroen 2CV6: $5-10.
57 Simca 1000: $5-10.
57 Simca 1000 Rally: $10-15.
58 Lancia Flaminia: $10-15.
59 Alpine A110: $5-10.
59A Alpine Police: $5-10.
60 BMW 700LS: $8-12.
61 Fiat 600: $8-12.
62 Volkswagen 1200: $8-12.
62 Volkswagen 1300: $8-12.
63 Volkswagen 1500: $8-12.
64 Opel Kapitän: $10-15.
65 Renault R4 Van: $20-30.
66 Fiat 1500 Cabriolet: $10-15.
67 Ford Anglia: $8-12.
68 Renault R8: $8-15.
68 Renault Gordini: $5-10.
69 Corvair Monza: $25-30.
70 BMW 2002: $10-15.
71 Peugeot 404: $10-15.
72 Penhard 24CT: $10-15.
73 Simca 1000: $8-12.
74 Ford Consul: $8-12.
75 Morris Mini-Minor: $10-20.
76 Panhard PL17: $10-15.
77 Ford Taunus 12M: $8-12.
78 Renault NN1: $15-20.
79 Simca 1500: $8-12.
80 Fiat 2300 Coupe: $8-12.
21 Citroen 1200 KG Van: $20-30.
22 Citroen 2CV Van: $20-30.
83 Morris 1100: $8-12.

84 Ford Cortina: $8-12.
85 Panhard 24BT: $10-15.
86 Simca 1500 Break: $10-15.
87 Citroen ID19 Break: $10-15.
88 Citroen ID 19 Cabriolet: $20-25.
89 Austin 1100: $8-12.
90 MG 1100: $10-15.
91 Simca & Henon Caravan: $20-25.
92 Chrysler & Boat Trailer: $35-45.
92 Fiat or Simca & Boat Trailer: $10-15.
93 Peugeot & Digue Caravan: $10-15.
93 Corvair & Digue Caravan: $35-45.
94 Renault Estafette Bus: $30-40.
94 Simca & Voilier Trailer: $10-15.
95 Berliet Auto Transporter: $15-20.
96 Transporter & 5 Cars: $50-75.
97 Berliet Ladder Truck: $10-15.
98 Saviem Bus: $10-15.
99 Car & Henon Caravan: $10-15.
100 Saviem Cattle Truck: $15-20.
101 Saviem Garbage Truck: $15-20.
102 Saviem Milk Truck: $15-20.
103 BMW & Horse Trailer: $25-30.
104 Peugeot & Matra F.2: $15-20.
105 Tractor & Cattle Trailer: $15-20.
106 Tractor & Cargo Trailer: $15-20.
107 Land Rover & Trailer: $25-30.
108 Mercedes-Benz & Porsche: $20-25.
109 Fiat Dino & Ferrari: $20-25.
110 Corvair & CD: $35-45.
110 Mercedes-Benz & Porsche: $20-25.
111 Continental Bulldozer: $10-15.
112 Power Shovel: $10-15.
113 Berliet Dump Truck: $10-15.
114 Berliet Excavator: $15-20.
115 Berliet Low Loader: $15-20.
116 Berliet Bucket Truck: $15-20.
117 Renault Tractor: $5-10.
118 Land Rover & Police Trailer: $25-30.
119 Trotters & Sulkies: $10-15.
120 Land Rover & Trailer: $25-30.
121 Land Rover & Machine Gun: $25-30.
122 Land Rover & Rocket Trailer: $25-30.
123 Land Rover with Rockets: $25-30.
124 Mercedes-Benz Truck: $10-15.
125 Mercedes-Benz Truck & Trailer: $20-25.

126 Mercedes-Benz Cement Truck: $10-15.
127 Richier Road Grader: $40-50.
128 Richier Road Roller: $10-15.
129 Peugeot Road Service Van: $10-20.
131 Saviem Cherry Picker: $10-15.
132 Saviem Moving Van: $8-12.
133 Saviem Racer Transporter: $10-15.
137 Citroen Mehari: $5-10.
138 Matra Formula 2: $8-12.
139 Citroen Ami-8: $8-12.
140 Renault R12: $5-10.
141 Porsche Targa: $8-12.
142 Ferrari 275GTB: $10-15.
143 Matra 530A: $10-15.
144 Triumph TR5: $10-15.
145 Lancia Flavia: $10-15.
146 Fiat 525 1928: $15-20.
147 Peugeot 204 Coupe: $10-15.
148 Fiat 124: $8-12.
149 Porsche Carrera 6: $10-15.
150 Mercedes SSK: $15-20.
151 Simca 1100: $5-10.
152 Land Rover Police: $10-15.
153 Land Rover Safari: $10-15.
154 Land Rover Wrecker: $10-15.
155 Land Rover Expedition: $10-15.
156 Jaguar E-Type: $10-15.
157 Citroen Dyane: $8-12.
158 Citroen DS21: $10-15.
158P Citroen DS21 Police: $15-25.
159 Peugeot 404 Van: $15-20.
160 Peugeot 504: $8-12.
161 CD Le Mans: $10-15.
162 Renault R6: $5-10.
163 Fiat Dino Coupe: $8-12.
167 Renault 15TS: $5-10.
168 Renault 17TS: $5-10.
169 Citroen GS: $5-10.
170 Maserati Ghibli: $8-12.
171 Alpine A220: $5-10.
172 Mercedes-Benz C-111: $5-10.
173 Ligier JS2: $5-10.
174 Ligier JS3: $5-10.
175 Mercedes-Benz 350SL: $5-10.
176 Alpine A310: $5-10.
177 Opel 1900GT: $5-10.

178 Renault 5TL: $5-10.
179 Alfa Romeo Montreal: $8-12.
180 Porsche 917: $5-10. [end of file]
181 Alfa Romeo 33: $5-10.
182 Bertone Camargue: $5-10.
183 Lancia Stratos: $5-10.
184 Porsche Carrera RSR: $5-10.
186 Ferrari Dino: $5-10.
187 Citroen Présidentielle: $5-10.
188 Peugeot 104: Value $5-10.
189 Matra Simca Bagheera: $5-10.
190 Car with Luggage: $5-10.
191 Chevron B23: $5-10.
192 Ferrari 312P: $5-10.
193 Fiat X1/9: $5-10.
195 De Tomaso Pantera: $5-10.
196 Matra-Simca Short: $5-10.
197 Matra-Simca Long: $5-10.
198 Alpine A440: $5-10.
199 Mercedes-Benz with Crane: $10-15.
200 Car with Ski Rack: $5-10.
201 Lola T-294: $5-10.
202 Driving School Car: $5-15.
203 Car & Boat Trailer: $5-10.
204 Racing Car Transporter: $8-12.
205 Taxi: $5-10.
207 Citroen CX 2200: $5-10.
208 Citroen Présidentielle & Cycles: $8-12.
209 Police Van & Cycles: $8-12.
210 Fire Ambulance & Lifeboat: $8-12.
211 Tour de France Ambulance: $8-12.
212 Tour de France Press Car: $8-12.
214 Peugeot 504 Police Car: $5-10.
215 Fiat X1/9 Abarth: $4-8.
216 Renault 17 Rally: $5-10.
217 Renault 5 Rally: $5-10.
218 Alpine A310 Rally: $5-10.
219 Renault 30TS: $5-10.
220 Saviem Fire Tanker: $10-15.
221 Peugeot 604: $5-10.
222 Peugeot 504 Safari: $5-10.
223 Simca 1308GT: $5-10.
224 Official Car & Cycles: $10-15.
225 Police Car & Cycles: $10-15.
226 Tour Cycliste Set: $10-15.
227 Renault 14: $5-10.

228 Renault 20TL: $5-10.
229 Car & Caravan Trailer: $8-12.
230 BMW Police Motorcycle: $4-8.
231 Car & Cycle Trailer: $8-12.
233 Peugeot Mail Truck: $10-15.
235 Peugeot Bus & Boat Trailer: $10-15.
236 Peugeot Bus & Matra Bagheera: $10-15.
237 Renault Police Van & Cycles: $10-15.
238 Citroen Police Van & Cycles: $20-25.
239 Alpine Police Car: $5-10.
240 Renault 5 Doctor: $8-12.
241 Renault R4 Fire Van: $8-12.
242 Renault R4 Police Van: $8-12.
243 Renault R4 Mail Van: $10-15.
245 Peugeot J7 Police Van: 8-12.
246 Estafette School Bus: $8-12.
247 Citroen Police Van: $10-15.
248 Peugeot Bus with Skis: $8-12.
249 Peugeot Bus with Kayak: $8-12.
250 Estafette Minibus: $8-12.
251 Peugeot Road Service Van: $8-12.
252 Peugeot Fire Ambulance: $8-12.
253 Peugeot Mail Van: $8-12.
254 Renault Estafette: $8-12.
255 Alpine Police Car: $5-10.
256 Citroen Police Car: $8-12.
257 Mercedes-Benz Ambulance: $8-12.
300-400 Series Models: $4-8 each.
Mini-Jet Series Models: $3-5 each.
500 Series Micro Cars, Plastic: $8-12.
500 Series Micro Cars, Metal: $10-15.
515 Citroen Van: $10-15.
520 Unic Dump Truck: $10-15.
521 & Other Larger Trucks: $15-20 each.
526 Auto Transporter & 5 Cars: $25-30.
528 Saviem Bus: $15-20.
500-1500 1/43 Series: $10-15 each.
601 Matra Formula 2: $15-20.
603 DKW Junior: $20-25.
604 Volkswagen 1500: $20-25.
606 Simca 1500: $20-25.
607 Fiat 1500: $15-20.
609 Citroen 2CV Van: $15-20.
610 Renault 4L: $15-20.
612 Citroen 2CV AZ-Luxe: $15-20.
613 Volkswagen 1300: $15-20.

600 Series Mini-Jet Sets: $3-6 each.
700 Renault R4 Coca-Cola Van: $10-15.
701 Peugeot 404 Coupe: $25-35.
702 Fiat 2300 Coupe: $15-20.
703 Simca 1100 Coupe: $15-20.
704 Ford Taunus 12M: $15-20.
705 Ford Cortina: $15-20.
706 Fiat 124: $15-20.
707 Simca 1100S: $15-20.
708 Volkswagen 1600: $15-20.
708 Renault 5TL: $10-15.
709 Mercedes-Benz C-111: $10-15.
710 Ligier JS3: $5-10.
711 Renault 5TL: $10-15.
711 Renault R4 Van: $5-20.
712 Porsche 917: $8-12.
712 through 773, 792: $5-10 each.
778 through 780, 782: $5-15 each.
781 Renault 18TL: $8-12.
793 Talbot Solara: $5-10.
794 Citroen BX: $5-20.
798 Renault 9: $10-15.
801 Peugeot 204 Coupe: $25-30.
801 Citroen Visa Trophée: $5-10.
802 Renault Paris-Dakar: $5-10.
803 Opel Rekord 1700: $15-20.
803 Peugeot 505 Dinin: $5-10.
804 Peugeot 304: $12-18.
804 Renault Fuego Rexona: $5-10.
805 Renault 12: $10-15.
805 Renault 18 Police: $5-10.
806 Citroen DS21: $10-20.
806 Ligier JS3: $5-10.
807 Citroen SM: $10-15.
807 Talbot 1100S: $5-10.
808 Chrysler 180: $10-15.
808 Renault 5TL: $5-10.
809 Alpine A220: $6-12.
809 Mercedes-Benz C-111: $5-10.
810 Citroen GS: $8-15.
811 Opel GT: $8-15.
812 Alpine A310: $5-15.
813 Lola T-294: $5-10.
814 Bertone Camargue: $5-10.
815 Alfa Romeo 33: $5-10.
816 Alfa Romeo Montreal: $8-12.

818 Ligier JS2: $5-10.
818 Ligier JS2 Le Mans: $4-8.
820 Maserati Ghibli: $8-12.
821 Mercedes-Benz 350SL: $8-12.
822 Renault 15TS: $8-12.
823 Renault 17TS: $8-12.
824 Ferrari Dino: $8-12.
825 Matra Bagheera: $8-12.
826 Peugeot 104: $8-12.
829 De Tomaso Pantera: $6-10.
832 Matra-Simca Short: $6-10.
833 Matra-Simca Long: $6-10.
833 Citroen CX Taxi: $5-8.
834 Chevron B23: $4-8.
835 Ferrari 312P: $6-10.
836 Fiat X1/9: $6-10.
838 Citroen Présidentielle: $8-15.
839 Porsche Carrera RSR: $8-12.
840 Alpine A440: $6-8.
841 Renault 16TX: $6-10.
842 Peugeot 504: $6-8.
842 Renault 18 Police: $6-8.
843 Citroen 2CV6: $6-8.
845 Citroen CX: $6-12.
846 Renault 17 Rally: $5-8.
847 Fiat X1/9 Abarth: $5-8.
849 Peugeot 504 Police: $8-12.
850 Renault Driving School: $8-12.
850-851 Portuguese Versions: ?
851 Car with Ski Rack: $8-12.
852 Renault Taxi: $8-12.
852 Volvo Taxi: $6-8.
853 Renault 5TL Rally: $5-8.
853 Mercedes or Volvo Taxi: $6-8.
854 BMW Turbo: $10-15.
854 Mercedes-Benz Taxi: $6-8.
855 Alpine A310 Rally: $5-8.
856 Renault 30TS: $6-10.
857 Peugeot 604: $6-10.
858 Alpine A442 Turbo: $5-8.
859 Peugeot 504 Safari: $6-8.
860 Simca 1308GT: $5-10.
860 Talbot 1510: $6-8.
861 Renault 14TL: $6-12.
862 Renault 20TL: $6-10.
863 Lancia Stratos: $5-8.

864 Porsche 924: $6-10.
865 Renault R4 Fire: $8-12.
866 Renault R4 Police: $8-12.
867 Renault R4 Mail: $10-15.
868 BMW 633CF Coupe: $6-8.
869 BMW 633 Prototype: $5-8.
870 De Tomaso Pantera: $8-12.
871 Alpine A310 Police: $6-8.
872 Renault 18TL Police: $8-10.
873 Ford Fiesta: $6-8.
874 Mercedes-Benz Ambulance: $10-20.
875 Renault 5 Doctor: $8-12.
876 Simca 1308 Europe 1: $10-15.
876 Ferrari GTS: $8-10.
877 Ligier JS2 Le Mans: $5-8.
878 Volkswagen Golf: $5-8.
879 Peugeot 305SR: $5-8.
880 Simca Horizon: $8-10.
881 Renault 18TL: $6-10.
882 Citroen Visa: $6-10.
883 VW Golf Police: $8-10.
884 VW Golf ADAC: $8-10.
885 Porsche 924 Police: $8-12.
886 Volvo 264: $8-12.
887 Ford Mustang: $6-10.
888 Alfa Romeo 6: $6-10.
889 Peugeot 505: $6-10.
890 Mercedes-Benz 280SE: $6-10.
891 Renault Fuego: $6-10.
892 Ford Escort: $6-10.
893 Talbot Solara: $8-10.
895 Citroen BX: $8-15.
896 Volvo 264 Wagon: $6-12.
897 Renault 18TL Break: $6-12.
898 Renault 9: $6-10.
899 VW Golf Rally: $6-8.

QUIRALU

1 Simca Trianon: $75-85.
2 Simca Versailles: $75-85.
3 Simca Régence: $75-85.
4 Peugeot 403: $75-85.
5-6-7 Peugeot 403: $85-95.
8-9 Mercedes-Benz 300SL: $100-125.
10-11 Simca Marly Break: $75-85.

12 Simca Marly Ambulance: $100-120.
13-14 Porsche Carrera: $300-350.
15 Jaguar XK 140: $100-120.
16 Messerschmitt: $75-85.
17 Rolls-Royce: $100-120.
18 Vespa 400: $75-85.
19 Velam Isetta: $75-85.
20 Étoile Filante, decals: $90-100.
21 same, cast-in trim lines: $85-95.
22 Peugeot Primagaz Van: $300-350.
23 Peugeot Thomson Van: $300-350.
24 Peugeot Army Ambulance: $350-375.
25 Berliet Covered Truck: $250-300.
26 Berliet Dump Truck: $250-300.
27 GBO Covered Trailer: $100-125.

RAMI

All Models $40-50 each except:
13 Packard Landaulet: $45-55.
19 Hautier Electric: $45-55.
22 Scotte Steamer: $45-55.
37 Delage Torpedo: $45-55.
38 Mercedes SSK: $45-55.

SAFIR

Old-time Cars: $10-15 each except:
11 Citroen Fire Truck: $15-20.
12 Citroen Ambulance: $15-20.
13 Citroen Mail Truck: $15-25.
101 Gregoire Triple Berline: $15-20.
Super Champion 1/43 Sports & Racing:
30-35 Lolas: $10-15 each.
40-45, 50-55 Porsches: $15-20 each.
60-65 Ferraris: $15-20 each.
70-75 Porsches: $15-20 each.
80-83 Formula 1 Cars: $15-20.
Berliet Trucks: $8-12 each except:
Fire Truck, Circus Truck: $10-15 each.
Mercedes-Benz Trucks: $8-12 each.
Trucks & Trailers: $12-18 each except:
Fire Truck & Trailer: $15-25.
Circus Truck & Trailer: $15-25.
Tank Truck & Trailer: $15-25.
Dodge Trucks: $8-15 each.
Dodge Trucks & Trailers: $10-15 each.

Jeeps: $8-12 each except:
4 Red Cross Jeep: $10-15.
Circus Jeep: $10-15.
Fire Jeep: $10-15.
Jeeps and Trailers: $12-18 each.
Champion 1/66 Racing Cars:
First Series: $8-12 each.
Second Series: $5-10 each.
Champion 1/66 Sports Cars:
First Series: $5-12 each.
Second Series: $8-12 each.
Champion 1/66 Trucks: $5-10 each.
Other 1/66 Champions: $5-10 each.
Racing Plastic Models: $10-15 each.

OTHER BRANDS

Ador Caravan: ?
Bonux Peugeot 203: $10-15.
Bonux Road Roller: $4-8.
Bonux Old-timers: $4-8, except:
Bonux Double-deck Bus: $10-15.
Bourbon Peugeot Van: ?
Bourbon Berliet Tanker: $30-40?
B. S.: $4-8 each?
Calabut Carousel: ?
Cofalu Peugeots with Bicycles: $10-20?
Cofalu Go-Kart: $10-20?
D.E.L. Old-timers: $10-15 each?
Desormeaux Old-timers: $100 or more.
Eria Cars: ?
Faracars STP: $75-95?
Gege Cars: $60-75 each?
Gulliver Berliet Bus: $100 or more.
Gulliver Berliet Truck: $75-95.
Gulliver Renault Cars: $100 or more.
J.E.P. Cars: $65-75.
J.F. Citroens: $50-75 each?
Jouef Panamericaine, Aronde: ?
Jouef Farmall Tractor: $4-8?
Jouef Chausson Bus: $20-30?
Jouef HO Cars: $15-25?
Jouet Mecanique Panhard: ?
Joustra Trucks: $35-45?
Lavirolette Coupe: ?
Les Rouliers Étoile Filante: $40-50?

Poclain Heavy Equipment: ?
P. R. Promotional Vans: $100 or more.
Primo Renault: ?
Rhodanienne Ambulance: ?
Rolux Limousine, Staff Car: ?
Salza Tour de France Models: ?
Shell Ferrari: $5-10?
Makers Unknown: ?
Gitanes: ?

Jadali HO Series: $30-40?
Jadali Old-timers: $75-95?
Les Routiers Series: $40-50 each, except:
Les Routiers 11 Byrrh Tanker: $50-75?
Midget Toys 1/86 Series: $30-45 each.
Midget Toys 1/43 Vespa: $50-65.
J. P. Cars: Market prices if in production; otherwise ?

French-English Glossary

Note: The French like hyphenated words, so you may need to look up the pieces separately; they also add -e and -ée endings, and -s and -x plurals.

aérodynamique: streamlined, aerodynamic
affût: gun carriage
agricole: farm, agricultural
allemand: German
amiral: admiral
amphibie: amphibian
arbre de transmission: driveshaft
arrière: rear, back
arroseuse-balayeuse: street sprinkler-sweeper
autocar: bus
auto-école: driving school
autoroute: superhighway
avant: front

baché: covered (truck, Jeep)
bagages: luggage
balayeuse: street sweeper
basse: low
bateau: boat
benne à ordures: garbage truck
benne basculante: dump truck
benne basculante sur le côte: side tipper
benne carrière: quarry dump truck
berline: sedan
bétaillère: cattle truck, livestock truck
bétonnière: cement truck, cement mixer
bicolore: two-tone
blindé(e): armored

bois: wood
boîte de vitesses: gearbox
break: station wagon
brise-mottes: harrow

cabriolet: convertible
calandre: grille
camion: truck
camionnette: light truck
canon: cannon, gun
canon anti-aérien: anti-aircraft gun
canon anti-char: antitank gun
canon de campagne: field gun
capot: hood
caravane: house trailer, caravan trailer
caréné: streamlined
carosserie: body, bodywork
char: army tank, armored car
charrue: plow
charbon: coal
chargeur: loader
chasse-neige: snowplow
chemin de fer: railroad
chenilles: tracks, treads
cheval: horse
chevaux: horses, horsepower
chimique: chemical
chromé: chromed

ciment: cement
cirque: circus
citerne: tank, tank truck
civil: civilian
commercial: commercial (vehicle, truck)
compresseur: compressor, road roller
clignotant: flashing light
couleur: color
course: racing
Croix-Rouge: Red Cross
cuisine: kitchen
cylindre: cylinder

débâché: top down
décapotable: convertible
dépanneuse: wrecker, tow truck
direction: steering

eau: water
échelle: scale, ladder
éclairage: lighting, lights
électrogène: generator
élévateur: conveyor, elevator
élysée: Elysium, paradise
empennage: tailfin
essence: gasoline
essieu: axle
excavatrice: excavator
expédition: shipping

faucheuse: mower
ferme: farm
fermé, fermée: closed, locked up
fourche: fork
fourgon: van
fourgonnette: light van
frigorifique: refrigerated

garde-boue: fender
glace: glass, window
grand, grande: grand, great, big
grand pavois: flying colors, flagship
grande échelle: aerial ladder, large-scale
grue: crane

herse: harrow

horlogerie: clockwork
huile: oil

impériale: doubledeck (bus)
incendie: fire (truck)
injecté: diecast

jouet: toy

lait: milk
laitier: milk tank truck
léger, légère: light(weight)
limousine: sedan
livraison: delivery
longueur: length
lourd: heavy
luxe: luxury

maraîcher: farm truck
mécanique: mechanical
militaire: military, army
miroir: mirror, glass pane?
miroitier: glass truck, mirror truck
mitrailleuse: machine gun
modèles réduits: scale models
moteur: motor
motocyclette: motorcycle
moto-pompe: pump, pumper
mouvement: mechanism
moyen: medium, middle
multibenne: multibucket, bucket truck

niveleuse: road grader
non: no, not
numéro: number

obusier: howitzer
ouvert: open
ouvrant: opening

pare-brise: windshield
peinture: paint
pelle, pelleteuse: shovel, excavator
petit, petite: small, little
phare: light, headlight
pile: battery

place: seat, place
plateau, plateforme: flatbed
plâtre et farine: plaster and flour
plein ciel: open sky, open air
plomb: lead
pneu: tire
pompiers: fire department, firefighters
porte: door
porte-bagages: luggage rack
postale, poste: mail, postal
premier secours: first aid
projecteur: searchlight

radiateur: radiator
rampe: ramp, loading ramp
rayon: wheel spoke
remise: garage, hired carriage
remorque: trailer
remorque à foin: hay trailer
remorque surbaissée: low loader trailer
ressort: spring, clockwork
ridelle: stake, rack
roue: wheel
roue de secours: spare wheel
rouleau: roller
rouleau vibreur: vibrating roller

secours: help, aid, first aid
semi-remorque: semi-trailer
socle: mount, swivel
sortie: issued
surbaissé: low (low loader), underslung

terre: earth
toit: top, roof
toit bois: wooden top
toit ouvrant: opening roof panel, sun roof
tôle: sheet metal
tonneau: barrel (body style with rear seats)
touring secours: road service
tout terrain, tous terrains: off-road, all-terrain
tracteur: tractor
traction avant: front-wheel drive
transport d'autos: auto transporter
travaux publics: public works
triporteur: delivery tricycle

vapeur: steam
vehicule: vehicle
vélo: bicycle
vente ambulante: vendor's truck
vis-à-vis: face-to-face (seats)
vitre: window, glass pane
voiture: car
voiturette: light car, small car
voiture blindée: armored car
voiture de course: racing car
voiture de record: speed record car
volant: steering wheel

Colors, in the order usually listed:

gold: or
silver: argent
white: blanc, blanche
ivory: ivoire
cream: crème, vanille
pink: rose, saumon (salmon pink)
red: rouge, rouge brique (brick red)
maroon: marron, bordeaux (wine-red)
orange: orange
yellow: jaune, jaune citron (lemon yellow)
green: vert, vert bouteille (bottle green), vert émeraude (emerald)
blue: bleu, bleu ciel (sky blue)
purple: violet, mauve, prune
tan: beige, moutarde (mustard tan)
brown: brun
gray: gris
black: noir

pale: pâle
light: clair
bright: vif
dark: foncé
metallic: métal

Special thanks to colleagues Louis Auld and Samuel Schulman for their help!